# A CASEBOOK ON THE BEAT

CROWELL LITERARY CASEBOOKS

Under the General Editorship of

William Van O'Connor

# A CASEBOOK ON THE BEAT

*Edited by* **THOMAS PARKINSON**

*University of California*

Thomas Y. Crowell Company

*New York, Established 1834*

Designed by Laurel Wagner
Cover design by Orest Neimanis

Manufactured in the United States of America
by Vail-Ballou Press, Inc., Binghamton, N.Y.

Library of Congress Catalog Card Number: 60-9938

## PREFACE

The aim of this book is to present a body of material essential to understanding the writing often placed under the rubric "Beat Generation" or more simply "beat." The first section of the book is composed of selections from the poetry and fiction of nine writers, along with pieces of expository prose in which they explain or otherwise clarify their motives as writers and persons. The second section presents a variety of comments, ranging from the aggressively partisan writing of Lawrence Lipton to the equally aggressive attacks of Norman Podhoretz and Paul O'Neil. The bibliography is intended as a guide to further reading, both in the works of the several beat writers and in commentaries. The Suggested Problems are designed for classroom use, but they also indicate lines of thought suggested by the material that might further elucidate the problems posed by this considerable body of work.

Since the editor has been rather deeply involved in the literature here treated, he has felt it necessary to present his own views not as editorial views but as one of several comments. His essay "Phenomenon or Generation" is therefore included in the second section of the book, where its force will be less coercive and guiding than it would be if it were printed as an introduction.

The shaping of this book was greatly eased by suggestions from Allen Ginsberg and the cooperation of Lawrence Ferlinghetti. A special debt of gratitude is owed to Miss Bess Lowry of the Humanities Reference Service of the University of California Library, who was tirelessly cheerful and helpful.

THOMAS PARKINSON

*Berkeley, California*

# CONTENTS

# CONTENTS

## APPENDICES

# SOME WRITERS OF THE BEAT GENERATION

# ALLEN GINSBERG

## HOWL

*For Carl Solomon*

### 1

I saw the best minds of my generation destroyed by madness,
  starving hysterical naked,
dragging themselves through the negro streets at dawn looking
  for an angry fix,
angelheaded hipsters burning for the ancient heavenly connection to the starry dynamo in the machinery of night,
who poverty and tatters and hollow-eyed and high sat up smoking in the supernatural darkness of cold-water flats floating
  across the tops of cities contemplating jazz,
who bared their brains to Heaven under the El and saw Moham-
  medan angels staggering on tenement roofs illuminated,
who passed through universities with radiant cool eyes hallucinat-
  ing Arkansas and Blake-light tragedy among the scholars of
  war,
who were expelled from the academies for crazy & publishing
  obscene odes on the windows of the skull,
who cowered in unshaven rooms in underwear, burning their
  money in wastebaskets and listening to the Terror through
  the wall,
who got busted in their pubic beards returning through Laredo
  with a belt of marijuana for New York,
who ate fire in paint hotels or drank turpentine in Paradise Alley,
  death, or purgatoried their torsos night after night
with dreams, with drugs, with waking nightmares, alcohol and
  cock and endless balls,
incomparable blind streets of shuddering cloud and lightning in

Reprinted from Allen Ginsberg, *"Howl" and Other Poems*, Pocket Poets Series No. 4 (San Francisco, Calif.: City Lights Books, 1959), pp. 9–22. Copyright 1959 by Allen Ginsberg; reprinted by permission of City Lights Books.

the mind leaping toward poles of Canada & Paterson, [9] *
illuminating all the motionless world of Time between,
Peyote solidities of halls, backyard green tree cemetery dawns,
wine drunkenness over the rooftops, storefront boroughs of
teahead joyride neon blinking traffic light, sun and moon and
tree vibrations in the roaring winter dusks of Brooklyn, ashcan rantings and kind king light of mind,
who chained themselves to subways for the endless ride from
Battery to holy Bronx on benzedrine until the noise of
wheels and children brought them down shuddering mouth-
wracked and battered bleak of brain all drained of brilliance
in the drear light of Zoo,
who sank all night in submarine light of Bickford's floated out
and sat through the stale beer afternoon in desolate Fugazzi's,
listening to the crack of doom on the hydrogen jukebox,
who talked continuously seventy hours from park to pad to bar to
Bellevue to museum to the Brooklyn Bridge,
a lost battalion of platonic conversationalists jumping down the
stoops off fire escapes off windowsills off Empire State out
of the moon,
yacketayakking screaming vomiting whispering facts and memories and anecdotes and eyeball kicks and shocks of hospitals
and jails and wars,
whole intellects disgorged in total recall for seven days and nights
with brilliant eyes, meat for the Synagogue cast on the pavement,
who vanished into nowhere Zen New Jersey leaving a trail of ambiguous picture postcards of Atlantic City Hall,
suffering Eastern sweats and Tangerian bone-grindings and mi-
graines of China under junk-withdrawal in Newark's bleak
furnished room,
who wandered around and around at midnight in the railroad
yard wondering where to go, and went, leaving no broken
hearts, [10]
who lit cigarettes in boxcars boxcars boxcars racketing through
snow toward lonesome farms in grandfather night,
who studied Plotinus Poe St. John of the Cross telepathy and bop
kaballa because the cosmos instinctively vibrated at their
feet in Kansas,
who loned it through the streets of Idaho seeking visionary indian angels who were visionary indian angels,

* [Bracketed figures throughout text indicate page numbers on which selections appeared in their original sources.]

who thought they were only mad when Baltimore gleamed in
  supernatural ecstasy,
who jumped in limousines with the Chinaman of Oklahoma on
  the impulse of winter midnight streetlight small town rain,
who lounged hungry and lonesome through Houston seeking jazz
  or sex or soup, and followed the brilliant Spaniard to con-
  verse about America and Eternity, a hopeless task, and so
  took ship to Africa,
who disappeared into the volcanoes of Mexico leaving behind
  nothing but the shadow of dungarees and the lava and ash
  of poetry scattered in fireplace Chicago,
who reappeared on the West Coast investigating the F.B.I. in
  beards and shorts with big pacifist eyes sexy in their dark
  skin passing out incomprehensible leaflets,
who burned cigarette holes in their arms protesting the narcotic
  tobacco haze of Capitalism,
who distributed Supercommunist pamphlets in Union Square
  weeping and undressing while the sirens of Los Alamos
  wailed them down, and wailed down Wall, and the Staten
  Island ferry also wailed,
who broke down crying in white gymnasiums naked and trembling before the machinery of other skeletons,
who bit detectives in the neck and shrieked with delight in police-
  cars for committing no crime but their own wild cooking
  pederasty and intoxication, [11]
who howled on their knees in the subway and were dragged off
  the roof waving genitals and manuscripts,
who let themselves be . . . . . . in the . . . by saintly motorcyclists, and screamed with joy,
who blew and were blown by those human seraphim, the sailors,
  caresses of Atlantic and Caribbean love,
who balled in the mornings in the evenings in rosegardens and
  the grass of public parks and cemeteries scattering their
  semen freely to whomever come who may,
who hiccupped endlessly trying to giggle but wound up with a
  sob behind a partition in a Turkish Bath when the blonde &
  naked angel came to pierce them with a sword,
who lost their loveboys to the three old shrews of fate the one
  eyed shrew of the heterosexual dollar the one eyed shrew
  that winks out of the womb and the one eyed shrew that
  does nothing but sit on her ass and snip the intellectual
  golden threads of the craftsman's loom,
who copulated ecstatic and insatiate with a bottle of beer a

sweetheart a package of cigarettes a candle and fell off the
bed and continued along the floor and down the hall and
ended fainting on the wall with a vision of ultimate c . . .
and come eluding the last gyzym of consciousness,

who sweetened the snatches of a million girls trembling in the
sunset, and were red eyed in the morning but prepared to
sweeten the snatch of the sunrise, flashing buttocks under
barns and naked in the lake,

who went out whoring through Colorado in myriad stolen night-
cars, N.C., secret hero of these poems, cocksman and Adonis
of Denver—joy to the memory of his innumerable lays of
girls in empty lots & diner backyards, moviehouses, rickety
rows on mountaintops in caves or with gaunt waitresses in
familiar roadside lonely petticoat upliftings [12] & especially
secret gas-station solipsisms of johns, & hometown alleys
too,

who faded out in vast sordid movies, were shifted in dreams,
woke on a sudden Manhattan, and picked themselves up out
of basements hungover with heartless Tokay and horrors of
Third Avenue iron dreams & stumbled to unemployment
offices,

who walked all night with their shoes full of blood on the snow-
bank docks waiting for a door in the East River to open to
a room full of steamheat and opium,

who created great suicidal dramas on the apartment cliff-banks
of the Hudson under the wartime blue floodlight of the
moon & their heads shall be crowned with laurel in oblivion,

who ate the lamb stew of the imagination or digested the crab
at the muddy bottom of the rivers of Bowery,

who wept at the romance of the streets with their pushcarts full
of onions and bad music,

who sat in boxes breathing in the darkness under the bridge, and
rose up to build harpsichords in their lofts,

who coughed on the sixth floor of Harlem crowned with flame
under the tubercular sky surrounded by orange crates of
theology,

who scribbled all night rocking and rolling over lofty incanta-
tions which in the yellow morning were stanzas of gibberish,

who cooked rotten animals lung heart feet tail borsht & tortillas
dreaming of the pure vegetable kingdom,

who plunged themselves under meat trucks looking for an egg,

who threw their watches off the roof to cast their ballot for

Eternity outside of Time, & alarm clocks fell on their heads
every day for the next decade,

who cut their wrists three times successively unsuccessfully, gave
up [13] and were forced to open antique stores where they
thought they were growing old and cried,

who were burned alive in their innocent flannel suits on Madison
Avenue amid blasts of leaden verse & the tanked-up clatter
of the iron regiments of fashion & the nitroglycerine shrieks
of the fairies of advertising & the mustard gas of sinister intelligent editors, or were run down by the drunken taxicabs
of Absolute Reality,

who jumped off the Brooklyn Bridge this actually happened and
walked away unknown and forgotten into the ghostly daze
of Chinatown soup alleyways & firetrucks, not even one free
beer,

who sang out of their windows in despair, fell out of the subway
window, jumped in the filthy Passaic, leaped on negroes,
cried all over the street, danced on broken wineglasses barefoot smashed phonograph records of nostalgic European
1930's German jazz finished the whiskey and threw up groaning into the bloody toilet, moans in their ears and the blast
of colossal steamwhistles,

who barreled down the highways of the past journeying to each
other's hotrod-Golgotha jail-solitude watch or Birmingham
jazz incarnation,

who drove crosscountry seventytwo hours to find out if I had a
vision or you had a vision or he had a vision to find out
Eternity,

who journeyed to Denver, who died in Denver, who came back
to Denver & waited in vain, who watched over Denver &
brooded & loned in Denver and finally went away to find
out the Time, & now Denver is lonely for her heroes,

who fell on their knees in hopeless cathedrals praying for each
other's salvation and light and breasts, until the soul illuminated its hair for a second, [14]

who crashed through their minds in jail waiting for impossible
criminals with golden heads and the charm of reality in their
hearts who sang sweet blues to Alcatraz,

who retired to Mexico to cultivate a habit, or Rocky Mount to
tender Buddha or Tangiers to boys or Southern Pacific to
the black locomotive or Harvard to Narcissus to Woodlawn
to the daisychain or grave,

who demanded sanity trials accusing the radio of hypnotism &
were left with their insanity & their hands & a hung jury,

who threw potato salad at CCNY lecturers on Dadaism and subsequently presented themselves on the granite steps of the
madhouse with shaven heads and harlequin speech of suicide, demanding instantaneous lobotomy,

and who were given instead the concrete void of insulin metrasol
electricity hydrotherapy psychotherapy occupational therapy
pingpong & amnesia,

who in humorless protest overturned only one symbolic ping-
pong table, resting briefly in catatonia,

returning years later truly bald except for a wig of blood, and tears
and fingers, to the visible madman doom of the wards of
the madtowns of the East,

Pilgrim State's Rockland's and Greystone's foetid halls, bickering
with the echoes of the soul, rocking and rolling in the midnight solitude-bench dolmen-realms of love, dream of life a
nightmare, bodies turned to stone as heavy as the moon,

with mother finally ******, and the last fantastic book flung out
of the tenement window, and the last door closed at 4 AM
and the last telephone slammed at the wall in reply and the
last furnished room emptied down to the last piece of mental
furniture, a yellow paper rose twisted on a wire hanger in
the closet, and even that imaginary, nothing but a hopeful
little bit of hallucination— [15]

ah, Carl, while you are not safe I am not safe, and now you're
really in the total animal soup of time—

and who therefore ran through the icy streets obsessed with a
sudden flash of the alchemy of the use of the ellipse the catalog the meter & the vibrating plane,

who dreamt and made incarnate gaps in Time & Space through
images juxtaposed, and trapped the archangel of the soul
between 2 visual images and joined the elemental verbs and
set the noun and dash of consciousness together jumping
with sensation of Pater Omnipotens Aeterna Deus

to recreate the syntax and measure of poor human prose and
stand before you speechless and intelligent and shaking with
shame, rejected yet confessing out the soul to conform to the
rhythm of thought in his naked and endless head,

the madman bum and angel beat in time, unknown, yet putting
down here what might be left to say in time come after death,

and rose reincarnate in the ghostly clothes of jazz in the goldhorn
     shadow of the band and blew the suffering of America's
     naked mind for love into an eli eli lamma lamma sabacthani
     saxophone cry that shivered the cities down to the last radio
with the absolute heart of the poem of life butchered out of their
     own bodies good to eat a thousand years. [16]


     2


What sphinx of cement and aluminum bashed open their skulls
     and ate up their brains and imagination?
Moloch! Solitude! Filth! Ugliness! Ashcans and unobtainable
     dollars! Children screaming under the stairways! Boys sob-
     bing in armies! Old men weeping in the parks!
Moloch! Moloch! Nightmare of Moloch! Moloch the loveless!
     Mental Moloch! Moloch the heavy judger of men!
Moloch the incomprehensible prison! Moloch the crossbone soul-
     less jailhouse and Congress of sorrows! Moloch whose build-
     ings are judgement! Moloch the vast stone of war! Moloch
     the stunned governments!
Moloch whose mind is pure machinery! Moloch whose blood is
     running money! Moloch whose fingers are ten armies! Moloch
     whose breast is a cannibal dynamo! Moloch whose ear is a
     smoking tomb!
Moloch whose eyes are a thousand blind windows! Moloch whose
     skyscrapers stand in the long streets like endless Jehovahs!
     Moloch whose factories dream and croak in the fog! Moloch
     whose smokestacks and antennae crown the cities!
Moloch whose love is endless oil and stone! Moloch whose soul
     is electricity and banks! Moloch whose poverty is the specter
     of genius! Moloch whose fate is a cloud of sexless hydro-
     gen! Moloch whose name is the Mind!
Moloch in whom I sit lonely! Moloch in whom I dream Angels!
     Crazy in Moloch! C . . . sucker in Moloch! Lacklove and
     manless in Moloch!
Moloch who entered my soul early! Moloch in whom I am a
     consciousness without a body! Moloch who frightened me
     out of my natural ecstasy! Moloch whom I abandon! Wake
     up in Moloch! Light streaming out of the sky! [17]
Moloch! Moloch! Robot apartments! invisible suburbs! skeleton
     treasuries! blind capitals! demonic industries! spectral na-

tions! invincible madhouses! granite cocks! monstrous bombs!
They broke their backs lifting Moloch to Heaven! Pavements,
trees, radios, tons! lifting the city to Heaven which exists and
is everywhere about us!

Visions! omens! hallucinations! miracles! ecstasies! gone down the
American river!

Dreams! adorations! illuminations! religions! the whole boatload
of sensitive bullshit!

Breakthroughs! over the river! flips and crucifixions! gone down
the flood! Highs! Epiphanies! Despairs! Ten years' animal
screams and suicides! Minds! New loves! Mad generation!
down on the rocks of Time!

Real holy laughter in the river! They saw it all! the wild eyes! the
holy yells! They bade farewell! They jumped off the roof!
to solitude! waving! carrying flowers! Down to the river! into
the street! [18]


3

Carl Solomon! I'm with you in Rockland
    where you're madder than I am
I'm with you in Rockland
    where you must feel very strange
I'm with you in Rockland
    where you imitate the shade of my mother
I'm with you in Rockland
    where you've murdered your twelve secretaries
I'm with you in Rockland
    where you laugh at this invisible humor
I'm with you in Rockland
    where we are great writers on the same dreadful typewriter
I'm with you in Rockland
    where your condition has become serious and is reported
    on the radio
I'm with you in Rockland
    where the faculties of the skull no longer admit the worms
    of the senses
I'm with you in Rockland
    where you drink the tea of the breasts of the spinsters of
    Utica
I'm with you in Rockland
    where you pun on the bodies of your nurses the harpies of
    the Bronx

I'm with you in Rockland
>where you scream in a straightjacket that you're losing the
game of the actual pingpong of the abyss
I'm with you in Rockland
>where you bang on the catatonic piano the soul is innocent
and immortal it should never die ungodly in an armed
madhouse [19]
I'm with you in Rockland
>where fifty more shocks will never return your soul to its
body again from its pilgrimage to a cross in the void
I'm with you in Rockland
>where you accuse your doctors of insanity and plot the
Hebrew socialist revolution against the fascist national
Golgotha
I'm with you in Rockland
>where you will split the heavens of Long Island and resur-
rect your living human Jesus from the superhuman tomb
I'm with you in Rockland
>where there are twentyfive-thousand mad comrades all to-
gether singing the final stanzas of the Internationale
I'm with you in Rockland
>where we hug and kiss the United States under our bed-
sheets the United States that coughs all night and won't
let us sleep
I'm with you in Rockland
>where we wake up electrified out of the coma by our own
souls' airplanes roaring over the roof they've come to drop
angelic bombs the hospital illuminates itself imaginary
walls collapse O skinny legions run outside O starry-
spangled shock of mercy the eternal war is here O victory
forget your underwear we're free
I'm with you in Rockland
>in my dreams you walk dripping from a sea-journey on
the highway across America in tears to the door of my
cottage in the Western night [20]

## FOOTNOTE TO HOWL

Holy! Holy! Holy! Holy! Holy! Holy! Holy! Holy! Holy! Holy!
Holy! Holy! Holy! Holy! Holy!
The world is holy! The soul is holy! The skin is holy! The nose is
holy! The tongue and cock and hand and asshole holy!
Everything is holy! everybody's holy! everywhere is holy! every-
day is in eternity! Everyman's an angel!
The bum's as holy as the seraphim! the madman is holy as you
my soul are holy!
The typewriter is holy the poem is holy the voice is holy the
hearers are holy the ecstasy is holy!
Holy Peter holy Allen holy Solomon holy Lucien holy Kerouac
holy Huncke holy Burroughs holy Cassady holy the unknown
buggered and suffering beggars holy the hideous human an-
gels!
Holy my mother in the insane asylum! Holy the cocks of the
grandfathers of Kansas!
Holy the groaning saxophone! Holy the bop apocalypse! Holy
the jazzbands marijuana hipsters peace & junk & drums!
Holy the solitudes of skyscrapers and pavements! Holy the cafe-
terias filled with the millions! Holy the mysterious rivers of
tears under the streets!
Holy the lone juggernaut! Holy the vast lamb of the middleclass!
Holy the crazy shepherds of rebellion! Who digs Los Angeles
IS Los Angeles!
Holy New York Holy San Francisco Holy Peoria & Seattle Holy
Paris Holy Tangiers Holy Moscow Holy Istanbul!
Holy time in eternity holy eternity in time holy the clocks in space
holy the fourth dimension holy the fifth International holy
the Angel in Moloch! [21]
Holy the sea holy the desert holy the railroad holy the locomotive
holy the visions holy the hallucinations holy the miracles holy
the eyeball holy the abyss!
Holy forgiveness! mercy! charity! faith! Holy! Ours! bodies! suffering! magnanimity!
Holy the supernatural extra brilliant intelligent kindness of the
soul! [22]

## AMERICA

America I've given you all and now I'm nothing.
America two dollars and twentyseven cents January 17, 1956.
I can't stand my own mind.
America when will we end the human war?
Go fuck yourself with your atom bomb.
I don't feel good don't bother me.
I won't write my poem till I'm in my right mind.
America when will you be angelic?
When will you take off your clothes?
When will you look at yourself through the grave?
When will you be worthy of your million Trotskyites?
America why are your libraries full of tears?
America when will you send your eggs to India?
I'm sick of your insane demands.
When can I go into the supermarket and buy what I need with
    my good looks?
America after all it is you and I who are perfect not the next
    world.
Your machinery is too much for me.
You made me want to be a saint.
There must be some other way to settle this argument.
Burroughs is in Tangiers I don't think he'll come back it's sinister.
Are you being sinister or is this some form of practical joke?
I'm trying to come to the point.
I refuse to give up my obsession.
America stop pushing I know what I'm doing.
America the plum blossoms are falling.
I haven't read the newspapers for months, everyday somebody
    goes on trial for murder.
America I feel sentimental about the Wobblies.
America I used to be a communist when I was a kid I'm not
    sorry. [31]

Reprinted from Allen Ginsberg, "Howl" and Other Poems, Pocket Poets
Series, No. 4 (San Francisco, Calif.: City Lights Books, 1959), pp. 31–34.
Copyright 1959 by Allen Ginsberg; reprinted by permission of City Lights
Books.

I smoke marijuana every chance I get.
I sit in my house for days on end and stare at the roses in the closet.
When I go to Chinatown I get drunk and never get laid.
My mind is made up there's going to be trouble.
You should have seen me reading Marx.
My psychoanalyst thinks I'm perfectly right.
I won't say the Lord's Prayer.
I have mystical visions and cosmic vibrations.
America I still haven't told you what you did to Uncle Max after he came over from Russia.

I'm addressing you.
Are you going to let your emotional life be run by Time Magazine?
I'm obsessed by Time Magazine.
I read it every week.
Its cover stares at me every time I slink past the corner candystore.
I read it in the basement of the Berkeley Public Library.
It's always telling me about responsibility. Businessmen are serious. Movie producers are serious. Everybody's serious but me.
It occurs to me that I am America.
I am talking to myself again.

Asia is rising against me.
I haven't got a chinaman's chance.
I'd better consider my national resources.
My national resources consist of two joints of marijuana millions of genitals an unpublishable private literature that goes 1400 miles an hour and twentyfive-thousand mental institutions.
I say nothing about my prisons nor the millions of underprivileged who live in my flowerpots under the light of five hundred suns. [32]
I have abolished the whorehouses of France, Tangiers is the next to go.
My ambition is to be President despite the fact that I'm a Catholic.

America how can I write a holy litany in your silly mood?
I will continue like Henry Ford my strophes are as individual as his automobiles more so they're all different sexes.
America I will sell you strophes $2500 apiece $500 down on your old strophe

America free Tom Mooney
America save the Spanish Loyalists
America Sacco & Vanzetti must not die
America I am the Scottsboro boys.
America when I was seven momma took me to Communist Cell
    meetings they sold us garbanzos a handful per ticket a ticket
    costs a nickel and the speeches were free everybody was an-
    gelic and sentimental about the workers it was all so sincere
    you have no idea what a good thing the party was in 1935
    Scott Nearing was a grand old man a real mensch Mother
    Bloor made me cry I once saw Israel Amter plain. Everybody
    must have been a spy.
America you don't really want to go to war.
America it's them bad Russians.
Them Russians them Russians and them Chinamen. And them
    Russians.
The Russia wants to eat us alive. The Russia's power mad. She
    wants to take our cars from out our garages.
Her wants to grab Chicago. Her needs a Red Readers' Digest.
    Her wants our auto plants in Siberia. Him big bureaucracy
    running our fiillingstations. [33]
That no good. Ugh. Him make Indians learn read. Him need big
    black niggers. Hah. Her make us all work sixteen hours a
    day. Help.
America this is quite serious.
America this is the impression I get from looking in the television
    set.
America is this correct?
I'd better get right down to the job.
It's true I don't want to join the Army or turn lathes in precision
    parts factories, I'm nearsighted and psychopathic anyway.
America I'm putting my queer shoulder to the wheel. [34]

## SUNFLOWER SUTRA

I walked on the banks of the tincan banana dock and sat down
under the huge shade of a Southern Pacific locomotive to
look at the sunset over the box house hills and cry.

Jack Kerouac sat beside me on a busted rusty iron pole, companion, we thought the same thoughts of the soul, bleak
and blue and sad-eyed, surrounded by the gnarled steel
roots of trees of machinery.

The oily water on the river mirrored the red sky, sun sank on top
of final Frisco peaks, no fish in that stream, no hermit in
those mounts, just ourselves rheumy-eyed and hungover like
old bums on the riverbank, tired and wily.

Look at the Sunflower, he said, there was a dead gray shadow
against the sky, big as a man, sitting dry on top of a pile of
ancient sawdust—

—I rushed up enchanted—it was my first sunflower, memories of
Blake—my visions—Harlem

and Hells of the Eastern rivers, bridges clanking Joes Greasy
Sandwiches, dead baby carriages, black treadless tires forgotten and unretreaded, the poem of the riverbank, condoms
& pots, steel knives, nothing stainless, only the dank muck and
the razor sharp artifacts passing into the past—

and the gray Sunflower poised against the sunset, crackly bleak
and dusty with the smut and smog and smoke of olden locomotives in its eye—

corolla of bleary spikes pushed down and broken like a battered
crown, seeds fallen out of its face, soon-to-be-toothless mouth
of sunny air, sunrays obliterated on its hairy head like a
dried wire spiderweb,

leaves stuck out like arms out of the stem, gestures from the [28]
sawdust root, broke pieces of plaster fallen out of the black
twigs, a dead fly in its ear,

Unholy battered old thing you were, my sunflower O my soul, I
loved you then!

Reprinted from Allen Ginsberg, *"Howl"* and *Other Poems,* Pocket Poets
Series, No. 4 (San Francisco, Calif.: City Lights Books, 1959), pp. 28–30.
Copyright 1959 by Allen Ginsberg; reprinted by permission of City Lights
Books.

The grime was no man's grime but death and human locomotives,
all that dress of dust, that veil of darkened railroad skin, that
  smog of cheek, that eyelid of black mis'ry, that sooty hand
  or phallus or protuberance of artificial worse-than-dirt—
  industrial—modern—all that civilization spotting your crazy
  golden crown—
and those blear thoughts of death and dusty loveless eyes and
  ends and withered roots below, in the home-pile of sand and
  sawdust, rubber dollar bills, skin of machinery, the guts and
  innards of the weeping coughing car, the empty lonely tin-
  cans with their rusty tongues alack, what more could I name,
  the smoked ashes of some cock cigar, the cunts of wheel-
  barrows and the milky breasts of cars, wornout asses out of
  chairs & sphincters of dynamos—all these
entangled in your mummied roots—and you there standing before me in the sunset, all your glory in your form!
A perfect beauty of a sunflower! a perfect excellent lovely sunflower existence! a sweet natural eye to the new hip moon,
  woke up alive and excited grasping in the sunset shadow sunrise golden monthly breeze!
How many flies buzzed round you innocent of your grime, while
  you cursed the heavens of the railroad and your flower
  soul?
Poor dead flower? when did you forget you were a flower? when
  did you look at your skin and decide you were an impotent
  dirty old locomotive? the ghost of a locomotive? the specter
  and shade of a once powerful mad American locomotive?
  [29]
You were never no locomotive, Sunflower, you were a sunflower!
And you Locomotive, you are a locomotive, forget me not!
So I grabbed up the skeleton thick sunflower and stuck it at my
  side like a scepter,
and deliver my sermon to my soul, and Jack's soul too, and anyone who'll listen,
—We're not our skin of grime, we're not our dread bleak dusty
  imageless locomotive, we're all beautiful golden sunflowers
  inside, we're blessed by our own seed & golden hairy naked
  accomplishment-bodies growing into mad black formal sunflowers in the sunset, spied on by our eyes under the shadow
  of the mad locomotive riverbank sunset Frisco hilly tincan
  evening sitdown vision. [30]

*Berkeley 1955*

## KADDISH

Strange now to think of you, gone without corsets and eyes, while
    I walk on the sunny pavement of Greenwich Village
downtown Manhattan, clear winter noon, and I've been up all
    night, talking, talking, reading the Kaddish aloud, listening
    to Ray Charles blues shout blind on the phonograph
the rhythm the rhythm—and your memory in my head three
    years after—And read Adonais' last triumphant stanzas aloud
    —wept, realizing how we suffer—
And how Death is that remedy all singers dream of, sing, remem-
    ber, prophesy as in the Hebrew Anthem, or the Buddhist
    Book of Answers—and my own imagination of a withered
    leaf—at dawn—
Dreaming back thru life, Your time—and mine accelerating
    toward Apocalypse,
the final moment—flower burning in the Day—and what comes
    after,
looking back on the mind itself that saw an American city [19]
a flash away, and the great dream of Me or China, or you and a
    phantom Russia, or a crumpled bed that never existed—
like a poem in the dark—escaped back to Oblivion—
No more to say, and nothing to weep for but the Beings in the
    Dream, trapped in its disappearance,
sighing, screaming with it, buying and selling pieces of phantom,
    worshipping each other,
worshipping the God included in it all—longing or inevitabil-
    ity?—while it lasts, a Vision—anything more?
It leaps about me, as I go out and walk the street, look back over
    my shoulder, Seventh Avenue, the battlements of window
    office buildings shouldering each other high, under a cloud,
    tall as the sky an instant—and the sky above—an old blue
    place,
or down the Avenue to the South, to—as I walk toward the Lower

Part I originally appeared in Big Table # 2, Vol. 1 (Summer, 1959), pp.
19–23; parts II–IV in Big Table # 3, Vol. 1 ([Fall], 1959), pp. 7–10. Copyright 1960 by Allen Ginsberg, Kaddish: Poems 1957–60. Published by City
Lights Books.

East Side—where you walked fifty years ago, little girl—
from Russia, eating the first poisonous tomatoes of America—
frightened on the dock—
then struggling in the crowds of Orchard Street toward what?—
toward Newark—
toward candy store, first home-made sodas of the century, hand-
churned ice cream in backroom on musty brownfloor
boards—
Toward education marriage nervous breakdown, operation, teaching school, and learning to be mad, in a dream—What is
this life?
Toward the Key in the window—and the great Key lays its head
of light on top of Manhattan, and over the floor, and lays
down on the sidewalk—in a single vast beam, moving—as I
walk down First toward the Yiddish Theater—and the place
of poverty
you knew, and I know, but without caring now—Strange to have
moved thru Paterson, and the West, and Europe and here
again,
with the cries of Spaniards now in the doorstoops doors and
dark boys on the street, fire escapes old as you [20]
—Though you're not old now, that's left here with me—
Myself, anyhow, maybe as old as the universe—and I guess that
dies with us—enough to cancel all that comes—What came
is gone forever every time—
That's good! That leaves it open for no regret—no fear radiators,
lacklove, torture even toothache in the end—
Though while it comes it is a lion that eats the soul—and the
lamb, the soul, in us, alas, offering itself in sacrifice to
change's fierce hunger—hair and teeth—and the roar of
bonepain, skull bare, break rib, rot skin, braintricked Im-
placability.
Ai! ai! we do worse! We are in a fix! And you're out, Death let
you out, Death had the Mercy, you're done with your century, done with God, done with the path thru it—Done
with yourself at last—Pure—Back to the Babe dark before
your Father, before us all—before the world—
There, rest. No more suffering for you. I know where you've
gone, it's good.
No more flowers in the summer fields of New York, no joy now,
no more fear of Louis,
and no more of his sweetness and glasses, his high school decades,

debts, loves, frightened telephone calls, conception beds, relatives, hands—

No more of sister Elanor—she gone before you—we kept it secret—you killed her, or she killed herself to bear with you—an arthritic heart—But Death's killed you both—No matter—

Nor your memory of your mother, 1915 tears in silent movies weeks and weeks—forgetting, agrieve watching Marie Dressler address humanity, Chaplin dance in youth,

or Boris Gudinov, Chaliapin's at the Met, hauling his voice of a weeping Czar—by standing room with Elanor and Max— watching also the Capitalists take seats in Orchestra, white furs, diamonds,

with the YPSL's hitch-hiking thru Pennsylvania, in black baggy gym skirt pants, photograph of four girls holding each [21] other round the waist, and laughing eye, too coy, virginal solitude of 1920

all girls grown old, or dead, now, and that long hair in the grave —lucky to have husbands later—

You made it—I came too—Eugene my brother before (still grieving now and will dream on to his last stiff hand, as he goes thru his cancer—or kill—later perhaps—soon he will think—)

And it's the last moment I remember, when I see them all, thru myself, now—though not you

I didn't foresee what you felt—what more hideous gape of bad mouth came first—to you—and were you prepared?

To go where? In that Dark—that—in that God? a radiance? A Lord in the Void? Like an eye in the black cloud in a dream? Adonoi at last, with you?

Beyond my remembrance! Incapable to guess! Not merely the yellow skull in the grave, or a box of worm dust, and a stained ribbon—Deathshead with Halo? can you believe it?

Is it only the sun that shines once for the mind, only the flash of existence, that none ever was?

Nothing beyond what we have—what you had—that so pitiful— yet Triumph,

to have been here, and changed, like a tree, broken, or flower— fed to the ground—but mad, with its petals, colored, thinking Great Universe, shaken, cut in the head, leaf stript, hid in an egg crate hospital, cloth wrapped, sore—freaked in the moon brain, Naughtless.

No flower like that flower, which knew itself in the garden, and fought the knife—lost

Cut down by an idiot Snowman's icy—even in the Spring—strange
ghost thought—some Death—Sharp icicle in his hand—
crowned with old roses—a dog for his eyes—cock of a sweatshop—heart of electric irons.

All the accumulations of life, that wear us out—clocks, bodies,
consciousness, shoes, breasts—begotten sons—your Com-
munism—"Paranoia" into hospitals. [22]

You once kicked Elanor in the leg, she died of heart failure later.
You of stroke. Asleep? Within a year, the two of you, sisters
in death. Is Elanor happy?

Max grieves alive in an office on Lower Broadway, lone large
mustache over midnight Accountings, not sure. His life
passes—as he sees—and what does he doubt now? Still
dream of making money, or that might have made money,
hired nurse, had children, found even your Immortality,
Naomi?

I'll see him soon. Now I've got to cut through—to talk to you—
as I didn't when you had a mouth.

Forever. And we're bound for that, Forever—like Emily Dickin-
son's horses—headed to the End.

They know the way—These Steeds—run faster than we think—
it's our own life they cross—and take with them.

Magnificent, mourned no more, marred of heart, mind behind,
married dreamed, mortal changed—Ass and face done with
murder.

In the world, given, flower maddened, made no Utopia, shut
under pine, almed in Earth, balmed in Lone, Jehovah, accept.

Nameless, One Faced, Forever, beyond me, beginningless, endless, Father in death. Though I am not there for this Prophecy, I am unmarried, I'm hymnless, I'm Heavenless, headless in
blisshood I would still adore

Thee, Heaven, after Death, only One blessed in Nothingness,
not light or darkness, Dayless Eternity—

Take this, this Psalm, from me, burst from my hand in a day,
some of my Time, now given to Nothing—to praise Thee—

But Death

This is the end, the redemption from Wilderness, way for the
Wonderer, House sought for All, black handkerchief washed
clean by weeping—page beyond Psalm—Last chance of mine
and Naomi—to God's perfect Darkness—Death, stay thy phan-
toms! [23]

## II

Only to have not forgotten the beginning in which she drank
   cheap sodas in the morgues of Newark,
only to have seen her weeping on grey tables in long wards of her
   universe
only to have known the weird ideas of Hitler at the door, the
   wires in her head, the three big sticks
rammed down her back, the voices in the ceiling shrieking out
   her ugly early lays for 30 years,
only to have seen the time-jumps, memory lapse, the crash of
   wars, the roar and silence of a vast electric shock,
only to have seen her painting crude pictures of Elevateds running over the rooftops of the Bronx
her brothers dead in Riverside or Russia, her lone in Long Island
   writing a last letter—and her image in the sunlight at the
   window [7]
"The key is in the sunlight at the window in the bars the key
   is in the sunlight,"
only to have come to that dark night on iron bed by stroke when
   the sun gone down on Long Island
and the vast Atlantic outside roars the great call of Being to its
   own
to come back out of the Nightmare—divided creation—with her
   head lain on a pillow of the hospital to die
—in one last glimpse—all Earth one everlasting Light in the
   familiar blackout—no tears for this vision—
But that the key should be left behind—at the window—the key
   in the sunlight—to the living—that can take
that slice of light in hand—and turn the door—and look back see
Creation glistening backwards to the same grave, size of universe,
size of the tick of the hospital's clock on the archway over the
   white door—


## III

O mother
what have I left out
O mother
what have I forgotten
O mother
farewell

with a long black shoe
farewell
with old dress and broken stocking
farewell
with six dark hairs on the wen of your breast
farewell
with six vaginas and a long black beard around the vagina [8]
with your sagging belly
with your fear of Hitler
with your mouth of bad short stories
with your fingers of rotten mandolines
with your arms of fat Paterson porches
with your belly of strikes and smokestacks
with your chin of Trotsky and the Spanish War
with your voice singing for the decaying overbroken workers
with your nose of bad lay with your nose of the smell of the
    pickles of Newark
with your eyes
with your eyes of Russia
with your eyes of no money
with your eyes of false China
with your eyes of Aunt Elanor
with your eyes of starving India
with your eyes pissing in the park
with your eyes of your failure at the piano
with your eyes of your relatives in California
with your eyes of Ma Rainey dying in an ambulance
with your eyes of Czechoslovakia attacked by robots
with your eyes going to painting class at night in the Bronx
with your eyes of the killer Grandma you see on the fire-escape
with your eyes running naked out of the apartment screaming
    into the hall
with your eyes being led away by policemen to an ambulance
with your eyes strapped down on the operating table
with your eyes with the pancreas removed
with your eyes of appendix operation
with your eyes of abortion
with your eyes of ovaries removed
with your eyes of shock [9]
with your eyes of lobotomy
with your eyes of divorce
with your eyes of stroke

with your eyes alone
with your eyes
with your eyes
with your death full of flowers


*IV*

Caw caw caw crows shriek in the white sun over grave stones in
Long Island
Lord Lord Lord Naomi underneath this grass my halflife and
my own as hers
caw caw my eye be buried in the same ground where I stand
in Angel
Lord Lord great Eye that stares on All and moves in a black
cloud
caw caw strange cry of Beings flung up into sky over the waving
trees
Lord Lord O Grinder of giant Beyonds my voice in a boundless
field is Sheol
caw caw the call of Time rent out of foot and wing an instant in
the universe
Lord Lord an echo in the sky the wind through ragged leaves the
roar of memory
caw caw all years my birth a dream caw caw New York the bus
the broken shoe that vast highschool caw caw all Visions of
the Lord
Lord Lord Lord caw caw caw Lord Lord Lord caw caw caw
Lord. [10]


## POETRY, VIOLENCE, AND THE TREMBLING LAMBS


Recent history is the record of a vast conspiracy to impose one
level of mechanical consciousness on mankind and exterminate
all manifestations of that unique part of human sentience, identical in all men, which the individual shares with his Creator. The

Reprinted from *The Village Voice*, Vol. IV, No. 44 (Wednesday, August 25,
1959), pp. 1, 8. First printed in the San Francisco *Chronicle, This World*
section, July 26, 1959. Reprinted by permission of Allen Ginsberg.

suppression of contemplative individuality is nearly complete.

The only immediate historical data that we can know and act on are those fed to our senses through systems of mass communication.

These media are exactly the places where the deepest and most personal sensitivities and confessions of reality are most prohibited, mocked, suppressed.

### National Subconscious

At the same time there is a crack in the mass consciousness of America—sudden emergence of insight into a vast national subconscious netherworld filled with nerve gases, universal death bombs, malevolent bureaucracies, secret police systems, drugs that open the door to God, ships leaving Earth, unknown chemical terrors, evil dreams at hand.

Because systems of mass communication can communicate only officially acceptable levels of reality, no one can know the extent of the secret unconscious life. No one in America can know what will happen. No one is in real control. America is having a nervous breakdown.

Poetry is the record of individual insights into the secret soul of the individual—and, because all individuals are One in the eyes of their Creator, into the soul of the World. The world has a soul.

### Some Insight

America is having a nervous breakdown. San Francisco is one of many places where a few individuals, poets, have had the luck and courage and fate to glimpse something new through the crack in mass consciousness; they have been exposed to some insight into their own nature, the nature of God.

Therefore there has been great exaltation, despair, prophecy, strain, suicide, secrecy, and public gaiety among the poets of the city.

Those of the general populace whose individual perception is sufficiently weak to be formed by [1] stereotypes of mass communication disapprove and deny the insight. The police and newspapers have moved in, mad movie manufacturers from Hollywood are at this moment preparing bestial stereotypes of the scene.

The poets and those who share their activities, or exhibit some sign of dress, hair, or demeanor of understanding, or hipness, are ridiculed. Those of us who have used certain benevolent drugs (marijuana) to alter our consciousness in order to gain insight are hunted down in the street by police. Peyote, an historic vision-producing agent, is prohibited on pain of arrest. Those who have used opiates and junk are threatened with permanent jail and death. To be a junky in America is like having been a Jew in Nazi Germany.

A huge sadistic police bureaucracy has risen in every state, encouraged by the central government, to persecute the illuminati, to brainwash the public with official lies about the drugs, and to terrify and destroy those addicts whose spiritual search has made them sick.

Deviants from the mass sexual stereotype, quietists, those who will not work for money, or fib and make arms for hire, or join armies in murder and threat, those who wish to loaf, think, rest in visions, act beautifully on their own, speak truthfully in public, inspired by Democracy—what is their psychic fate now in America? An America, the greater portion of whose economy is yoked to mental and mechanical preparations for war?

Literature expressing these insights has been mocked, misinterpreted, and suppressed by a horde of middlemen whose fearful allegiance to the organization of mass stereotype communication prevents them from sympathy (not only with their own inner nature but) with any manifestation of unconditioned individuality. I mean journalists, commercial publishers, book-review fellows, multitudes of professors of literature, etc., etc. Poetry is hated. Whole schools of academic criticism have risen to prove that human consciousness of unconditioned Spirit is a myth. A poetic renaissance glimpsed in San Francisco has been responded to with ugliness, anger, jealousy, vitriol, sullen protestations of superiority.

And violence. By police, by customs officials, post-office employees, by trustees of great universities. By anyone whose love of Power has led him to a position where he can push other people around over a difference of opinion—or Vision.

### Great Stakes

The stakes are too great—an America gone mad with materialism, a police-state America, a sexless and soulless America prepared to battle the world in defense of a false image of its

Authority. Not the wild and beautiful America of the comrades of Whitman, not the historic America of Blake and Thoreau where the spiritual independence of each individual was an America, a universe, more huge and awesome than all the abstract bureaucracies and Authoritative Officialdoms of the World combined.

Only those who have entered the world of Spirit know what a vast laugh there is in the illusory appearance of worldly authority. And all men at one time or other enter that Spirit, whether in life or death.

### Trembling Lambs

How many hypocrites are there in America? How many trembling lambs, fearful of discovery? What Authority have we set up over ourselves, that we are not as we Are? Who shall prohibit an art from being published to the world? What conspirators have power to determine our mode of consciousness, our sexual enjoyments, our different labors and our loves? What fiends determine our wars?

When will we discover an America that will not deny its own God? Who takes up arms, money, police, and a million hands to murder the consciousness of God? Who spits in the beautiful face of Poetry which sings of the Glory of God and weeps in the dust of the world? [8]

## NOTES WRITTEN ON FINALLY RECORDING "HOWL"

By 1955 I wrote poetry adapted from prose seeds, journals, scratchings, arranged by phrasing or breath groups into little short-line patterns according to ideas of measure of American speech I'd picked up from W. C. Williams' imagist preoccupations. I suddenly turned aside in San Francisco, unemployment compensation leisure, to follow my romantic inspiration—Hebraic-Melvillean bardic breath. I thought I wouldn't write a *poem*, but just write what I wanted to without fear, let my imagination go, open secrecy, and scribble magic lines from my real

Reprinted from Fantasy, Spoken Word Series, 7006. Copyright 1959 by Fantasy Records, Inc. Reprinted by permission of the author.

mind—sum up my life—something I wouldn't be able to show anybody, writ for my own soul's ear and a few other golden ears. So the first line of *Howl*, "I saw the best minds etc.," the whole first section typed out madly in one afternoon, a tragic custard-pie comedy of wild phrasing, meaningless images for the beauty of abstract poetry of mind running along making awkward combinations like Charlie Chaplin's walk, long saxophone-like chorus lines I knew Kerouac would hear *sound* of—taking off from his own inspired prose line really a new poetry.

I depended on the "who" to keep the beat, a base to keep measure, return to and take off from again onto another streak of invention: "who lit cigarettes in boxcars boxcars boxcars," continuing to prophesy what I really knew despite the drear consciousness of the world: "who were visionary indian angels." Have I really been attacked for this sort of joy? So the poem got awesome, I went on to what my imagination believed true to Eternity (for I'd had a beatific illumination years before during which I'd heard Blake's ancient voice and saw the universe unfold in my brain), & what my memory could reconstitute of the data of celestial experiences.

But how sustain a long line in poetry (lest it lapse into prosaic)? It's natural inspiration of the moment that keeps it moving, disparate thinks put down together, shorthand notations of visual imagery, juxtapositions of hydrogen jukebox—abstract *haikus* sustain the mystery & put iron poetry back into the line: the last line of *Sunflower Sutra* is the extreme, one stream of single word associations, summing up. Mind is shapely, Art is shapely. Meaning Mind practiced in spontaneity invents forms in its own image and gets to Last Thoughts. Loose ghosts wailing for body try to invade the bodies of living men. I hear ghostly Academies in Limbo screeching about Form.

Ideally each line of *Howl* is a single breath unit. My breath is long—that's the Measure, one physical-mental inspiration of thought contained in the elastic of a breath. It probably bugs Williams now, but it's a natural consequence, my own heightened conversation, not cooler average-daily-talk short breath. I get to mouth more madly this way.

So these poems are a series of experiments with the formal organization of the long line. Explanations follow. I realized at the time that Whitman's form had rarely been further explored (improved on even) in the U.S.—Whitman always a mountain too vast to be seen. Everybody assumes (with Pound?) (except Jeffers) that his line is a big freakish uncontrollable necessary prosaic goof. No attempt's been made to use it in the light of early XX Century organization of new speech-rhythm prosody to *build up* large organic structures.

I had an apartment on Nob Hill, got high on Peyote, & saw an image of the robot skullface of Moloch in the upper stories of a big hotel glaring into my window; got high weeks later again, the Visage was still there in red smokey downtown Metropolis, I wandered down Powell street muttering, "Moloch Moloch" all night and wrote *Howl* II nearly intact in cafeteria at foot of Drake Hotel, deep in the hellish vale. Here the long line is used as a stanza form broken into exclamatory units punctuated by a base repetition, Moloch.

The rhythmic paradigm for Part III was conceived and half-written same day as the beginning of *Howl*, I went back later and filled it out. Part I, a lament for the Lamb in America with instances of remarkable lamblike youths; Part II names the monster of mental consciousness that preys on the Lamb; Part III a litany of affirmation of the Lamb in its glory: "O starry-spangled shock of Mercy." The structure of Part III, pyramidal, with a graduated longer response to the fixed base.

I remembered the archetypal rhythm of Holy Holy Holy weeping in a bus on Kearny Street, & wrote most of it down in notebook there. That exhausted this set of experiments with a fixed base. I set it as *Footnote to Howl* because it was an extra variation of the form of Part II. (Several variations on these forms, including stanzas of graduated litanies followed by fugues, will be seen in *Kaddish*.)

A lot of these forms developed out of an extreme rhapsodic wail I once heard in a madhouse. Later I wondered if short quiet lyrical poems could be written using the long line. *Cottage in Berkeley* & *Supermarket in California* (written same day) fell in place later that year. Not purposely, I simply followed my Angel in the course of compositions.

What if I just simply wrote, in long units and broken short lines, spontaneously noting prosaic realities mixed with emotional upsurges, solitaries? *Transcription of Organ Music* (sensual data), strange writing which passes from prose to poetry & back, like the mind.

What about poem with rhythmic buildup power equal to *Howl* without use of repetitive base to sustain it? *The Sunflower Sutra* (composition time 20 minutes, me at desk scribbling, Kerouac at cottage door waiting for me to finish so we could go off somewhere party) did that, it surprised me, one long Who.

Next what happens if you mix long and short lines, single breath remaining the rule of measure? I didn't trust free flight yet, so went back to fixed base to sustain the flow, *America*. After that, a regular formal type long poem in parts, short and long breaths mixed at random, no fixed base, sum of earlier experiments—*Baggage Room at Greyhound*. *In Back of the Real* shows what I was doing with short lines (see sentence 1 above) before I accidentally wrote *Howl*.

Later I tried for a strong rhythm built up using free short syncopated lines, *Europe! Europe!* a phophecy written in Paris (*Kaddish*, City Lights, 1960).

Last, the Proem to *Kaddish* (NY 1959 work)—finally, completely free composition, the long line breaking up within itself into short staccato breath units—notations of one spontaneous phrase after another linked within the line by dashes mostly: the long line now perhaps a variable stanzaic unit, measuring groups of related ideas, grouping them—a method of notation. Ending with a hymn in rhythm similar to the synagogue death lament. Passing into dactylic? says Williams? Perhaps not: at least the ear hears itself in Promethean natural measure, not in mechanical count of accent.

All these poems are recorded now as best I can, tho with scared love, imperfect to an angelic trumpet in mind. I have quit reading in front of live audiences for a while. I began in obscurity to communicate a live poetry, it's become more a trap & duty than the spontaneous ball it was first.

A word on the Academies: poetry has been attacked by an ignorant and frightened bunch of bores who don't understand how it's made, & the trouble with these creeps is they wouldn't know poetry if it came up and buggered them in broad daylight.

A word on the Politicians: my poetry is Angelical Ravings, and has nothing to do with dull materialistic vagaries about who should shoot who. The secrets of individual imagination—which are transconceptual & non-verbal—I mean Unconditioned Spirit —are not for sale to this consciousness, are no use to this world, except perhaps to make it shut its trap & listen to the music of the Spheres. Who denies the music of the spheres denies poetry, denies man, & spits on Blake, Shelley, Christ, & Buddha. Meanwhile have a ball. The Universe is a new flower. America will be discovered. Who wants a war against roses will have it. Fate tells big lies, and the gay Creator dances on his own body in Eternity.

# JACK KEROUAC

## OCTOBER IN THE RAILROAD EARTH

There was a little alley in San Francisco back of the Southern
Pacific station at Third and Townsend in redbrick of drowsy
lazy afternoons with everybody at work in offices in the air you
feel the impending rush of their commuter frenzy as soon they'll
be charging en masse from Market and Sansome buildings on
foot and in buses and all well-dressed thru workingman Frisco
of Walkup ?? truck drivers and even the poor grime-bemarked
Third Street of lost bums even Negroes so hopeless and long left
East and meanings of responsibility and *try* that now all they do
is stand there spitting in the broken glass sometimes fifty in one
afternoon against one wall at Third and Howard and here's all
these Millbrae and San Carlos neat-necktied producers and commuters of America and Steel civilization rushing by with San
Francisco *Chronicles* and green *Call-Bulletins* not even enough
time to be disdainful, they've got to catch 130, 132, 134, 136 all
the way up to 146 till the time of evening supper in homes of
the railroad earth when high in the sky the magic stars ride above
the following hotshot freight trains—it's all in California, it's all a
sea, I swim out of it in afternoons of sun hot meditation in my
jeans with head on handkerchief on brakeman's lantern or (if
not working) on book, I look up at blue sky of perfect lostpurity
and feel the warp of wood of old America beneath me and have
insane conversations with Negroes in several-story windows above
and everything is pouring in, the switching moves of boxcars in
that little alley which is so much like the alleys of Lowell and I
hear far off in the sense of coming night that engine calling our
mountains.

But it was that beautiful cut of clouds I could always see above
the little S.P. alley, puffs floating by from Oakland [119] or the
Gate of Marin to the north or San Jose south, the clarity of Cal

to break your heart. It was the fantastic drowse and drum hum of lum mum afternoon nathin' to do, ole Frisco with end of land sadness—the people—the alley full of trucks and cars of businesses nearabouts and nobody knew or far from cared who I was all my life three thousand five hundred miles from birth-O opened up and at last belonged to me in Great America.

Now it's night in Third Street the keen little neons and also yellow bulblights of impossible-to-believe flops with dark ruined shadows moving back of torn yellow shades like a degenerate China with no money—the cats in Annie's Alley, the flop comes on, moans, rolls, the street is loaded with darkness. Blue sky above with stars hanging high over old hotel roofs and blowers of hotels moaning out dusts of interior, the grime inside the word in mouths falling out tooth by tooth, the reading rooms tick tock bigclock with creak chair and slantboards and old faces looking up over rimless spectacles bought in some West Virginia or Florida or Liverpool England pawnshop long before I was born and across rains they've come to the end of the land sadness end of the world gladness all you San Franciscos will have to fall eventually and burn again. But I'm walking and one night a bum fell into the hole of the construction job where they're tearing a sewer by day the husky Pacific & Electric youths in torn jeans who work there often I think of going up to some of 'em like say blond ones with wild hair and torn shirts and say "You oughta apply for the railroad it's much easier work you don't stand around the street all day and you get much more pay" but this bum fell in the hole you saw his foot stick out, a British MG also driven by some eccentric once backed into the hole and as I came home from a long Saturday afternoon local to Hollister out of San Jose miles away across verdurous fields of prune and juice joy here's this British MG backed and legs up wheels up into a pit and bums and cops [120] standing around right outside the coffee shop—it was the way they fenced it but he never had the nerve to do it due to the fact that he had no money and nowhere to go and O his father was dead and O his mother was dead and O his sister was dead and O his whereabout was dead was dead—but and then at that time also I lay in my room on long Saturday afternoons listening to Jumpin' George with my fifth of tokay no tea and just under the sheets laughed to hear the crazy music "Mama, he treats your daughter mean," Mama, Papa, and don't you come in here I'll kill you etc. getting high by myself in room glooms and all wondrous knowing about the

Negro the essential American out there always finding his solace his meaning in the fellaheen street and not in abstract morality and even when he has a church you see the pastor out front bowing to the ladies on the make you hear his great vibrant voice on the sunny Sunday afternoon sidewalk full of sexual vibratos saying "Why yes Mam but de gospel do say that man was born of woman's womb—" and no and so by that time I come crawling out of my warmsack and hit the street when I see the railroad ain't gonna call me till 5 AM Sunday morn probably for a local out of Bay Shore in fact always for a local out of Bay Shore and I go to the wailbar of all the wildbars in the world the one and only Third-and-Howard and there I go in and drink with the madmen and if I get drunk I git.

The whore who come up to me in there the night I was there with Al Buckle and said to me "You wanta play with me tonight Jim, and?" and I didn't think I had enough money and later told this to Charley Low and he laughed and said "How do you know she wanted money always take the chance that she might be out just for love or just out for love you know what I mean man don't be a sucker." She was a good-looking doll and said "How would you like to oolyakoo with me mon?" and I stood there like a jerk and in fact bought drink got drink drunk that night and in the 299 Club I was [121] hit by the proprietor the band breaking up the fight before I had a chance to decide to hit him back which I didn't do and out on the street I tried to rush back in but they had locked the door and were looking at me thru the forbidden glass in the door with faces like undersea —I should have played with her shurrouruuruuruuruuruuruurk-diei.

Despite the fact I was a brakeman making 600 a month I kept going to the Public restaurant on Howard Street which was three eggs for 26 cents 2 eggs for 21 this with toast (hardly no butter) coffee (hardly no coffee and sugar rationed) oatmeal with dash of milk and sugar the smell of soured old shirts lingering above the cookpot steams as if they were making skidrow lumberjack stews out of San Francisco ancient Chinese mildewed laundries with poker games in the back among the barrels and the rats of the earthquake days, but actually the food somewhat on the level of an old-time 1890 or 1910 section-gang cook of lumber camps far in the North with an oldtime pigtail Chinaman cooking it and cussing out those who didn't like it. The prices were in-

credible but one time I had the beefstew and it was absolutely
the worst beefstew I ever et, it was incredible I tell you—and as
they often did that to me it was with the most intensest regret
that I tried to convey to the geek back of counter what I wanted
but he was a tough sonofabitch, ech, ti-ti, I thought the counterman was kind of queer especially he handled gruffly the hopeless
drooldrunks, "What now you doing you think you can come in
here and cut like that for God's sake act like a man won't you
and eat or get out-t-t-t-"—I always did wonder what a guy like
that was doing working in a place like that because, but why
some sympathy in his horny heart for the busted wrecks, all
up and down the street were restaurants like the Public catering
exclusively to bums of the black, winos with no money, who
found 21 cents left over from wine panhandlings and so stumbled
in for their [122] third or fourth touch of food in a week, as
sometimes they didn't eat at all and so you'd see them in the
corner puking white liquid which was a couple quarts of rancid
sauterne rotgut or sweet white sherry and they had nothing on
their stomachs, most of them had one leg or were on crutches
and had bandages around their feet, from nicotine and alcohol
poisoning together, and one time finally on my way up Third
near Market across the street from Breens, when in early 1952
I lived on Russian Hill and didn't quite dig the complete horror
and humor of railroad's Third Street, a bum a thin sickly little-
bum like Anton Abraham lay face down on the pavement with
crutch aside and some old remnant newspaper sticking out and
it seemed to me he was dead. I looked closely to see if he was
breathing and he was not, another man with me was looking
down and we agreed he was dead, and soon a cop came over
and took and agreed and called the wagon, the little wretch
weighed about 50 pounds in his bleeding count and was stone
mackerel snotnose cold dead as a bleeding doornail—ah I tell
you—and who could notice but other half dead deadbums bums
bums bums dead dead times X times X times all dead bums forever dead with nothing and all finished and out—there—and
this was the clientele in the Public Hair restaurant where I ate
many's the morn a 3-egg breakfast with almost dry toast and
oatmeal a little saucer of, and thin sickly dishwater coffee, all to
save 14 cents so in my little book proudly I could make a notation and of the day and prove that I could live comfortably in
America while working seven days a week and earning 600 a
month I could live on less than 17 a week which with my rent of

4.20 was okay as I had also to spend money to eat and sleep sometimes on the other end of my Watsonville chaingang run but preferred most times to sleep free of charge and uncomfortable in cabooses of the crummy rack—my 26-cent breakfast, my pride—and that incredible semiqueer counterman who dished out the food, threw it at you, [123] slammed it, had a languid frank expression straight in your eyes like a 1930's lunchcart heroine in Steinbeck and at the steamtable itself labored coolly a junkey-looking Chinese with an actual stocking in his hair as if they'd just Shanghai'd him off the foot of Commercial Street before the Ferry Building was up but forgot it was 1952, dreamed it was 1860 goldrush Frisco—and on rainy days you felt they had ships in the back room.

I'd take walks up Harrison and the boomcrash of truck traffic towards the glorious girders of the Oakland Bay Bridge that you could see after climbing Harrison Hill a little like radar machine of eternity in the sky, huge, in the blue, by pure clouds crossed, gulls, idiot cars streaking to destinations on its undinal boom across shmoshwaters flocked up by winds and news of San Rafael storms and flash boats—there O I always came and walked and negotiated whole Friscos in one afternoon from the overlooking hills of the high Fillmore where Orient-bound vessels you can see on drowsy Sunday mornings of poolhall goof like after a whole night playing drums in a jam session and a morn in the hall of cuesticks I went by the rich homes of old ladies supported by daughters or female secretaries with immense ugly gargoyle Frisco millions fronts of other days and way below is the blue passage of the Gate, the Alcatraz mad rock, the mouths of Tamalpais, San Pablo Bay, Sausalito sleepy hemming the rock and bush over yonder, and the sweet white ships cleanly cutting a path to Sasebo.—Over Harrison and down to the Embarcadero and around Telegraph Hill and up the back of Russian Hill and down to the play streets of Chinatown and down Kearney back across Market to Third and my wild-night neon twinkle fate there, ah, and then finally at dawn of a Sunday and they did call me, the immense girders of Oakland Bay still haunting me and all that eternity too much to swallow and not knowing who I am at [124] all but like a big plump longhaired baby worwalking up in the dark trying to wonder who I am the door knocks and it's the desk keeper of the flop hotel with silver rims and white hair and clean clothes and sickly potbelly said he was from Rocky Mount and looked like yes, he had been desk clerk of the Nash Buncome Association hotel down there in 50 successive heatwave summers without the sun and only palmos of the lobby with cigar crutches in the albums of the South and him with his dear mother waiting in a buried log cabin of graves with all that mashed past historied underground afoot with the stain of the bear the blood of the tree and cornfields long plowed under and Negroes whose voices long faded from the middle of the wood and the dog barked his last, this man had voyageured to the West Coast too like all the other loose American elements and was pale and sixty and complaining of sickness, might at one time been a handsome squire to women with money but now a forgotten clerk and maybe spent a little time in jail for a few forgeries or harmless cons and might also have been a railroad clerk and might have wept and might have never made it, and that day I'd say he saw the bridgegirders up over the hill of traffic of Harrison like me and woke up mornings with same lost, is now beckoning on my door and breaking in the world on me and he is standing on the frayed carpet of the hall all worn down by black steps of sunken old men for last 40 years since earthquake and the toilet stained, beyond the last toilet bowl and the last stink and stain I guess yes is the end of the world the bloody end of the world, so now knocks on my door and I wake up, saying "How what howp howelk howel of the knavery they've meaking, ek and won't let me slepit? Whey they dool? Whand out wisis thing that comes flarminging around my dooring in the mouth of the night and there everything knows that I have no mother, and no sister, and no father and no bot sosstle, but not crib" I got up and sit up and says "Howowow?" and he says [125] "Telephone?" and I have to put on my jeans heavy with knife, wallet, I look closely at my railroad watch hanging on little door flicker of closet door face to me ticking silent the time, it says 4:30 AM of a Sunday morn, I go down the carpet of the skidrow hall in jeans and with no shirt and yes with shirt tails hanging gray workshirt and pick up phone and ticky sleepy night desk with cage and spittoons and keys hanging and old towels piled clean ones but frayed at edges and bearing names of every hotel of the moving prime, on the phone is the Crew Clerk, "Kerroway?" "Yeah." "Kerroway it's gonna be the Sherman Local at 7 AM this morning." "Sherman Local right." "Out of Bay Shore, you know the way?" "Yeah." "You had that same job last Sunday— Okay Kerroway-y-y-y-y." And we mutually hang up and I say to myself okay it's the Bay Shore bloody old dirty hagglous old coveted old madman Sherman who hates me so much especially when we were at Redwood Junction kicking boxcars and he always insists I work the rear end tho as one-year man it would be easier for me to follow pot but I work rear and he wants me to be right there with a block of wood when a car or cut of cars kicked stops, so they won't roll down that incline and start catastrophes, O well anyway I'll be learning eventually to like the railroad and Sherman will like me some day, and anyway another day another dollar.

And there's my room, small, gray in the Sunday morning, now all the franticness of the street and night before is done with, bums sleep, maybe one or two sprawled on sidewalk with empty poorboy on a sill—my mind whirls with life.

So there I am in dawn in my dim cell—2½ hours to go till the time I have to stick my railroad watch in my jean watchpocket and cut out allowing myself exactly 8 minutes to the station and the 7:15 train No. 112 I have to catch for the ride five miles to Bay Shore through four tunnels, emerging from the sad Rath scene of Frisco gloom gleak in the rainymouth fogmorning to a sudden valley with grim [126] hills rising to the sea, bay on left, the fog rolling in like demented in the draws that have little white cottages disposed real-estatically for come-Christmas blue sad lights—my whole soul and concomitant eyes looking out on this reality of living and working in San Francisco with that pleased semi-loin-located shudder, energy for sex changing to pain at the portals of work and culture and natural foggy fear.—There I am in my little room wondering how I'll really manage to fool myself into feeling that these next 2½ hours will be well filled, fed, with work and pleasure thoughts.—It's so thrilling to feel the coldness of the morning wrap around my thickquilt blankets as I lay there, watch facing and ticking me, legs spread in comfy skidrow soft sheets with soft tears or sew lines in 'em, huddled in my own skin and rich and not spending a cent on—I look at my littlebook—and I stare at the words of the Bible.—On the floor I find last red afternoon Saturday's *Chronicle* sports page with news of football games in Great America the end of which I bleakly see in the gray light entering—the fact that Frisco is built of wood satisfies me in my peace, I know nobody'll disturb me for 2½ hours and all bums are asleep in their own bed of eternity awake or not, bottle or not—it's the joy I feel that counts for me.—On the floor's my shoes, big lumberboot flopjack work-shoes to colomp over rockbed with and not turn the ankle—solidity shoes that when you put them on, yokewise, you know you're working now and so for same reason shoes not be worn for any reason like joys of restaurant and shows.—Night-before shoes are on the floor beside the Clunkershoes a pair of blue canvas shoes à la 1952 style, in them I'd trod soft as ghost the indented hill sidewalks of Ah Me Frisco all in the glitter night, from the top of Russian Hill I'd looked down at one point on all roofs of North Beach and the Mexican night-club neons, I'd descended to them on the old steps of Broadway under which they were newly laboring a mountain [127] tunnel—shoes fit for watersides, embarcaderos, hill and plot lawns of park and tiptop vista.—Workshoes covered with dust and some oil of engines—the crumpled jeans nearby, belt, blue railroad hank, knife, comb, keys, switch keys and caboose coach key, the knees white from Pajaro Riverbottom finedusts, the ass black from slick sandboxes in yardgoat after yardgoat—the gray workshorts, the dirty undershirt, sad shorts, tortured socks of my life.—And the Bible on my desk next to the peanut butter, the lettuce, the raisin bread, the crack in the plaster, the stiff-with-old-dust lace drape now no longer laceable but hard as—after all those years of hard dust eternity in that Cameo skid inn with red eyes of rheumy oldmen dying there staring without hope out on the dead wall you can hardly see thru windowdusts and all you heard lately in the shaft of the rooftop middle way was the cries of a Chinese child whose father and mother were always telling him to shush and then screaming at him, he was a pest and his tears from China were most persistent and worldwide and represented all our feelings in brokendown Cameo tho this was not admitted by bum one except for an occasional harsh clearing of throat in the halls or moan of nightmarer—by things like this and neglect of a hard-eyed alcoholic oldtime chorusgirl maid the curtains had now absorbed all the iron they could take and hung stiff and even the dust in them was iron, if you shook them they'd crack and fall in tatters to the floor and spatter like wings of iron on the bong and the dust would fly into your nose like filings of steel and choke you to death, so I never touched them. My little room at 6 in the comfy dawn (at 4:30) and before me all that time, that fresh-eyed time for a little coffee to boil water on my hot plate, throw some coffee in, stir it, French style, slowly carefully pour it in my white tin cup, throw sugar in (not California beet sugar like I should have been using but New Orleans cane sugar, because beet racks I carried from Oakland out to Watsonville many's the time, [128] a 80-car freight train with nothing but gondolas loaded with sad beets looking like the heads of decapitated women)—ah me how but it was a hell and now I had the whole thing to myself, and make my raisin toast by sitting it on a little wire I'd especially bent to place over the hotplate, the toast crackled up, there, I spread the margarine on the still red hot toast and it too would crackle and sink in golden, among burnt raisins and this was my toast—then two eggs gently slowly fried in soft margarine in my little skidrow frying pan about half as thick as a dime in fact less a little piece of tiny tin you could bring on a camp trip—the eggs slowly fluffed in there and swelled from butter steams and I threw garlic salt on them, and when they were ready the yellow of them had been slightly filmed with a cooked white at the top from the tin cover I'd put over the frying pan, so now they were ready, and out they came, I spread them out on top of my already prepared potatoes which had been boiled in small pieces and then mixed with the bacon I'd already fried in small pieces, kind of raggely mashed bacon potatoes, with eggs on top steaming, and on the side lettuce, with peanut butter dab nearby on side.—I had heard that peanut butter and lettuce contained all the vitamins you should want, this after I had originally started to eat this combination because of the deliciousness and nostalgia of the taste—my breakfast ready at about 6:45 and as I eat already I'm dressing to go piece by piece and by the time the last dish is washed in the little sink at the boiling hotwater tap and I'm taking my lastquick slug of coffee and quickly rinsing the cup in the hot water spout and rushing to dry it and plop it in its place by the hot plate and the brown carton in which all the groceries sit tightly wrapped in brown paper, I'm already picking up my brakeman's lantern from where it's been hanging on the door handle and my tattered timetable's long been in my backpocket folded and ready to go, everything tight, keys, timetable, lantern, knife, handkerchief, [129] wallet, comb, railroad keys, change and myself. I put the light out on the sad dab mad grub little diving room and hustle out into the fog of the flow, descending the creak hall steps where the old men are not yet sitting with Sunday morn papers because still asleep or some of them I can now as I leave hear beginning to disfawdle to wake in their rooms with their moans and yorks and scrapings and horror sounds, I'm going down the steps to work, glance to check time of watch with clerk cage clock—a hardy two or three oldtimers sitting already in the dark brown lobby under the tockboom clock, toothless, or grim, or elegantly mustached—what thought in the world swirling in them as they see the young eager brakeman bum hurrying to his thirty dollars of the Sunday—what memories of old homesteads, built without sympathy, hornyhanded fate dealt them the loss of wives, childs, moons—libraries collapsed in their time—oldtimers of the telegraph wired wood Frisco in the fog gray top time sitting in their brown sunk sea and will be there when this afternoon my face flushed from the sun, which at eight'll flame out and make sunbaths for us at Redwood, they'll still be here the color of paste in the green underworld and still reading the same editorial over again and won't understand where I've been or what for or what—I have to get out of there or suffocate, out of Third Street or become a worm, it's alright to live and bed-wine in and play the radio and cook little breakfasts and rest in but O my I've got to tog now to work, I hurry down Third to Townsend for my 7:15 train—it's 3 minutes to go, I start in a panic to jog, goddam it I didn't give myself enough time this morning, I hurry down under the Harrison ramp to the Oakland-Bay Bridge, down past Schweibacker-Frey the great dim red neon printshop always spectrally my father the dead executive I see there, I run and hurry past the beat Negro grocery stores where I buy all my peanut butter and raisin bread, past the redbrick railroad alley now mist and wet, across Townsend, the train is leaving! [130]

Fatuous railroad men, the conductor old John J. Coppertwang 35 years pure service on ye olde S.P. is there in the gray Sunday morning with his gold watch out peering at it, he's standing by the engine yelling up pleasantries at old hoghead Jones and young fireman Smith with the baseball cap is at the fireman's seat munching sandwich—"We'll how'd ye like old Johnny O yestiddy, I guess he didn't score so many touchdowns like we thought." "Smith bet six dollars on the pool down in Watsonville and said he's rakin' in thirty four." "I've been in that Watsonville pool—." They've been in the pool of life fleartiming with one another, all the long poker-playing nights in brownwood railroad places, you can smell the mashed cigar in the wood, the spittoon's been there for more than 750,099 yars and the dog's been in and out and these old boys by old shaded brown light have bent and muttered and young boys too with their new brakeman passenger uniform the tie undone the coat thrown back the flashing youth smile of happy fatuous well-fed goodjobbed careered futured pensioned hospitalized taken-care-of railroad men—35, 40 years of it and then they get to be conductors and in the middle of the night they've been for years called by the Crew Clerk yelling "Cassady? It's the Maximush localized week do you for the right lead" but now as old men all they have is a regular job, a regular train, conductor of the 112 with gold-watch is helling up his pleasantries at all fire dog crazy Satan hoghead Willis why the wildest man this side of France and Frankincense, he was known once to take his engine up that steep grade—7:15, time to pull, as I'm running thru the station hearing the bell jangling and the steam chuff they're pulling out, O I come flying out on the platform and forget momentarily or that is never did know what track it was and whirl in confusion a while wondering what track and can't see no train and this is the time I lose there, 5, 6, 7 seconds when the train tho underway is only slowly upchugging to go and a man a fat executive could easily run up and grab it [131] but when I yell to Assistant Stationmaster "Where's 112?" and he tells me the last track which is the track I never dreamed I run to it fast as I can go and dodge people à la Columbia halfback and cut into track fast as off-tackle where you carry the ball with you to the left and feint with neck and head and push of ball as tho you're gonna throw yourself all out to fly around that left end and everybody psychologically chuffs with you that way and suddenly you contract and you like whiff of smoke are buried in the hole in tackle, cutback play, you're flying into the hole almost before you yourself know it, flying into the track I am and there's the train about 30 yards away even as I look picking up tremendously momentum the kind of momentum I would have been able to catch if I'd a looked a second earlier—but I run, I know I can catch it. Standing on the back platform are the rear brakeman and an old deadheading conductor ole Charley W. Jones, why he had seven wives and six kids and one time out at Lick not I guess it was Coyote he couldn't seen on account of the steam and out he come and found his lantern in the igloo regular anglecock of my herald and they gave him fifteen benefits so now there he is in the Sunday har har owlala morning and he and young rear man watch incredulously this student brakeman running like a crazy trackman after their departing train. I feel like yelling "Make your airtest now make your airtest now!" knowing that when a passenger pulls out just about at the first crossing east of the station they pull the air a little bit to test the brakes, on signal from the engine, and this momentarily slows up the train and I could manage it, and could catch it, but they're not making no air-test the bastards, and I hek knowing I'm going to have to run like a sonofabitch. But suddenly I get embarrassed thinking what are all the people of the world gonna say to see a man running so devilishly fast with all his might sprinting thru life like Jesse Owens just to catch a goddam train and all of them with their hysteria wondering if I'll get killed [132] when I catch the back platform and glam, I fall down and go boom and lay supine across the crossing, so the old flagman when the train has flowed by will see that everything lies on the earth in the same stew, all of us angels will die and we don't ever know how or our own diamond, O heaven will enlighten us and open your youeeeeeoueee—open our eyes, open our eyes—I know I won't get hurt, I trust my shoes, hand grip, feet, solidity of yipe and cripe of gripe and grip and strength and need no mystic strength to measure the musculature in my rib rack—but damn it all it's a social embarrassment to be caught sprinting like a maniac after a train especially with two men gaping at me from rear of train and shaking their heads and yelling I can't make it even as I halfheartedly sprint after them with open eyes trying to com-municate that I can and not for them to get hysterical or laugh, but I realize it's all too much for me, not the run, not the speed of the train which anyway two seconds after I gave up the com-plicated chase did indeed slow down at the crossing in the air-test before chugging up again for good and Bay Shore. So I was late for work, and old Sherman hated me and was about to hate me more.

The ground I would have eaten in solitude, cronch—the rail-road earth, the flat stretches of long Bay Shore that I have to negotiate to get to Sherman's bloody caboose on track 17 ready to go with pot pointed to Redwood and the morning's 3-hour work—I get off the bus at Bay Shore Highway and rush down the little street and turn in—boys riding the pot of a switcheroo in the yardgoat day come yelling by at me from the headboards and footboards "Come on down ride with us" otherwise I would have been about 3 minutes even later to my work but now I hop on the little engine that momentarily slows up to pick me up and it's alone not pulling anything but tender, the guys have been up to the other end of the yard to get back on some track of necessity—[133] that boy will have to learn to flag himself without nobody helping him as many's the time I've seen some of these young goats think they have everything but the plan is late, the word will have to wait, the massive arboreal thief with the crime of the kind, and air and all kinds of ghouls—ZONKed! made tremendous by the flare of the whole prime and encrudalatures of all kinds—San Franciscos and shroudband Bay Shores the last and the last furbelow of the eek plot pall prime tit top work oil twicks and wouldn't you?—the railroad earth I would have eaten alone, cronch, on foot head bent to get to Sherman who ticking watch observes with finicky eyes the time to go to give the hiball sign get on going it's Sunday no time to waste the only day of his long seven-day-a-week work-life he gets a chance to rest a little bit at home when "Eee Christ" when "Tell that sonofabitch student this is no party picnic damn this shit and throb tit you tell them something and how do you what the hell expect to underdries out tit all you bright tremendous trouble anyway, we's LATE" and this is the way I come rushing up late. Old Sherman is sitting in the crummy over his switch lists, when he sees me with cold blue eyes he says "You know you're supposed to be here 7:30 don't you so what the hell you doing gettin' in here at 7:50 you're twenty goddam minutes late, what the fuck you think this your birthday?" and he gets up and leans off the rear bleak platform and gives the high sign to the enginemen up front we have a cut of about 12 cars and they sat it easy and off we go slowly at first, picking up momentum to the work, "Light that goddam fire" says Sherman he's wearing brandnew workshoes just about bought yestiddy and I notice his clean coveralls that his wife washed and set on his chair just that morning probably and I rush up and throw coal in the potbelly flop and take a fusee and two fusees and light them crack em Ah fourth of the July when the angels would smile on the horizon and all the racks where the mad are lost are returned to us forever from Lowell of my soul prime and [134] single meditatee longsong hope to heaven of prayers and angels and of course the sleep and interested eye of images and but now we detect the missing buffoon there's the poor goodman rear man ain't even on the train yet and Sherman looks out sulkily the back door and sees his rear man waving from fifteen yards aways to stop and wait for him and being an old railroad man he certainly isn't going to run or even walk fast, it's well understood, conductor

Sherman's got to get up off his switch-list desk chair and pull the
air and stop the goddam train for rear man Arkansaw Charley,
who sees this done and just come up lopin' in his flop overalls
without no care, so he was late too, or at least had gone gossip-
ping in the yard office while waiting for the stupid head brakeman, the tagman's up in front on the presumably pot. "First thing
we do is pick up a car in front at Redwood so all's you do get
off at the crossing and stand back to flag, not too far." "Don't
I work the head end?" "You work the hind end we got not much
to do and I wanta get it done fast," snarls the conductor. "Just
take it easy and do what we say and watch and flag." So it's peace-
ful Sunday morning in California and off we go, tack-a-tick, lao-
tichi-couch, out of the Bay Shore yards, pause momentarily at
the main line for the green, ole 71 or ole whatever been by and
now we get out and go swamming up the tree valleys and town
vale hollows and main street crossing parking-lot last-night attendant plots and Stanford lots of the world—to our destination
in the Poo which I can see, and, so to while the time I'm up in
the cupolo and with my newspaper dig the latest news on the
front page and also consider and make notations of the money
I spent already for this day Sunday absolutely not jot spent a
nothing—California rushes by and with sad eyes we watch it
reel the whole bay and the discourse falling off to gradual gils
that ease and graduate to Santa Clara Valley then and the fig
and behind is the fog immemoriates while the mist closes and
we come running out to the bright sun of the Sabbath Californiay
—[135]

At Redwood I get off and standing on sad oily ties of the
brakie railroad earth with red flag and torpedoes attached and
fusees in backpocket with timetable crushed against and I leave
my hot jacket in crummy standing there then with sleeves rolled
up and there's the porch of a Negro home, the brothers are sitting
in shirtsleeves talking with cigarettes and laughing and little
daughter standing amongst the weeds of the garden with her
playpail and pigtails and we the railroad men with soft signs
and no sound pick up our flower, according to same goodman
train order that for the last entire lifetime of attentions ole conductor industrial worker harlotized Sherman has been reading
carefully son so's not to make a mistake:

"Sunday morning October 15 pick up flower
car at Redwood, Dispatcher M.M.S." [136]

## CONCLUSION OF THE RAILROAD EARTH

I'd put a block of wood under the wheels of the car and watch it writhe and crack as the car eased up on it and stopped and sometimes didnt at all but just rolled on leaving the wood flattened to the level of the rail with upthrusted crackee ends— afternoons in Lowell long ago I'd wondered what the grimy men were doing with big boxcars and blocks of wood in their hands and when far above the ramps and rooftops of the great gray warehouse of eternity I'd see the immortal canal clouds of redbrick time, the drowse so heavy in the whole July city it would hang even in the dank gloom of my father's shop outside where they kept big rolltrucks with little wheels and flat silvery platforms and junk in corners and boards, the ink dyed into the oily wood as deep as a black river folded therein forever, contrasts for the whitepuff creamclouds outdoors that you just can see standing in the dust moted hall door over the old 1830 Lowell Dickens redbrick floating like in an old cartoon with little bird designs floating by too, all of a gray daguerrotype mystery in the whorly spermy waters of the canal—thus in the same way the afternoons in the S.P. redbrick alley, remembering my wonder at the slow grinding movement and squee of gigantic boxcars and flats and gons rolling by with that overpowering steel dust crenching closh and clack of steel on steel, the shudder of the whole steely proposition, a car going by with a brake on and so the whole brakebar—*monstre emporduement de fer en enfer* the frightening fog nights in California when you can see thru the mist the monsters slowly passing and hear the whee whee squee, those merciless wheels that one time Conductor Ray Miles on my student trips said, "When those wheels go over your leg they dont care about you" same way with that wood that I sacrifice—what those grimy men had been doing some of em standing on top of the boxcars and signalling far down the redbrick canal alleys of Lowell and some old men [37] slowly like bums moving around over rails with nothing to do, the big cut

Reprinted from *Evergreen Review*, Vol. 3, No. 11 (January–February, 1960), pp. 37–59. Copyright 1960 by Jack Kerouac, and reprinted by permission of The Sterling Lord Agency.

of cars squeeing by with that teethgritting cree cree and gigantic hugsteel bending rails into earth and making ties move, now I knew from working as on the Sherman Local on Sundays we dealt with blocks of wood because of an incline in the ground that made kicked cars keep going and you had to ride them brake them and stop them up with blocks. Lessons I learned there, like, "Put, tie a good brake on him, we dont want to start chasin the sonofabitch back to the City when we kick a car again him," okay, but I'm playing the safety rules of the safety book to the T and so now here I am the rear man on the Sherman Local, we've set out our Sunday morning preacher blossom flower car and made curtsies bows to the sabbath God tin th eeou ddkk everything has been arranged in that fashion and according to old traditions reaching back to Sutter's Mill and the times when the pioneers sick of hanging around the hardware store all week had put on their best vestments and smoked and jaw-bleaked in front of the wooden church and old railroad men of the 19th century the inconceivably ancient S.P. of another era with stovepipe hats and flowers in their lapels and had made the moves with the few cars into the goldtown milkboolick with the formality and the diffiereeiout cheoue theoueh thtnthtytoutt-kokt,—They give the sign and kick a car, with wood in hand I run out, the old conductor yells "You'd better brake him he's going too fast can you get im?" "Okay" and I run and take it easy on a jog and wait and here's the big car looming over me has just switched into its track from the locomotive tracks where (the lead) all the angling and arrowing's been done by the conductor who throws the switch, reads the taglist, throws the switch —so up the rungs I glo and according to safety rules with one hand I hang on, with the other I brake, slowly, according to a joint, easing up, till I reach the cut of cars waiting and into it gently my braked boxcar bangs, zommm—vibrations, things inside shake, the cradle rockababy merchandise zomms with it, all the cars at this impact go forward about a foot and crush woodblocks earlier placed, I jump down and place a block of wood and just neatly glue it under the steel lip of that monstrous wheel [38] and everything stops. And so I turn back to take care of the next kicked car which is going down the other track and also quite fast, I jog, finding wood en route, run up the rung, stop it, safety rule hanging on one hand forgetting the conductor's "Tie a good brake on it," something I should have learned then as a year later in Guadaloupe hundreds of miles down the line

I tied poor brakes on three flats, the flat handbrakes that have old rust and loose chains, poorly with one hand safety wise hanging on in case unexpected joint would jolt me off and under merciless wheels whose action with blocks of wood my bones would belie—bam, at Guadaloupe they kicked a cut of cars against my poorly braked flats and everything began parading down the incline back to San Luis Obispo, if it hadn't been for the alert old conductor looking out of the crummy switch lists to see this parade and running out to throw switches in front of it and unlocking switch locks as fast as the cars kept coming, a kind of comic circus act with him in floppy clown pants and hysterical horror darting from switch stand to switch stand and the guys in back hollering, the pot taking off after the cut and catching it almost pushing it but the couplers closing just in time and the engine braking everything to a stop, 30 feet almost in front of the final derail which the old winded conductor couldnt have finally made, we'd all have lost our jobs, my safety rule brakes had not taken momentum of steel and slight land inclines into consideration . . . if it had been Sherman at Guadaloupe I would have been hated Keoroowaaayy

Guadaloupe is 275.5 miles down the shining rail from San Francisco, down on the subdivision named after it, the Guadaloupe—the whole Coast Division begins at those sad dead end blocks of Third and Townsend where grass grows from soot beds like green hair of old tokay heroes long slanted into the ground like the railroad men of the 19th century whom I saw in the Colorado plains at little train order stations slanted into the ground of the hard dry dustcake, boxed, mawklipped, puking grit, fondled by the cricket, gone aslant so far sunk gravewise boxdeep into the foot of the sole of the earth Oh, you'd [39] think they had never suffered and dropped real sweats to that unhumped earth, had never voiced juicy sorrow words from blackcaked lips now make no more noise than the tire of an old tin lizzy the tin of which is zinging in the sun winds this afternoon, ah spectral Cheyenne Wellses and train order Denver Rio Grandes Northern Pacifics and Atlantic Coast Lines and Wunposts of America, all gone—The Coast Division of the ole S.P. which was built in umpteen o too too and used to run a little crazy crooked mainline up and down the hills of Bayshore like a crazy cross country track for European runners, this was their gold carrying bandito held up railroad of the old Zorro night of inks and furly caped riders—But now 'tis the modern ole Coast Division S.P. and begins at those dead end blocks and at 4:30 the frantic Market Street and Sansome Street commuters as I say come hysterically running for their 112 to get home on time for the 5:30 televisions Howdy Doody dof rthwir gun tooting near casday'd hopalong childreneees—1.9 miles to 23rd Street, another 1.2 to Newcomb, another 1.0 to Paul Avenue and etcetera these being the little piss stops on that 5 mile short run thru 4 tunnels to mighty Bayshore, Bayshore at milepost 5.2 shows you as I say that gigantic valley wall sloping in with sometimes in extinct winter dusks the huge fogs milking furling meerolling in with out t sound but as if you could hear the radar hum, the oldfashioned dullmasks mouth of Potato Patch Jack London old scrollwoaves crawling in across the gray bleak North Pacific with a wild fleck, a fish, the wall of a cabin, the old arranged wallworks of a sunken ship, the fish swimming in the pelvic bones of old lovers lay tangled at the bottom of the sea like slugs no longer discernible bone by bone but melted into one squid of time, that fog, that terrible and bleak Seattle ish fog that potatopatch wise comes bringing messages from Alaska and from the Aleutian mongol, and from the seal, and from the wave, and from the smiling porpoise, that fog at Bayshore you can see waving in and filling in rills and rolling down and making milk on hillsides and you think, "It's hypocrisy of men makes these hills grim"—To the left at the Bayshore mountain wall there s all your San Fran Bay pointing across the broadflat blues to the Oakland [40] lostness and the train the mainline train runs and clack and clackity clicks and makes the little Bayshore yard office a passing fancy things so important to the railroad men the little yellowish shack of clerks and paper onion skin train order lips and clearances of conductors and waybills tacked and typed and stamped from Kearney Neb. on in with mooing cows that have moved over 3 different railroads and all ye such facts, that passed in a flashed and the train negotiates, on, passing Visitacion Tower, that by old Okie railroad men of now-California aint at all mexicanized in pronunciation, Vi Zi Tah Sioh, but is simply called, Visitation, like on Sunday morning, and oft you hear, "Visitation Tower, Visitation Tower," ah ah ah ah aha—mile post 6.9, the following 8.6 Butler Road far from being a mystery to me by the time I became a brakeman was the great sad scene of yard clerking nights when at the far end of a 80 car freight the numbers of which with my little lamp I was taking down as I crunched over the gravel and all backtired, measuring how far I had to go by the sad streetlamp of Butler Road shining up ahead at the wall's end of long black sadmouth longcars of ye iron reddark railroad night—with stars above, and the smashby Zipper and the fragrance of locomotive coal-smoke as I stand aside and let them pass and far down the line at night around that South San Fran airport you can see that sonofabitch red light waving Mars signal light waving in the dark big red markers blowing up and down and sending fires in the keenpure lostpurity lovelyskies of old California in the late sad night of autumn spring comefefall winter's summer-time tall, like trees—all of it, and Butler Road no mystery to me, no blind spot in this song, but well known, I could also measure how far I had to go by the end of the gigantic rose neon six miles long you'd think saying WEST COAST BETHLEHEM STEEL as I'd be taking down the numbers of boxcars JC 74635 (Jersey Central) D&RG 38376 and NYC and PR and all the others, my work almost done when that huge neon was even with me and at the same time this meant the sad little streetlamp of Butler Road was only 50 feet away and no cars beyond that because that was the crossing where they'd cut them and then fold them over into another [41] track of the South City yards, things of brake significance switch significance I only got to learn later—So SF milepost 9.3 and what a bleak little main street, o my goodness, the fog'd roll in fine from there and the little neon cocktails with a little cherry on a toothpick and the bleak foglike green Chronicles in 10c sidewalk tin clonks, and yr bars with fat slick haired ex troopers inside drinking and October in the poolhall and all, where I'd go for a few bars of candy or desultory soups between chores as yardclerk when I was a yardclerk digging the lostness on that side, the human, and then having to go to the other end, a mile towards the Bay, to the great Armour & Swift slaughterplants where I'd take down the numbers of meat reefers and sometimes have to step aside and wait while the local came in and did some switching and the tagman or conductor would always tell me which ones were staying, which ones going—always at night, and always soft ground of like manure but really rat ground underneath, the countless rats I saw and threw rocks at till I felt like being sick, I'd hurry fleeing as from nightmare from that hole and sometimes fabricated phoney numbers instead of going too near a gigantic woodpile which was so full of rats it was like their tenement—and the sad cows mooing inside where little ratty Mexicans and Californians with bleak unpleasant unfriendly faces and going-to-work jalopies were milling around in their bloody work—till finally I worked it on a Sunday, the Armour & Swift yards, and saw that the Bay was 60 feet away and I'd never known it, but a dump yard a recka of crap and rat havens worse than ever tho beyond it the waters did ripple bluely and did in the sat morning clarity show clear flat mirrors clear to Oakland and the Alameda places across the way—and in the hard wind of that Sunday morning I heard the mutter of the tinware walls of brokendown abandoned slaughter house warehouses, the crap inside and dead rats killed by that local on off nights and some even I might have hit with my jacketful of protective rocks, but mostly systematically killed rats laying around in the keen heartbreaking cloud haunted wildwind day with big silver airplanes of civilized hope taking off across the stinking swamp and filthy tin flats for places in the air—gah, [42] bah, ieoeoeoeoe—it has a horrible filthy moaning sound you'd hear eiderdowning in that flydung those hideaway silos and murdered tinpaint aisles, scum, of salt, and bya abaya and harbors of the rat, the axe, the sledgehammer, the moo cows and all that, one big South San Francisco horror there's your milepost 9.3—After that the rushing train takes you to San Bruno clear and far around a long bend circling the marsh of the SSF airport and then on in to Lomita Park milepost 12.1 where the sweet commuter trees are and the redwoods crash and talk about you when you pass in the engine the boilers of which redly cast your omnipotent shadow out on the night—you see all the lil ranchstyle California homes and in the evening people sipping in livingrooms open to the sweetness, the stars, the hope that lil children must see when they lay in little beds and bedtime and look up and a star throbs for them above the railroad earth, and the train calls, and they think tonite the stars will be out, they come, they leave, they lave, they angelicize, ah me, I must come from a land where they let the children cry, ah me I wish I was a child in California when the sun's gone down and the Zipper crashes by and I could see thru the redwood or the fig tree my throbbing hope-light shining just for me and making milk on Permanente hillsides horrible Kafka cement factories or no, rats of South City slaughterhouses or no, no, or no, I wish I was a little child in a crib in a little ranchstyle sweet house with my parents sipping in the livingroom with their picture window pointing out on the little backyard of lawning chairs and the fence, the ranchstyle brown pointed full fence, the stars above, the pure dry golden smelling night, and just beyond a few weeds, and blocks of wood, and rubber tires, bam the main line of the Ole SP and the train flashing by, toom, tboom, the great crash of the black engine, the grimy red men inside, the tender, then the long snake freight-train and all the numbers and tall the and d dout ttye ething flashing by, gcrachs, thunder, the world, sisx going ab all of it finally terminated by the sweet little caboose with its brown smoky light inside where old conductor bends over waybills and up in the cupolo the rear man sits looking out once in a while and saying to himself all black, and the rear markers, [43] red, the lamps in the caboose rear porch, and the thing all gone howling around the bend to Burlingame to Mountain View to the sweet San Joses of the night the further down Gilroys Carnaderos Corporals and that bird of Chittenden of the dawn, your Logans of the strange night all be-lit and insected and mad, your Watsonvilles sea marshes you long long line and mainline track sticky to the touch in the midnight star

Mile post 46.9 is San Jose scene of a hundred interested bums lounging in the weeds along the track with their packs of junk, their buddies, their private watertanks, their cans of water to make coffee or tea or soup with, and their bottle of tokay wine or usually muskatel—The Muskat California is all around them, in the sky blue, tatteredly white clouds are being shoved across the top of the Santa Clara Valley from Bayshore where a high fogwind came and thru South City gaps too and the peace lies heavy in the sheltered valley where the bums have found a temporary rest—Hot drowse in the dry weeds, just hollows of dry reed stick up and you walk against them crashing—"Well boy, how's about a shot of rum to Watsonville." "This aint rum boy, this is a new kinda shit"—a colored hobo sitting on a shitty old newspaper of last year and's been used by Rat Eye Jim of the Denver viaducts who came thru here last spring with a package of dates on his back—"Things ain't been as bad as this since 1906!" Now it's 1952 October and the dew is on the grain of this real ground. One of the boys picks up a piece of tin from the ground (that got bounced off a gon in a sudden sprrram of freights ramming together in the yard from the bucklin slack) (bowm!)—pieces of tin go flying off, fall in the weeds, outside track No. 1—the hobo puts the tin on rocks over the

fire and uses it to toast some bread but's drinking tokay and talking to the other boys and toast burns just like in tile kitchen
tragedies—the bum comes curses angrily because he lost some
bread, and kicks a rock, and says "Twenty eight years I spent
inside the walls of Dannemora and I had my fill of excitin pan-
oramas of the great actions like when drunken canneman wrote
me that letter fum minneapoly and it was jess about chicago
sponges—I turd him looka jock you caint—well [44] I wrote
im a letter ennyways." Aint been a soul listening because no one
listens to a bum all the other bums are blagdengabsting and you
cant find nor finangilate yr way out of that—all talking at the
same time and all of them confused. You have to go back to the
railroad man to understand—like, say, you ask a man "Where's
track 109?"—nu—if it's a bum he'll say "Cart right over there
dadday, and see if the old boy in the blue bandana knows, I'm
Slim Holmes Hubbard from Ruston Louisiana and I got no time
and got no knowledge to make me ways of knowin what where
that track 109—only thing's I got, is—I want a dime, if you can
spare a dime I'll go along my way peacefully—if you cant I'll
go along my way peacefully—ya cant win—ya cant lose—and
from between here to Bismark Idaho I got nothing but lost and
lost and lost everything I ever had." You've got to admit these
bums into your soul when they talk like that—most of them rasp
"Track 109 Chillicothe Ioway" thru the stubbles and spits of
their beard—and wander off dragassing packs so huge, profound,
heavy—dismembered bodies are in there you'd think—red eyes,
wild wild hair, the railroad men look at them with amazement
and at first sight then never look again—what would wives say
—If you ask a railroad man what track is 109, he stop, stop chewing his gum, shift his package his coatlamp or lunch and turn,
and spit, and squint at the mountains to the east and roll his
eyes very slowly in the private cavern of his eyebone between
brow bone and cheek bone, and say, still deliberating and having deliberated "They call it track 109 but they should call it 110,
it's right next to the ice platform you know the ice house up
there—" "Yeah—" "There it is, from track one on the main line
here we start the numbers but the ice house make em jump they
make a turn and you have to go across track 110 to get to 109—
But you never have to go to 109 too often—so it's just like 109
was jess missing from the yard . . . numbers, see . . ." "Yeah"
—I know it for sure—"I know it for sure now." "And there she
is—" "Thanks—I gotta get there fast"—"That's the trouble with

the railroad, you always gotta get there fast—'cause if you dont it's like turning down a local on the phone and say you want to turn over and go to sleep (like Mike Ryan did last Monday" [45] he's sayin to himself)—And we walk wave and are gone.

This is the cricket in the reed. I sat down in the Pajaro river-bottoms and lit fires and slept with my coat on top of my brakeman's lantern and considered the California life staring at the blue sky——

The conductor is in there hanging around waiting for his train orders—when he gets them he'll give the engineer the hi-ball sign, a little side to side wave of the palmed hand, and off we go—the old hoghead gives orders for steam, the young fireman complies, the hoghead kicks and pulls at his big lever throttle and sometimes jumps up to wrestle with it like hugely an angel in hell and pulls the whistle twice toot toot we're leaving, and you hear the first chug of the engine—chug—a failure like—chug a lut—zoom—chug CHUG—the first movement—the train's underway——

San Jose—because the soul of the railroad is the chain gang run, the long freight train you see snaking down the track with a puff puff en jyne pulling is the traveler the winner the arterial moody mainline maker of the rail—San Jose is 50 miles south of Frisco and is the center of the Coast Division chain gang or long road run activity, known as the horn because the pivot point for rails going down from Frisco toward Santa Barbara and L.A. and rails going and shining back to Oakland via Newark and Niles on sub lines that also cross the mighty main line of the Fresno bound Valley Division—San Jose is where I should have been living instead of Third Street Frisco, for these reasons: 4 o'clock in the morning, in San Jose, comes a call on the phone it is the Chief Dispatcher calling from 4th and Townsend in the sad Frisco, "Keroowayyyy? it's deadhead on 112 to San Jose for a drag east with Conductor Degnan got that?" "Yeh dedaehead 112 drag east right," meaning, go back to bed and rise again around 9, you're being paid all this time and boy dont worry about a durg and doogaddm things, at 9 all's you gotta do is get ups and you already done made how many dollars? anyways in your sleep and put on your gig clothes and cut out and take a little bus and go down to the San Jose yard office down by the airport there and in the yard [46] office are hundreds of interested railroad men and tackings of tickers and telegraph and the engines are being lined up and numbered and markered out there, and new engines keep rushing up from the roundhouse, & everywhere in the gray air tremendous excitements of movement of rolling stocks and the making of great wages—you go down there, find your conductor who'll just be some old baggypants circus comedian with a turned up hatbrim and red face and red handkerchief and grimy waybills and switchlists in his hand and far from carrying a student big brakeman lantern like you's got his little old 10 year old tiny lantern from some old boomer bought and the batteries of which he has to keep buying at Davegas instead of like the student getting free at the yard office, because after 20 years on the rr you gotta find some bway to be different and also tlighten the burdens you carry around with yourself, he's there, leaning, by spittoons, with others, you go up hat over eyes, say "Conductor Degnan?" "I'm Degnan, well it doesn't look like anything'll bevore noon so just take it easy and be around" so you go into the blue room they call it, where blue flies buzz and hum around old zawful dirty couch tops stretched on benches with the stuffing coming out and attracting and probably breeding further, flies, and there you lie down if it ain't already full of sleeping brakemen and you turn your shoetops up to the dirty old brown sad ceiling of time there, haunted by the clack of telegraphs and the chug of engines out doors enough to make you go in your pants, and turns your hatbrim over yr eyes, and go ahead and sleep—since 4 in the morning, since 6 in the morning when still the sleep was on yr eyes in that dark dream house you've been getting 1.90 per hour and it is now 10 A M and the train aint even made up and "not before noon" says Degnan so that by noon you'll already have been working (because counting from time of 112, deadhead time) six hours and so you'll leave San Jose with your train around noon or may be further at one and not get to the terminal great chaingang town of Watsonville where everything's going (L.A. ward) till 3 in the afternoon and with happy mishaps 4 or 5, nightfall, when down there waiting for the herder's sign enginemen and trainmen see the long red sad sun of waning day [47] falling on the lovely old landmark milepost 98.2 farm and day's done, run's done, they been being paid since down dawn of that day and only traveled about 50 miles—this will be so, so sleep in the blue room, dream of 1.90 per hour and also of your dead father and your dead love

and the mouldering in your bones and the eventual Fall of you
—the train wont be made up till noon and no one wants to bother
you *till*—lucky child and railroad angel softly in your steel prop-
ositioned sleep.

So much more to San Jose.

so if you live in
San Jose you have the advantage of 3 hours of extra sleep at
home not counting the further sleep on the blue room rot puff
leather scoooch—nevertheless I was using the 50 mile ride from
3rd Street as my library, bringing books and papers in a little
tattered black bag already 10 years old which I'd originally
bought on a pristine morning in Lowell in 1942 to go to sea
with, arriving in Greenland that summer, and so a bag so bad
a brakeman seeing me with it in the San Jose yard coffee shop
said whooping loud "A railroad loot bag if I ever saw one!"
and I didn't even smile or acknowledged and that was the beginning middle and extent of my social rapport on the railroad
with the good old boys who worked it, thereafter becoming
known as Kerouaayyy the Indian with the phoney name and
everytime we went by the Pomo Indians working sectionhand
tracks, gandy dancers with greasy black hair I waved and smiled
and was the only man on the S.P. who did so except old hog-
heads always do wave and smile and sectionhand bosses who
are old white bespectacled respectable old toppers and topers
of time and everybody respects, but the dark Indian and the
eastern Negro, with sledgehammers and dirtypants to them I
waved and shortly thereafter I read a book and found out that
the Pomo Indian battle cry is Ya Ya Henna, which I thought
once of yelling as the engine crashboomed by but what would
I be starting but derailments of my own self and engineer—
all the railroad opening up and vaster and vaster until finally
when I did quit it a year later I saw it again but now over the
waves of the sea, the entire Coast Division winding down along
the dun walls of bleak headland balboa amerikay, from a [48]
ship, and so the railroad opens up on the waves that are Chinese
and on the orient shroud and sea—it runs ragged to the plateau
clouds and Pucalpas and lost Andean heights far below the
world rim, it also bores a deep hole in the mind of man and
freights a lot of interesting cargo in and out the holes precipi-
tate and otherwise hidingplaces and imitative cauchemar of eternity, as you'll see

So one morning they called me at 3rd Street at about 4 A M and I took the early morning train to San Jose, arriving there 7:30 was told not to worry about anything till about 10 so I went out in my inconceivably bum's existence went looking for pieces of wire that I could bend in such a way over my hotplate so they would support little raisin breads to make toast and also looking if possible for better than that a chickenwire arrangement on which I could sit pots to heat water and pans to fry eggs since the hotplate was so powerful it often burned and blackcaked the bottom of my eggs if by chance I'd overlook the possibility while busy peeling my potatoes or otherwise involved —I'd walk around, San Jose had a junk yard across the track, I went in there and lookt around, stuff in there so useless the proprietor never came out, I who was earning 600 a month made off with a piece of chicken wire for my hotplate—here it was 11 and still no train made up, gray, gloomy, wonderful day—I wandered down the little street of cottages to the big boulevard of Jose and had Carnation ice cream and coffee in the morning, whole bevies and classrooms of girls came in with tightfitting and sloosesucking sweaters and everything on earth on, it was some academy of dames suddenly come to gossip coffee and I was there in my baseball hat black slick oiled and rusted jacket weather jacket with fur collar that I had used to lean my head on in the sands of Watsonville riverbottoms and grits of Sunnyvale across from Westinghouse near Schukl's student days ground where my first great moment of the railroad had taken place over by Del Monte's when I kicked my first car and Whitey said "You're the boss do it pull the pin with a will put your hand in there and pull 'cause you're the boss" and it was October night, dark, clean, clear, dry, piles of leaves [49] by the track in the sweet scented dark and beyond them crates of the Del Monte fruit and workers going around in crate wagons with under reaching stuckers and—never will forget Whitey saying that—by same reviousloout of ddou tkth, in spite and because of, wanted to save all me money for Mexico, I also refused to spend 75 cents or even 35 cents less for a pair of workgloves, instead, after initial losing of my first bought workglove while setting out that sweet San Mateo flower car on Sunday morning with the Sherman local I resolved to get all my other gloves from the ground and so went for weeks with my black hand clutching sticky cold iron of engines in the dewy cold night, till I finally found the first glove outside the San Jose yard office, a brown cloth glove with red Mephistophelean lining, picking it up limp and damp from the ground and smashed it on my knee and let it dry and wore it—final other glove found outside Watsonville yard office, a little leather imitation outside glove with inside warm lining and cut with scissors or razor at the wrist to facilitate putting it on and obviate yanking and yunking—these were my gloves, I'd lost as I say my first glove in San Mateo, the second with Conductor Degnan while waiting for the all clear signal from the pot (working rear because of his fear) by the track at Lick, the long curve, the traffic on 101 making it difficult to hear and in fact it was the old conductor who in the dark of that Saturday night did finally hear, I heard nothing, I ran to the caboose as it leapt ahead with the slack and got on counting my red lamps gloves fusees and whatnots and realizing with horror as the train pulled along I had dropped one of my gloves at Lick, damn!— now I had two new gloves from off the ground pickied—at noon of that day the engine still wasnt on, the old hoghead hadnt left home yet where he'd picked up his kid on a sunny sidewalk with open arms and kissed him the late red john time of afternoon before, so I was there sleeping on the horrible old couch when by god itn some way or other and after I'd gone out several times to check and climb around the pot which was now tied on and the conductor and rear man having coffee in the shop and even the fireman and then I went back for further musings or nappings on the seat cover expecting them to call [50] me, when in my dreams I hear a double toot toot and hear a great anxiety engine taking off and it's my engine but I dont realize it right away, I think it's some slomming woeful old blacktrackpot whack cracking along in a dream or dream reality when suddenly I wake up to the fact they didnt know I was sleeping in the blue room, and they got their orders, and gave the hiball, and there they go to Watsonville leaving the head man behind—as tradition goes, fireman and engineer if they dont see the head man on the engine and they've gotten the sign, off they go, they have nothing to do with these sleepy trainmen—I leap up grab lamp and in the gray day and running precisely over the spot where I'd found that brown glove with red lining and thinking of it in the fury of my worry and as I dash I see the engine way down the line 50 years picking up and chufgffouffing and the whole train's rumbling after and cars waiting at the crossing for the event, it's MY TRAIN—off I go loping and runking fast over the glove place, and over the road, and over the corner of the junk field where I'd searched for tin also that lazy morning, amazied mouth-gagaped railroad men about five of them are watching this crazy student running after his engine as it leaves for Watsonville—is he going to make it? Inside 30 seconds I was abreast with the iron ladder and shifting lantern t'other hand to grab holt of and get on and climb, and anyway the whole shebang restopped again at a red to allow old I think 71 get through the station yards, it was I think by now almost 3 o'clock I'd slept and earned or started to earn incredible overtimes and this nightmare trans-piring—so they got the red and stopped anyway and I had my train made and sat on the sand box to catch my breath, no comment whatever in the world on the bleak jawbones and cold blue okie eyes of that engineer and fire-man they must have been holding some protocol with the iron railroad in their hearts for all they cared about this softheaded kid who'd run down the cinders to his late lost work

Forgive me o Lord

At the rickety fenceback Del Monte fruitpacking company which is directly across the track from the San Jose passenger [51] station there is a curve in the track, a curve shmurve of eternity rememberable from the dreams of the railroad dark I had where I'm working unspeakable locals with Indians and sud-denly we come upon a great Indian caucus in an underground subterraneana somewhere right there in the vicinity of the Del Monte curve (where Indians work anyway) (packing the crates, the cans, the fruit in cans with syrup) and I'm with the heroes of the Portuguese bars of San Franciscos watching dances and hearing revolutionary speeches like the speeches of the revolu-tionary sod squat down heroes of Culiacan where by the bark of the wave in the drearylit drolling night I have heard them say *la tierra esta la notre* and knew they mean it and for this reason the dream of the Indians revolutionary meeting and celebrating in the bottom lip cellar of the railroad earth—the train goes around the curve there and gently I lean out of the grabiron darks and look and there's our little clearance and train order sitting in a piece of string which is stretched be-tween the two train order bamrods, as the train passes the train-men simply (usually the fireman) reaches out with whole arm so to make sure not to miss and hooks the string in passing (the string being taut) and off comes the string and the two bows which are rigid sorta ping a little and in yr arm is looped the train orders on yellow onionskin tied by string, the engineer upon receipt of this freight takes the string and slowly according to years of personal habit in the manner of undoing train order strings undoes the string and then according again to habit unfolds the paper to read and sometimes they even put glasses on like great professors of ivy universities to read as that big engine goes chug chugging across and down the green land of California and Mexicans of railside mexshacks standing with eyes shades watching us past, see the great bespectacles monk student in engineer of the night peering learnedly at this little slip in big grimy paw and it reads, date, "Oct 3 1952, Train Orders, to Train 2-9222, issued 2:04 PM, wait at Rucker till 3:58 for eastbound 914, do not go beyond Corporal till 4:08 and etc." all the various orders which the train order dispatchers and various thinking officials at switch towers and telephones are thinking up in the great metaphysical passage [52] of iron traffics of the rail —we all take turns reading, like they say to young students "Read it carefully dont leave it up to us to decide if there are any mistakes many's the time a student found a mistake that the engineer and fireman out of years of habit didnt see so read it carefully" so I go over the whole thing reading even over and over again checking dates the time, like, the time of the order should certainly be not later than time of departure from station (when I went loping over the junkfield with lantern and loot bag racing to catch my guilt late in the gray candy gloom) and ah bout allit tall sweet. The little curve at Del Monte, the train orders, then the train goes on to mile post 49.1 to the Western Pacific RR crossing, where you always you the track goes directly vertically across this alien track so there is a definite hump in the rail bed, but ckci a luck, as we go over, sometimes at dawn returning from Watsonville I'd be dozing in the engine and wondering just about where we were not knowing generally we were in the vicinity of San Jose or Lick and I'd hear the brock a brock and say to myself "The Western Pacific crossing!" and remember how one time a brakee said to me, "Cant sleep nights in this here new house I got here out on Santa Clara avenue for the clatter and racket of that damn engine out there in the midnight" "Why I thought you loved the railroad" "Well thee tell you the fact of the matter, is the Western Pacific happens to have a rail running out there" and with such, as tho it was inconceivable that there could be other railroads than the Southern Pacific—On we go ass the crossing and there we go along the stream, the Oconee of old Jose the

little blank blank Guadaloupe river dry and with Indians standing on the banks, that is Mexican children watching the train, and
great fields of prickly pear cactus and all green and sweet in the
gray afternoon and gonna be golden brown and rich when the
sun at five flames flares to throw the California waine over the
reasterwestern rearourr ikks into the pacific brine—on we go to
Lick, always I take my looks at favorite landmarks, some school
where boys are practising football in varsity and sub varsity and
freshman and sub freshman squads, four of em, under tutelage
of raven priests with piping glad voices in the wind, for it's October of footingball [53] heaven gin rooting ecaleiemeoo—then at
Lick there is on a hill a kind of monastery, you barefly see the
dreaming marijuana walls of it as you pass, up there, with a bird
wheeling to peace, there a field, cloisters, work, cloisterous paray-
ers and every form known to man of sweet mediating going on as
we wrangle and badkdkdinggle by with a boutshing engine and
long knosiseyij space-taking-up vaat mile elong freight any minute
I expect a hotbox in, as I look back anxiously, fit to work—the
dreams of monastery men up there on the hill at Lick, and I think,
"Ah creamy walls of either Rome, civilizations, or the last monas-
terial mediation with God in the didoudkekeghgj" god knows
what I'm thinking, and then and my thoughts rapidly change as
101 rears into sight, and Coyote, and the beginning of the sweet
fruit fields and prune orchards and the great strawberry fields
and the vast fields where you see far off the humble squatting
figures of Mexican brazeros in the great haze working to pluck
from the earth that which the America with his vast iron wages
no longer thinks feasible as an activity yet eats, yet goes on eating,
and the brass backs with arms of iron Mexico in the cactus plateau love, they'll do it for us, the railroad freight train and concomitant racks of beets is not even, the men on it, are not even
mindful of how those beets or in what mood, sweat, sweetness,
were picked—and laid to rest out of the earth in the steely
craydle—I see them their bent humble backs remembering my
own cottonpicking days in Selma California and I see far off
across the grapevines the hills to the west, then the sea, the great
sweet hills and further along you begin to see the familiar hill of
Morgan Hill, we pass the fields of Perry and Madrone and where
they make wine, anh ssljiut there's all sweet the, furrows of
brown, with blossoms and one time we took a siding to wait for
98 and I ran out there like the hound of the Baskervilles and got
me a few old prunes not longer finger to eat—the proprietor see-

ing me, trainman running guiltily back to engine with a stolen prune, always I was running, always was running, running to throw switches, running in my sleep and running now—happy.

The sweetness of the fields unspeakable—the names [54] themselves bloody edible like Lick Coyote Perry Madrone Morgan Hill San Martin Rucker Gilroy o sleepy Gilroy Carnadero Corporal Sargent Chittenden Logan Aromas and Watsonville Junction with the Pajaro River pasing thru it and we of the railroad pass over its wooded dry Indian draws at somewhere outside Chittenden where one morning all dew pink I saw a little bird sitting on a piece of stanchion strait up wood in the wild tangle, and it was the Bird of Chittenden, and the meaning of morning—sweet enough the fields outside San Jose like at say Lawrence and Sunnyvale and where they have vast harvest and fields with the bentback sad mexicano laborioring in his primavery—but once past San Jose somehow the whole California opens ever further, at sunset at Perry or Madrone it is like a dream, you see the little rickety farmhouse, the fields, the rows of green planted fruit, and beyond the green pale mist of hills and over that the red aureolaos of packific sunfall and in the silence the bark of a duog and that fine California night dew already rising ere maw's done wiped the hamburg juice off the frying pant and later on tonite beautiful little Carmelita o Jose will be gomezing along the road with her brown breasts inside cashmere sweater bouncing ever so slightly even with maidenform bra and her brown feet in thonged sandals also brown, and her dark eyes with pools in em of you wonder what mad meaning, and her arms like arms of handmaidens in the Plutonian bible—and ladels for her arms, in the form of trees, with juice, take a peach, take the fulsome orange, bite a hole in in, take the orange throw your head back use all your strength and drink and squeeze out the orange thru the hole, all the juice runs down your lip and on her arms—she has dust on her toes, and toe nail polish—she has a tiny brown waist, a little soft chin, soft neck like swan, little voice, little femininity and doesn't know it—her little voice is littletinkled—along comes the tired field hand Jose Cmamrrouooo and he see her in the vast sun red in the fruit field moving uqueen majesty to the well, the tower, he runs for her, the railroad crashes by he pays no attention standing on the engine student brakeman J. L. Kerouac and old hoghead W. H. Sears 12 years in California since leaving the fpeac Oklahoma dust farms, his father'd in [55] a broken down okie truck ordered departures from there, for the first nonces they were and tried to be cottonpickers and were mighty good at it but one day somebody told Sears to try railroading which he did and then he was now after several years a young fireman, an engineer—the beautify of the salvation fields of California making no difference to the stone of his eye as with glove famed throttle hand he guides the black beast down the star rail— switches rush up and melt into the rail, sidings part from it like lips, return like lover arms—my mind is on the brown knees of Carmelity, the dark spltot between her thighs where creation hides its majesty and all the boys with eager head do rush suffering and want the whole the hole the works the hair the seekme membrane the lovey sosoudkdk thdldout tkdyd jdodu, the ehtkae eou, she nevee able and down goes the sun and it's dark and they're layin in a grape row, nobody can see, or hear, only the dog hears OOO slowly against the dust of that eworkrkraoub earth he presses her little behind down to form a little depression in the earth from the force and weight of his tears slowly lunging her downthru and into the portals of her sweetness, and slowly the blood pounds in his indian head and comes to a rise and she softly pants with parted brownly lips and with little pear teeth showing and sticking out just far and just so gently almost biting, burning in the burn of his own, lips—he drives and thrives to pund, the grain, the grape nod in unison, the win is springing from the noggin of the ground, bottles will roll on 3rd Street to the sands of Santa Barbara, he's making it with the wouddlk tituthe then would and wouldn't you if you too could—the sweet flesh intermingling, the flowing blood wine dry husk leaf bepiled earth with the hard iron passages going oer, the engine's saying K RRRR OOO AAAWWOOOO and the crossing it's ye famous Krrot Krroot Krroo oooooaaaawwww Kroot—2 short one long, one short, 'sa thing I got to learn as one time the hoghead was busy telling a joke in the fireman's ear and we were coming to a crossing and he yelled at me "Go ahead go ahead" and made a pull sign with his hand and I lookied up and grabbed the string and looked out, big engineer, saw the crossing racing up and girls in sandals and tight [56] ass dresses waiting at the flashby RR crossing boards of Carnadero and I let it to, two short pulls, one long, one short, Krroo Krroo Krrrooooa Krut—so now it's purple in the sky, the whole rim America falling spilling over the west mountains into the eternal and orient sea, and there's yur sad field and lovers twined and the wine is in the earth already and in Watsonville up ahead at the end of my grimy run among a million others sits a bottle of tokay wine which I am going to buy to put some of that earth back in my belly after all this shudder of ferrous knock klock against my soft flesh and bone exultation—in other words, when work's done, I'm gonna have a drink of wine, and rest—The Gilroy Subdivision this is.

The first run I ever made on the Gilroy subdivision, that night dark and clean, standing by the engine with my lamp and loot-bag waiting for the big men to make up their minds here comes this young kid out of the dark, no railroad man but obviously a bummer but on the bum from college or good family or if not with cleanteeth smile and no broken down datebag river Jack from the bottoms of the world night—said, "This thing going to L.A.?"—"Well it's going about part of the way to there, about 50 miles to Watsonville then if you stick on it they might route you down to San Luis Obispo too and that's about halfway to L.A."—"Ba what d'I care about halfway to L.A. I want to go all the way to L.A.—what are you a railroad brakemenananana?" "Yeah, I'm a student"—"What's a student"—"Well it's a guy learning and getting, well I aint getting paid" (this being my student chain gang run all the way down)—"Ah well I dont like going up and down the same rail, if you ask me goin to sea is the real life, now that's where I'm headed or hitch hike to New York, either way, I wouldnt want to be a railroad man"—"What you talkin about man it's great and you're moving all the time and you make a lot of money and no body bothers you out there"— "Neverthefuckingless you keep going up and down the same rail dont you for krissakes" so I told him what how and where boxcar to get on, "Krissakes dont hurt yourself always remember when you try to go around proving you're a big adventurer of the American night and [57] wanta you hop freights like Joel McRea heroes of old movies Jesus you dumb son aa bitch hang on angel with your tightest hand and dont let your feet drag under that iron roundwheel it'll have less regard for the bone of your leg than it has for this toothpick in my mouty" "Ah you shitt tyuo shit you think I'm afraid of a goddamn railroad train I'm going off to join the goddam navy and be on carriers and there's your iron for you I'll land my airplane half on iron half on water and crashbang and jet to the moon too" "Good luck to you guy, dont fall off hang tight grip wrists dont fuck up and tout and when you gets to L.A. give my regards to Lana Turner"—the train was starting to leave and the kid had disappeared up the long black bed and snakeline redcars—I jumped up on the engine with the regular head man who was going to show me how the run runs, and the fireman, and hoghead—off we chugged, over the crossing, over to the Del Monte curve and where the head man showed me how you hang on with one hand and lean out and crook your arm and grab the train orders off the string—then out to Lick, the night, the stars—never will forget, the fireman wore a black leather jacket and a white skidrow San Frisco seaman Embarcadero cap, with visor, in the ink of this night he looked exactly like a revolutionary Bridges Curran Bryson hero of old waterfront smosh flops, I could see him with meaty hand waving a club in forgotten union publications rotting in gutters of back-alley bars, I could see him with hands deep in pocket along angrily thru the uneccentric unworkingbums of 3rd Street to his rendezvous with the fate of the fish at the waterfront gold blue pier edge where boys sit of afternoons dreaming under clouds on bits of piers with the slap of skeely love waters at their feet, white masts of ships, orange masts of ships with black hulls and all your orient trade pouring in under the Golden Gate, this guy I tell you was like a sea dog not a railroad firemen yet there he sat with his snow white cap in the grimeblack night and rode that fireman's seat like a jockey, chug and we were really racing, they were opening her up wanted to make good time to get past Gilroy before any orders would fuck them up, so across the onlitt tintight and with our big pot 3500 style engine [58] headlights throwing its feverish big lick tongue over the wurrling and in-curling and outflying track we go swinging and roaring and flying down that line like fucking mademan and the fireman doesnt exactly hold on to his white hat but he has hand on fire throttle and keeps close eye on valves and tags and steam bubblers and outside looks on the rail and the wind blows his nose back but t but ee god he bouncing on that seat exactly like a jocket riding a wild horse, why we had a hoghead that night which was my first night so wild he had the throttle opened fullblack and keep yanking at it with one heel against the iron skcum of the floor trying to open her up further and if possible tear the locomotive apart to get more out of her and leave the track and fly up in the night over the prune fields, what a magnificent opening night it was for me to ride a fast run like that with a bunch of speed demons and that magnificent fireman with his unpredestined im-

possible unprecedentable hat white in the black black railroad—
and all the time and the conversations they have, and the visions
in his hat I saw of the pubic hair restaurant on Howard, how I
saw that Frisco California white and gray of rain fogs and the
back alleys of bottles, breens, derbies, mustachios of beer, oysters,
flying seals, crossing hills, bleak bay windows, eoue diddle for
old churches with handoouts for seadogs bark ling and snurling in
aveneu e a 's of lost porrporttity time, ah—loved it all, and the
first night the finest night, the blood, "railroading gets in yr
blood" the old hog head is yelling at me as he bounces up and
down in his seat and the wind blows his striped cap visor back
and the engine like a huge beast is lurching side to side 70
miles per hour breaking all rulebooxxkss rules, zomm, zomm,
were crashing through the night and out there carmelity is coming, jose is making her electricities mix and interrun with his and
the whole earth charged with juices turns up the organo to the
flower, the unfoldment, the stars bend to it, the whole world's
coming as the big engine booms and balls by with the madmen
of the white cap california in there flossing and wow there's
is just no end to all this wine—— [59]

## ESSENTIALS OF SPONTANEOUS PROSE

SET-UP   The object is set before the mind, either in reality, as in
sketching (before a landscape or teacup or old face) or is set in
the memory wherein it becomes the sketching from memory of
a definite image-object.

PROCEDURE   Time being of the essence in the purity of speech,
sketching language is undisturbed flow from the mind of personal secret idea-words, *blowing* (as per jazz musician) on subject of image.

METHOD   No periods separating sentence-structures already arbitrarily riddled by false colons and timid usually needless com-
mas—but the vigorous space dash separating rhetorical breath-

Reprinted from *Evergreen Review*, Vol. 2, No. 5 (Summer, 1958), pp. 72–
73. Copyright 1958 by Jack Kerouac, and reprinted by permission of The
Sterling Lord Agency.

ing (as jazz musician drawing breath between outblown phrases) —"measured pauses which are the essentials of our speech"— "divisions of the *sounds* we hear"—"time and how to note it down." (William Carlos Williams)

SCOPING  Not "selectivity" of expression but following free deviation (association) of mind into limitless blow-on-subject seas of thought, swimming in sea of English with no discipline other than rhythms of rhetorical exhalation and expostulated statement, like a fist coming down on a table with each complete utterance, bang! (the space dash)—Blow as deep as you want—write as deeply, fish as far down as you want, satisfy yourself first, then reader cannot fail to receive telepathic shock and meaning-excitement by same laws operating in his own human mind.

LAG IN PROCEDURE  No pause to think of proper word but the infantile pileup of scatalogical buildup words till satisfaction is gained, which will turn out to be a great appending rhythm to a thought and be in accordance with Great Law of timing.

TIMING  Nothing is muddy that *runs in time* and to laws of *time* —Shakespearian stress of dramatic need to speak now in own unalterable way or forever hold tongue—*no revisions* (except obvious rational mistakes, such as names or *calculated* insertions in act of not writing but *inserting*).

CENTER OF INTEREST  Begin not from preconceived idea of what to say about image but from jewel center of interest in subject of image at *moment* of writing, and write outwards swimming in sea of language to peripheral release and exhaustion—Do not afterthink except for poetic or P. S. reasons. Never afterthink to "improve" or defray impressions, as, the best writing is always the most painful personal wrung-out tossed from cradle warm protective mind—tap from yourself the song of yourself, *blow!*— *now!*—*your* way is your only way—"good"—or "bad"—always honest, ("ludicrous"), spontaneous, "confessional" interesting, because not "crafted." Craft *is* craft.

STRUCTURE OF WORK  Modern bizarre structures (science fiction, etc.) arise from language being dead, "different" themes give illusion of "new" life. Follow roughly outlines in outfanning movement over subject, as river rock, so mindflow over jewel-center need (run your mind over it, *once*) arriving at pivot, where what was dim-formed "beginning" becomes sharp-necessitating "ending" and language shortens in race to wire of time-race of work, following laws of Deep Form, to conclusion, last words, last trickle—Night is The End.

MENTAL STATE   If possible write "without consciousness" in semi-trance (as Yeats' later "trance writing") allowing subconscious to admit in own uninhibited interesting necessary and so "modern" language what conscious art would censor, and write excitedly, swiftly, with writing-or-typing-cramps, in accordance (as from center to periphery) with laws of orgasm, Reich's "beclouding of consciousness." *Come* from within, out—to relaxed and said.


## BELIEF & TECHNIQUE FOR MODERN PROSE


*List of Essentials*

1. Scribbled secret notebooks, and wild typewritten pages, for yr own joy
2. Submissive to everything, open, listening
3. Try never get drunk outside yr own house
4. Be in love with yr life
5. Something that you feel will find its own form
6. Be crazy dumbsaint of the mind
7. Blow as deep as you want to blow
8. Write what you want bottomless from bottom of the mind
9. The unspeakable visions of the individual
10. No time for poetry but exactly what is
11. Visionary tics shivering in the chest
12. In tranced fixation dreaming upon object before you
13. Remove literary, grammatical and syntactical inhibition
14. Like Proust be an old teahead of time
15. Telling the true story of the world in interior monolog
16. The jewel center of interest is the eye within the eye
17. Write in recollection and amazement for yourself
18. Work from pithy middle eye out, swimming in language sea
19. Accept loss forever

Reprinted from *Evergreen Review*, Vol. 2, No. 8 (Spring, 1959), p. 57. Copyright 1960 by Jack Kerouac, and reprinted by permission of The Sterling Lord Agency.

20. Believe in the holy contour of life
21. Struggle to sketch the flow that already exists intact in mind
22. Dont think of words when you stop but to see picture better
23. Keep track of every day the date emblazoned in yr morning
24. No fear or shame in the dignity of yr experience, language & knowledge
25. Write for the world to read and see yr exact pictures of it
26. Bookmovie is the movie in words, the visual American form
27. In praise of Character in the Bleak inhuman Loneliness
28. Composing wild, undisciplined, pure, coming in from under, crazier the better
29. You're a Genius all the time
30. Writer-Director of Earthly movies Sponsored & Angeled in Heaven

## THE ORIGINS OF THE BEAT GENERATION

This article necessarily'll have to be about myself. I'm going all out.

That nutty picture of me on the cover of *On the Road* results from the fact that I had just gotten down from a high mountain where I'd been for two months completely alone and usually I was in the habit of combing my hair of course because you have to get rides on the highway and all that and you usually want girls to look at you as though you were a man and not a wild beast but my poet friend Gregory Corso opened his shirt and took out a silver crucifix that was hanging from a chain and said "Wear this and wear it outside your shirt and don't comb your hair!" so I spent several days around San Francisco going around with him and others like that, to parties, arties, parts, jam sessions, bars, poetry readings, churches, walking talking poetry in the streets, walking talking God in the streets (and at one point a strange gang of hoodlums got mad and said "What right does he got to wear that?" and my own gang of musicians and poets

Reprinted from *Playboy*, Vol. 6, No. 6 (June, 1959), pp. 31–32, 42, 79. Copyright 1959 by Jack Kerouac; originally appeared in *Playboy*. This article is based on a speech delivered by Jack Kerouac at the Brandeis University seminar at Hunter College.

told them to cool it) and finally on the third day *Mademoiselle* magazine wanted to take pictures of us all so I posed just like that, wild hair, crucifix, and all, with Gregory Corso, Allen Ginsberg and Phil Whalen, and the only publication which later did not erase the crucifix from my breast (from that plaid sleeveless cotton shirtfront) was *The New York Times,* therefore *The New York Times* is as beat as I am, and I'm glad I've got a friend. I mean it sincerely, God bless *The New York Times* for not erasing the crucifix from my picture as though it was [31] something distasteful. As a matter of fact, who's *really* beat around here, I mean if you wanta talk of Beat as "beat down" the people who erased the crucifix are really the "beat down" ones and not *The New York Times,* myself, and Gregory Corso the poet. I am not ashamed to wear the crucifix of my Lord. It is because I am Beat, that is, I believe in beatitude and that God so loved the world that he gave his only begotten son to it. I am sure no priest would've condemned me for wearing the crucifix outside my shirt everywhere and *no matter where* I went, even to have my picture taken by *Mademoiselle.* So you people don't believe in God. So you're all big smart know-it-all Marxists and Freudians, hey? Why don't you come back in a million years and tell me all about it, angels?

Recently Ben Hecht said to me on TV "Why are you afraid to speak out your mind, what's wrong with this country, what is everybody afraid of?" Was he talking to me? And all he wanted me to do was speak out my mind *against* people, he sneeringly brought up Dulles, Eisenhower, the Pope, all kinds of people like that habitually he would sneer at with Drew Pearson, *against* the world he wanted, this is his idea of freedom, he calls it freedom. Who knows, my God, but that the universe is not one vast sea of compassion actually, the veritable holy honey, beneath all this show of personality and cruelty. In fact who knows but that it isn't the solitude of the oneness of the essence of everything, the solitude of the actual oneness of the unbornness of the unborn essence of everything, nay the true pure foreverhood, that big blank potential that can ray forth anything it wants from its pure store, that blazing bliss, *Mattivajrakaruna* the Transcendental Diamond Compassion! No, I want to speak *for* things, for the crucifix I speak out, for the Star of Israel I speak out, for the divinest man who ever lived who was a German (Bach) I speak out, for sweet Mohammed I speak out, for Buddha I speak out, for Lao-tse and Chuang-tse I speak out, for D. T.

Suzuki I speak out . . . why should I attack what I love out of life. This is Beat. Live your lives out? Naw, *love* your lives out. When they come and stone you at least you won't have a glass house, just your glassy flesh.

That wild eager picture of me on the cover of *On the Road* where I look so Beat goes back much further than 1948 when John Clellon Holmes (author of *Go* and *The Horn*) and I were sitting around trying to think up the meaning of the Lost Generation and the subsequent Existentialism and I said "You know, this is really a beat generation" and he leapt up and said "That's it, that's right!" It goes back to the 1880s when my grandfather Jean-Baptiste Kerouac used to go out on the porch in big thunderstorms and swing his kerosene lamp at the lightning and yell "Go ahead, go, if you're more powerful than I am strike me and put the light out!" while the mother and the children cowered in the kitchen. And the light never went out. Maybe since I'm supposed to be the spokesman of the Beat Generation (I *am* the originator of the term, and around it the term and the generation have taken shape) it should be pointed out that all this "Beat" guts therefore goes back to my ancestors who were Bretons who were the most independent group of nobles in all old Europe and kept fighting Latin France to the last wall (although a big blond bosun on a merchant ship snorted when I told him my ancestors were Bretons in Cornwall, Brittany, "Why, we Wikings used to swoop down and steal your nets!") Breton, Wiking, Irishman, Indian, madboy, it doesn't make any difference, there is no doubt about the Beat Generation, at least the core of it, being a swinging group of new American men intent on joy . . . Irresponsibility? Who wouldn't help a dying man on an empty road? No and the Beat Generation goes back to the wild parties my father used to have at home in the 1920s and 1930s in New England that were so fantastically loud nobody could sleep for blocks around and when the cops came they always had a drink. It goes back to the wild and raving childhood of playing the Shadow under windswept trees of New England's gleeful autumn, and the howl of the Moon Man on the sandbank until we caught him in a tree (he was an "older" guy of 15), the maniacal laugh of certain neighborhood madboys, the furious humor of whole gangs playing basketball till long after dark in the park, it goes back to those crazy days before World War II when teenagers drank beer on Friday nights at Lake ballrooms and worked off their hangovers playing baseball on Saturday afternoon followed by a dive in the brook—and our fathers wore straw hats like W. C. Fields. It goes back to the completely senseless babble of the Three Stooges, the ravings of the Marx Brothers (the tenderness of Angel Harpo at harp, too).

It goes back to the inky ditties of old cartoons (Krazy Kat with the irrational brick)—to Laurel and Hardy in the Foreign Legion—to Count Dracula and his *smile* to Count Dracula shivering and hissing back before the Cross—to the Golem horrifying the persecutors of the Ghetto—to the quiet sage in a movie about India, unconcerned about the plot—to the giggling old Tao Chinaman trotting down the sidewalk of old Clark Gable Shanghai—to the holy old Arab warning the hotbloods that Ramadan is near. To the Werewolf of London a distinguished doctor in his velour smoking jacket smoking his pipe over a lamplit tome on botany and suddenly hairs grown on his hands, his cat hisses, and he slips out into the night with a cape and a slanty cap like the caps of people in breadlines—to Lamont Cranston so cool and sure suddenly becoming the frantic Shadow going mwee hee hee ha ha in the alleys of New York imagination. To Popeye the sailor and the Sea Hag and the meaty gunwales of boats, to Cap'n Easy and Wash Tubbs screaming with ecstasy over canned peaches on a cannibal isle, to Wimpy looking X-eyed for a juicy hamburger such as they make no more. To Jiggs ducking before a household of furniture flying through the air, to Jiggs and the boys at the bar and the corned beef and cabbage of old wood-fence noons—to King Kong his eyes looking into the hotel window with tender huge love for Fay Wray—nay, to Bruce Cabot in mate's cap leaning over the rail of a fogbound ship saying "Come aboard." It goes back to when grapefruits were thrown at crooners and harvestworkers at bar-rails slapped burlesque queens on the rump. To when fathers took their sons to the Twi League game. To the days of Babe Callahan on the waterfront, Dick Barthelmess camping under a London street-lamp. To dear old Basil Rathbone looking for the Hound of the Baskervilles (a dog big as the Gray Wolf who will destroy Odin)—to dear old bleary Doctor Watson with a brandy in his hand. To Joan Crawford her raw shanks in the fog, in striped blouse smoking a cigarette at sticky lips in the door of the waterfront dive. To train whistles of steam engines out above the moony pines. To Maw and Paw in the Model A clanking on to get a job in California selling used cars making a whole lotta money. To the glee of America, the honesty of America, the honesty of oldtime grafters in straw hats as well as the honesty of oldtime waiters in line at the Brooklyn Bridge in *Winterset*, the funny spitelessness of old bigfisted America like Big Boy Williams saying "Hoo? Hee? Huh?" in a movie about Mack Trucks and slidingdoor lunchcarts. To Clark Gable, his certain smile, his confident leer. Like my grandfather this America was invested with wild selfbelieving individuality and this had begun to disappear around the end of World War II with so many great guys dead (I can think of half a dozen from my own boyhood groups) when suddenly it began to emerge again, the hipsters began to appear gliding around saying "Crazy, man."

When I first saw the hipsters creeping around Times Square in 1944 I didn't like them either. One of them, Huncke [32] of Chicago, came up to me and said "Man, I'm beat." I knew right away what he meant somehow. At that time I still didn't like bop which was then being introduced by Bird Parker and Dizzy Gillespie and Bags Jackson (on vibes), the last of the great swing musicians was Don Byas who went to Spain right after, but then I began . . . but earlier I'd dug all my jazz in the old Minton Playhouse (Lester Young, Ben Webster, Joey Guy, Charlie Christian, others) and when I first heard Bird and Diz in the Three Deuces I knew they were serious musicians playing a goofy new sound and didn't care what I thought, or what my friend Seymour thought. In fact I was leaning against the bar with a beer when Dizzy came over for a glass of water from the bartender, put himself right against me and reached both arms around both sides of my head to get the glass and danced away, as though knowing I'd be singing about him someday, or that one of his arrangements would be named after me someday by some goofy circumstance. Charlie Parker was spoken of in Harlem as the greatest new musician since Chu Berry and Louis Armstrong.

Anyway, the hipsters, whose music was bop, they looked like criminals but they kept talking about the same things I liked, long outlines of personal experience and vision, nightlong confessions full of hope that had become illicit and repressed by War, stirrings, rumblings of a new soul (that same old human soul). And so Huncke appeared to us and said "I'm beat" with radiant light shining out of his despairing eyes . . . a word perhaps brought from some widwest carnival or junk cafeteria. It was a new language, actually spade (Negro) jargon but you soon learned it, like "hung up" couldn't be a more economical term to mean so many things. Some of these hipsters were raving mad and talked continually. It was jazzy. Symphony Sid's all-night modern jazz and bop show was always on. By 1948 it began to take shape. That was a wild vibrating year when a group of us would walk down the street and yell hello and even stop and talk to anybody that gave us a friendly look. The hipsters had eyes. That was the year I saw Montgomery Clift, unshaven, wearing a sloppy jacket, slouching down Madison Avenue with a companion. It was the year I saw Charley Bird Parker strolling down Eighth Avenue in a black turtleneck sweater with Babs Gonzales and a beautiful girl.

By 1948 the hipsters, or beatsters, were divided into cool and hot. Much of the misunderstanding about hipsters and the Beat Generation in general today derives from the fact that there are two distinct styles of hipsterism: the cool today is your bearded laconic sage, or schlerm, before a hardly touched beer in a beatnik dive, whose speech is low and unfriendly, whose girls say nothing and wear black: the "hot" today is the crazy talkative shining eyed (often innocent and openhearted) nut who runs from bar to bar, pad to pad looking for everybody, shouting, restless, lushy, trying to "make it" with the subterranean beatniks who ignore him. Most Beat Generation artists belong to the hot school, naturally since that hard gemlike flame needs a little heat. In many cases the mixture is 50–50. It was a hot hipster like myself who finally cooled it in Buddhist meditation, though when I go in a jazz joint I still feel like yelling "Blow baby blow!" to the musicians though nowadays I'd get 86d for this. In 1948 the "hot hipsters" were racing around in cars like in *On the Road* looking for wild bawling jazz like Willis Jackson or Lucky Thompson (the early) or Chubby Jackson's big band while the "cool hipsters" cooled it in dead silence before formal and excellent musical groups like Lennie Tristano or Miles Davis. It's still just about the same, except that it has begun to grow into a national generation and the name "Beat" has stuck (though all hipsters hate the word).

The word "beat" originally meant poor, down and out, deadbeat, on the bum, sad, sleeping in subways. Now that the word is belonging officially it is being made to stretch to include people who do not sleep in subways but have a certain new gesture, or attitude, which I can only describe as a new *more*. "Beat Generation" has simply become the slogan or label for a revolution in manners in America. Marlon Brando was not really first to portray it on the screen. Dane Clark with his pinched Dostoievskyan face and Brooklyn accent, and of course Garfield, were first. The private eyes were Beat, if you will recall. Bogart. Lorre was Beat. In *M*, Peter Lorre started a whole revival, I mean the slouchy street walk.

I wrote *On the Road* in three weeks in the beautiful month of May 1951 while living in the Chelsea district of lower West Side Manhattan, on a 100-foot roll and put the Beat Generation in words in there, saying at the point where I am taking part in a wild kind of collegiate party with a bunch of kids in an abandoned miner's shack "These kids are great but where are Dean Moriarty and Carlo Marx? Oh well I guess they wouldn't belong in this gang, they're too *dark*, too strange, too subterranean and I am slowly beginning to join a new kind of *beat* generation." The manuscript of *Road* was turned down on the grounds that it would displease the sales manager of my publisher at that time, though the editor, a very intelligent man, said "Jack this is just like Dostoievsky, but what can I do at this time?" It was too early. So for the next six years I was a bum, a brakeman, a seaman, a panhandler, a pseudo-Indian in Mexico, anything and everything, and went on writing because my hero was Goethe and I believed in art and hoped some day to write the third part of *Faust*, which I have done in *Doctor Sax*. Then in 1952 an article was published in *The New York Times* Sunday magazine saying, the headline, "'This is a Beat Generation'" (in quotes like that) and in the article it said that I had come up with the term first "when the face was harder to recognize," the face of the generation. After that there was some talk of the Beat Generation but in 1955 I published an excerpt from *Road* (melling it with parts of *Visions of Neal*) under the pseudonym "Jean-Louis," it was entitled *Jazz of the Beat Generation* and was copyrighted as being an excerpt from a novel-in-progress entitled *Beat Generation* (which I later changed to *On the Road* at the insistence of my new editor) and so then the term moved a little faster. The term and the cats. Everywhere began to appear strange hepcats and even college kids went around hep and cool and using the terms I'd heard on Times Square in the early Forties, it was growing somehow. But when the publishers finally took a dare and published *On the Road* in 1957 it burst open, it mushroomed, everybody began yelling about a Beat Generation. I was being interviewed everywhere I went for "what I meant" by such a thing. People began to call themselves beatniks, beats, jazzniks, bopniks, bugniks and finally I was called the "avatar" of all this.

Yet it was as a Catholic, it was not at the insistence of any of these "niks" and certainly not with their approval either, that I went one afternoon to the church of my childhood (one of them), Ste. Jeanne d'Arc in Lowell, Mass., and suddenly with tears in my eyes and had a vision of what I must have really meant with "Beat" anyhow when I heard the holy silence in the church (I was the only one in there, it was five P.M., dogs were barking outside, children yelling, the fall leaves, the candles were flickering alone just for me), the vision of the word Beat as being to mean beatific . . . There's the priest preaching on Sunday morning, all of a sudden through a side door of the church comes a group of Beat Generation characters in strapped raincoats like the I.R.A. coming in silently to "dig" the religion . . . I knew it then.

But this was 1954, so then what horror I felt in 1957 and later 1958 naturally to suddenly see "Beat" being taken up by everybody, press and TV and Hollywood borscht circuit to include [42] the "juvenile delinquency" shot and the horrors of a mad teeming billyclub New York and L.A. and they began to call *that* Beat, *that* beatific . . . bunch of fools marching against the San Francisco Giants protesting baseball, as if (now) in my name and I, my childhood ambition to be a big league baseball star hitter like Ted Williams so that when Bobby Thomson hit that home-run in 1951 I trembled with joy and couldn't get over it for days and wrote poems about how it is possible for the human spirit to win after all! Or, when a murder, a routine murder took place in North Beach, they labeled it a Beat Generation slaying although in my childhood I'd been famous as an eccentric in my block for stopping the younger kids from throwing rocks at the squirrels, for stopping them from frying snakes in cans or trying to blow up frogs with straws. Because my brother had died at the age of nine, his name was Gerard Kerouac, and he'd told me "Ti Jean never hurt any living being, all living beings whether it's just a little cat or squirrel or whatever, all, are going to heaven straight into God's snowy arms so never hurt anything and if you see anybody hurt anything stop them as best you can" and when he died a file of gloomy nuns in black from St. Louis de France parish had filed (1926) to his deathbed to hear his last words about Heaven. And my father too, Leo, had never lifted a hand to punish me, or to punish the little pets in our house, and this teaching was delivered to me by the men in my house and I have never had anything to do with violence, hatred, cruelty, and all that horrible nonsense which, nevertheless, because God is gracious beyond all human imagining, he will forgive in the long end . . . that million years I'm asking about you, America.

And so now they have beatnik routines on TV, starting with satires about girls in black and fellows in jeans with snapknives and sweatshirts and swastikas tattooed under their armpits, it will come to respectable m.c.s of spectaculars coming out nattily attired in Brooks Brothers jean-type tailoring and sweater-type pull-ons, in other words, it's a simple change in fashion and manners, just a history crust—like from the Age of Reason, from old Voltaire in a chair to romantic Chatterton in the moonlight— from Teddy Roosevelt to Scott Fitzgerald . . . So there's nothing to get excited about. Beat comes out, actually, of old American whoopee and it will only change a few dresses and pants and make chairs useless in the livingroom and pretty soon we'll have Beat Secretaries of State and there will be instituted new tinsels, in fact new reasons for malice and new reasons for virtue and new reasons for forgiveness . . .

But yet, but yet, woe, woe unto those who think that the Beat Generation means crime, delinquency, immorality, amorality . . . woe unto those who attack it on the grounds that they simply don't understand history and the yearnings of human souls . . . woe unto those who don't realize that America must, will, is, changing now, for the better I say. Woe unto those who believe in the atom bomb, who believe in hating mothers and fathers, who deny the most important of the Ten Commandments, woe unto those (though) who don't believe in the unbelievable sweetness of sex love, woe unto those who are the standard bearers of death, woe unto those who believe in conflict and horror and violence and fill our books and screens and livingrooms with all that crap, woe in fact unto those who make evil movies about the Beat Generation where innocent housewives are raped by beatniks! Woe unto those who are the real dreary sinners that even God finds room to forgive . . . woe unto those who spit on the Beat Generation, the wind'll blow it back. [79]

# GREGORY CORSO

## THE LAST WARMTH OF ARNOLD

Arnold, warm with God,
hides beneath the porch
remembering the time of escape, imprisoned in Vermont,
shoveling snow. Arnold was from somewhere else,
where it was warm; where he wore suede shoes
and played ping-pong.
Arnold knew the Koran.
And he knew to sing:
    Young Julien Sorel
    Knew his Latin well
    And was wise as he
    Was beautiful
    Until his head fell.

In the empty atmosphere
Arnold kept a tiplet pigeon, a bag of chicken corn.
He thought of Eleanor, her hands;
watched her sit sad in school
He got Carmine to lure her into the warm atmosphere;
he wanted to kiss her, live with her forever;
break her head with bargains.

Who is Arnold? Well,
I first saw him wear a black cap
covered with old Willkie buttons. He was 13.
And afraid. But with a smile. And he was always
willing to walk you home, to meet your mother, [20]
to tell her about Hester Street Park

about the cold bums there;
about the cold old Jewish ladies who sat,
hands folded, sad, keeping their faces

Reprinted from Gregory Corso, *Gasoline* (San Francisco, Calif.: City Lights Books, 1958), pp. 20–21. Copyright 1958 by Gregory Corso; reprinted by permission of City Lights Books.

away from the old Jewish Home.
Arnold grew up with a knowledge of bookies
and chicken pluckers.

And Arnold knew to sing:
    Dead now my 15th year
    F.D.R., whose smiling face
    Made evil the buck-toothed Imperialist,
    The moustached Aryan,
    The jut-jawed Caesar—
    Dead now, and I weep . . .
    For once I did hate that man
    and no reason
    but innocent hate
    —my cap decked with old Willkie buttons.

Arnold was kicked in the balls
by an Italian girl who got mad
because there was a big coal strike on
and it forced the Educational Alliance to close its doors.
Arnold, weak and dying, stole pennies from the library,
but he also read about Paderewski.
He used to walk along South Street
wondering about the various kinds of glue.
And it was about airplane glue he was thinking
when he fell and died beneath the Brooklyn Bridge. [21]

## THE MAD YAK

I am watching them churn the last milk
    they'll ever get from me.
They are waiting for me to die;
They want to make buttons out of my bones.
Where are my sisters and brothers?
That tall monk there, loading my uncle,
    he has a new cap.

And that idiot student of his—
    I never saw that muffler before.
Poor uncle, he lets them load him.
How sad he is, how tired!
I wonder what they'll do with his bones?
And that beautiful tail!
How many shoelaces will they make of that!


## POETS HITCHHIKING ON THE HIGHWAY


Of course I tried to tell him
but he cranked his head
    without an excuse.
I told him the sky chases
    the sun
And he smiled and said:
    'What's the use.'
I was feeling like a demon
    again
So I said: 'But the ocean chases
    the fish.'
This time he laughed
    and said: 'Suppose the
        strawberry were
            pushed into a mountain.'
After that I knew the
    war was on—
So we fought:
He said: 'The apple-cart like a
            broomstick-angel
    snaps & splinters
        old dutch shoes.'
I said: 'Lightning will strike the old oak
    and free the fumes!'
He said: 'Mad street with no name.'

Reprinted from Gregory Corso, *The Happy Birthday of Death* (Norfolk, Conn.: New Directions, 1960), p. 28. Copyright 1960 by New Directions. Reprinted by permission of New Directions.

I said: 'Bald killer! Bald killer! Bald killer!'
He said, getting real mad,
      'Firestoves! Gas! Couch!'
I said, only smiling,
      'I know God would turn back his head
      if I sat quietly and thought.'
We ended by melting away,
    hating the air!

## MARRIAGE

Should I get married? Should I be good?
Astound the girl next door with my velvet suit and faustus hood?
Don't take her to movies but to cemeteries
tell all about werewolf bathtubs and forked clarinets
then desire her and kiss her and all the preliminaries
and she going just so far and I understanding why
not getting angry saying You must feel! It's beautiful to feel!
Instead take her in my arms lean against an old crooked tomb-
    stone
and woo her the entire night the constellations in the sky—

When she introduces me to her parents
back straightened, hair finally combed, strangled by a tie,
should I sit knees together on their 3rd degree sofa
and not ask Where's the bathroom?
How else to feel other than I am,
often thinking Flash Gordon soap—
O how terrible it must be for a young man
seated before a family and the family thinking
We never saw him before! He wants our Mary Lou!
After tea and homemade cookies they ask What do you do for
    a living?

Should I tell them? Would they like me then?
Say All right get married, we're losing a daughter

but we're gaining a son—
And should I then ask Where's the bathroom?

O God, and the wedding! All her family and her friends
and only a handful of mine all scroungy and bearded
just wait to get at the drinks and food—
And the priest! he looking at me as if I masturbated
asking me Do you take this woman for your lawful wedded wife?
And I trembling what to say say Pie Glue!
I kiss the bride all those corny men slapping me on the back [29]
She's all yours, boy! Ha-ha-ha!
And in their eyes you could see some obscene honeymoon going
    on—
Then all that absurd rice and clanky cans and shoes
Niagara Falls! Hordes of us! Husbands! Wives! Flowers! Choco-
    lates!
All streaming into cozy hotels
All going to do the same thing tonight
The indifferent clerk he knowing what was going to happen
The lobby zombies they knowing what
The whistling elevator man he knowing
The winking bellboy knowing
Everybody knowing! I'd be almost inclined not to do anything!
Stay up all night! Stare that hotel clerk in the eye!
Screaming: I deny honeymoon! I deny honeymoon!
running rampant into those almost climactic suites
yelling Radio belly! Cat shovel!
O I'd live in Niagara forever! in a dark cave beneath the Falls
I'd sit there the Mad Honeymooner
devising ways to break marriages, a scourge of bigamy
a saint of divorce—

But I should get married I should be good
How nice it'd be to come home to her
and sit by the fireplace and she in the kitchen
aproned young and lovely wanting my baby
and so happy about me she burns the roast beef
and comes crying to me and I get up from my big papa chair
saying Christmas teeth! Radiant brains! Apple deaf!
God what a husband I'd make! Yes, I should get married!
So much to do! like sneaking into Mr Jones' house late at night
and cover his golf clubs with 1920 Norwegian books
Like hanging a picture of Rimbaud on the lawnmower

like pasting Tannu Tuva postage stamps all over the picket fence
like when Mrs Kindhead comes to collect for the Community
    Chest [30]
grab her and tell her There are unfavorable omens in the sky!
And when the mayor comes to get my vote tell him
When are you going to stop people killing whales!
And when the milkman comes leave him a note in the bottle
Penguin dust, bring me penguin dust, I want penguin dust—

Yet if I should get married and it's Connecticut and snow
and she gives birth to a child and I am sleepless, worn,
up for nights, head bowed against a quiet window, the past be-
    hind me,
finding myself in the most common of situations a trembling man
knowledged with responsibility not twig-smear nor Roman coin
    soup—
O what would that be like!
Surely I'd give it for a nipple a rubber Tacitus
For a rattle a bag of broken Bach records
Tack Della Francesca all over its crib
Sew the Greek alphabet on its bib
And build for its playpen a roofless Parthenon

No, I doubt I'd be that kind of father
not rural not snow no quiet window
but hot smelly tight New York City
seven flights up, roaches and rats in the walls
a fat Reichian wife screeching over potatoes Get a job!
And five nose running brats in love with Batman
And the neighbors all toothless and dry haired
like those hag masses of the 18th century
all wanting to come in and watch TV
The landlord wants his rent
Grocery store Blue Cross Gas & Electric Knights of Columbus
Impossible to lie back and dream Telephone snow, ghost park-
    ing—
No! I should not get married I should never get married!
But—imagine If I were married to a beautiful sophisticated
    woman [31]
tall and pale wearing an elegant black dress and long black
    gloves
holding a cigarette holder in one hand and a highball in the other

and we lived high up in a penthouse with a huge window
from which we could see all of New York and even farther on
   clearer days
No, can't imagine myself married to that pleasant prison dream—

O but what about love? I forget love
not that I am incapable of love
it's just that I see love as odd as wearing shoes—
I never wanted to marry a girl who was like my mother
And Ingrid Bergman was always impossible
And there's maybe a girl now but she's already married
And I don't like men and—
but there's got to be somebody!
Because what if I'm 60 years old and not married,
all alone in a furnished room with pee stains on my underwear
and everybody else is married! All the universe married but me!

Ah, yet well I know that were a woman possible as I am possible
then marriage would be possible—
Like SHE in her lonely alien gaud waiting her Egyptian lover
so I wait—bereft of 2,000 years and the bath of life. [32]

## POWER

*for Allen Ginsberg*

We are the imitation of Power
Every man is to be doubted
There is no mouth no eye no nose no ear no hand enough
The senses are insufficient
You need Power to dispel light
Not the closing of an eye

Since I observe memory and dream
And not the images of the moment
I am become more vivid

Reprinted from Gregory Corso, *The Happy Birthday of Death* (Norfolk, Conn.: New Directions, 1960), pp. 75–80. Copyright 1960 by New Directions. Reprinted by permission of New Directions.

And need not open the eye to see
With me light is always light
How powerful I am to imagine darkness!

Since I depend on heroes for opinion and acceptance
I live by proper truth and error
SHAZAM!
O but how sad is Ted Williams    gypped and chiseled
All alone in center field
Let me be your wise Buck Rogers!

Since I contradict the real with the unreal
Nothing is so unjust as impossibility
Outstepping myself as a man in Azerbaijan
I forge a rocket lion
And with a heart of wooing mathematics soar to passion a planet

O but there are times SHAZAM is not enough
There is a brutality in the rabbit
That leads the way to Paradise—far from God
There is a cruelness in the fawn
Its tiger-elegance gnawing clover to the bone [75]

I am a creature of Power
With me there is no ferocity
I am fair    careful    wise and laughable
I storm a career of love for myself
I am powerful humancy in search of compassion
My Power craves love    Beware my Power!

Know my Power
I resemble fifty miles of Power
I cut my fingernails with a red Power
In buses I stand on huge volumes of Spanish Power
The girl I love is like a goat splashing golden cream Power
Throughout the Spring I carried no Power

But my mission is outrageous!
I am here to tell you various failures of God
The unreasonableness of God
There is something unfair about this
It is not God that has made Power unbearable    it is Love
Love of Influence    Industry    Firearms    Protection
Man protected by man from man    this is Love
Good has no meaning and Sympathy no message    this is Love

THINK signs will never give way to DREAM signs    this is Love
We are ready to fight with howitzers!    this is Love
This has never been my Love
Thank God my Power

Who am I that sing of Power
Am I the stiff arm of Nicaragua
Do I wear green and red in Chrysler squads
Do I hate my people
What about the taxes
Do they forgive me their taxes
Am I to be shot at the racetrack—do they plot now
My monument of sculptured horses is white beneath the moon!
Am I Don Pancho Magnifico Pulque no longer a Power? [76]

No I do not sing of dictatorial Power
The hail of dictatorship is symbolic of awful Power
In my room I have gathered enough gasoline and evidence
To allow dictators inexhaustible Power

I *Ave* no particular Power but that of Life
Nor yet condemn fully any form of Power but that of Death
The inauguration of Death is an absurd Power
Life is the supreme Power
Whoever hurts Life is a penny candy in the confectionary of
    Power
Whoever complains about Life is a dazzling monster in the zoo
    of Power
The lovers of Life are deserved of Power's trophy
They need not jump Power's olympics nor prove pilgrimage
Each man is a happy spy of Power in the realm of Weakness

Power
What is Power
A hat is Power
The world is Power
Being afraid is Power
What is poetry when there is no Power
Poetry is powerless when there is no Power
Standing on a street corner waiting for no one is Power
The angel is not as powerful as looking and then not looking
Will Power make me mean and unforgettable?

Power is underpowered
Power is what is happening

Power is without body or spirit
Power is sadly fundamental
Power is attained by Weakness
Diesels do not explain Power
In Power there is no destruction
Power is not to be dropped by a plane [77]
A thirst for Power is drinking sand
I want no song Power
I want no dream Power
I want no driven-car Power
I want I want I want Power!

Power is without compensation
Angels of Power come down with cups of vengeance
They are demanding compensation
People! where is your Power
The angels of Power are coming down with their cups!

I am the ambassador of Power
I walk through tunnels of fear
With portfolios of Power under my arm
Look at me
The appearance of Power is there
I have come to survey your store of Power—where is it
Is it in your heart your purse
Is it beneath your kitchen sink
Beautiful people I remember your Power
I have not forgotten you in the snows of Bavaria
Skiing down on the sleeping villages with flares and carbines
I have not forgotten you rubbing your greasy hands on aircraft
Signing your obscure names on blockbusters
No! have not forgotten the bazooka you decked with palm
Fastened on the shoulder of a black man
Aimed at a tankful of Aryans
Nor have I forgotten the grenade
The fear and emergency it spread
Throughout your brother's trench
You are Power beautiful people [78]

In a playground where I write this poem feeling shot in the back
Wanting to change the old meaning of Power
Wanting to give it new meaning my meaning
I drop my unusual head dumb to the true joy of being good

And I wonder myself now powerless
Staggering back to the feeble boys of my youth
Are they now lesser men in the factories of universe
Are they there compressing the air
Pumping their bully profanations through long leafy tubes
I see them perched high on the shelves of God
Outpecking this offered hemisphere like a crumb—
O God! what uttered curse ushers me to them
Like a prisoner of war . . .
Be those ominous creaks of eternity their sad march?

How powerless I am in playgrounds
Swings like witches woosh about me
Sliding ponds like dinosaur tongues down to my unusual feet
To have me walk in the street would be *both* unusual

*1956*

*1958*
Power is still with me! Who got me hung on Power?
Am I stuffed in the grizzly maw of Power's hopped-up wheel
Will I always be like this   head in   legs out
Like one of Ulysses men in the mouth of Polyphemus
Am I the Power drag? Me   the Power head?
Just what Power am I for anyway!
The seized bee in a blaze of honey Power—
The spider in the center of its polar veil
With a fly-from-another-world Power—
Good noon nap on adoration lap with all cozy cruelty Power—
Towering melt like an avalanche of glass never ending chirring
     Power—
Stooped and hushed Chronicleleer of Spenserian gauderies
Is surely maybe my Power— [79]
Whenever I play the fiery lyre with cold-fingered minstrelry
A luscious Power gives me a heavened consequence good as sun-
     light—
Awful blank acreage once made pastoral by myths
Now abandoned to mankind's honest yet hopeless
Anthemion-elixir is in need of my Power
But the Power I have I built with my own help!
That bad wolf approach in dim-divine disguise Power
All mine! All illumination sheep Power!
That woodsy savant fetch-eyed scarce perspective from
Balm-volumed epics that prouds shy fantasy my Power!

That hand-grenade humor dropped down the hatch
Of an armoured suit my proposed bit come doomsday Power!
O joy to its march down the street!
Ha! The envy of diamonds in the windows!
The child of Power is laughter!

October you fat month of gloom and poetry
It's no longer your melodious graveyard air
Your night-yanked cypresses
Your lovely dead moon
It is October of me! My Power!
Alive with a joy a sparkle a laugh
That drops my woe and all woe to the floor
Like a shot spy [80]

## VARIATIONS ON A GENERATION

### 1

The most outstanding of all the great services the Beat Generation has thus far rendered is in connection with the use of 'measure' in poetry. When the Beat Generation came into existence,
poets, with prophetic insight, were already insisting upon the
overwhelming importance of supplementing their supplies of old
iambics by the use of mixtures containing spontaneity 'bop
prosody' surreal-real images jumps beats cool measures long
rapidic vowels, long long lines, and, the main content, soul. In
1950 these poets gave name to the generation, calling it the Beat
Generation; they did not know when they created that stupid
name what the vast extent of the future demand would be.

### 2

—What do you think about the Beat Generation?—
—I don't think it's anything. I don't think it exists. There's no
such thing as the Beat Generation.—
—You don't consider yourself beat?—

Reprinted from *Gemini*, Vol. 2, No. 6 (Spring, 1959), pp. 47–51, by permission of the author.

—Hell no! I don't consider myself beat, or beatified.—
—What are you if not beat?—
—An individual, nothing.—
—They say to be beat is to be nothing.—
—I don't care what they say, there's no Beat Generation.—
—Don't you care about the existence of the beat?—
—Hell no! man!—
—Don't you love your fellow men?—
—No I don't love my fellow man in fact I dislike them very much, except the individual if I get to know him; I don't want to govern or be governed.—
—But you are governed by laws of society.—
—But I'm trying to avoid that.—
—Ah, by avoiding society you become separate from society and being separate from society is being BEAT.—
—Oh, yeah?—
—Yeah.—
—I don't understand. I don't want to be in the society at all, I want to be outside it.—
—Face it, man, you're beat.—
—I am not! It's not even a conscious desire on my part, it's just the way I am, I am what I am.—
—Man, you're so beat you don't know.
—Oh, yeah?—
—Yeah.—
—Crazy, man.—
—Cool, here, light a joint.—

3

There was no mention of the use of "measure" in poetry; not one of them said a thing about the death of the iambic pentameter in America; they spoke about themselves, not about poetry. The Beat Generation is no longer about poetry. The Beat Generation is now about everything.

4

—And what do you think of the Beat Generation?—
—A generation is a human generation. Beat means to have all the blather knocked out of you by experience, suddenly seeing

things as they are. Beat doesn't mean a broken spirit, on the contrary, it's scourged of external blather! Wallace Stevens said the greatest misfortune is not to live in the physical world to feel that one's desire is too difficult to tell from one's despair.—

—But what do you think about the Beat Generation?—

—A certain style, when you look back on it, old photos, Fitzgerald in Paris, 1920, high society, prohibition, jazz; that's more what characterized a generation than what they believed in. The fundamental facts are always the same, the style changes, but the [47] facts, my boy, the facts remain.—

—Are you beat?—

—Well I'm not a square, you see a square is some guy who forces himself arbitrarily into a square auto-life mold, because squareness is not a shape that any living creature occurs in. There are all varieties of squares in America. Take for instance a sharecropper, only thing he'd share would be his manure, now that's kind of square, ain't it?—

—You're beat, then?—

—Beatness may result from any sort of fundamental experience, a particular form of insight whereby you realize that nine tenths of everything that moves and operates people is——!—

5

The Beat Generation is witty cheerful passionate sentimental poetical.

The Beat Generation is youth quarrels vexation American disappointment of a cherished hope, an enlightment, a testimonial of honor and distinction.

The Beat Generation foretells that all youth America will leave their homes and sojourn among strangers.

The Beat Generation is a dream of youth, a dream that will live to a great age like a pair of scissors, or a knife, or any other pointed deathical instrument.

Harlem stomp club seniors juniors cubs tiny-tims debs, gangs of eagles, gangs of Geronimo, Comanche.

The Beat Generation is song, front street-door song, Bible song, viper song, Lucifer is great, Lucifer is first free thinker, Lucifer is eternal rebel, hail Lucifer!

The Beat Generation is high, is good omen, is like frog.

## 6

—How do you see the Beat Generation?—

—The Angry Young Men are not technically equipped as the American poets are, the aims of the two movements are in a sense similar, but what English angry young man has had to face the enormous problem of building not merely a new society but a new language—Americanical, and with America the whole Mississippi of a new prosody to fit the ecstatic rhythm of the new American tongue. Fifty years ago America tore up the old metre rearranged searched into the classical past for examples of this vast tongue-shift—Provencal, Pound—and the oriental written language for example of the new sharpness of image—particular visions discovered when the eye was cleaned of its trite. This vast shift in prosody accomplished by Pound Williams and Eliot, this is now the great tradition, it is half a century old, all over the world maniacal voices of prophets have blotted out their own personal weeping music. In France Apollinaire who taught Eliot; Artaud who will teach the angels of the future. In Spain Lorca, the new found land of surrealist prosody discovered by the poet in New York. Myakovsky whose great heart exploded the ancient prosody of Russia and permanently murdered the illusory dictatorship of idiot politicians with its magnificent suicide. In America Walt Whitman the mountain too vast to be seen broods over the dance of walls that agitates her meadows—and his children Pound Williams Eliot have sat under his shadow inhabiting his beard like butterflies. A whole new generation of prosody has wept and wailed in the solitudinous cities of the West. It is the uproar of their voices and the countless intricacies of their measure which now descends like a great roc to stun and enlighten the new generation of Albion. Albion! Albion! Where is your music, lost in the dusty iambic attic of the 19th Century? Angry Young Men where is your revolution? Where is your prosody? Where is your actual tongues? Why are your stanzas so old? Why are your rhymes rhymes? Who dare talk of tradition when the ear is dead when invention is forgotten when the riot of 20th Century truth is lisped in the melancholy of Oxford pentameter? Beauty's speech must take the real tongue of the naked human form divine! Milton! thou shouldst be living at this hour! Samson Agonistes where is thy sting? The Establishment is none other than the very iamb with which thou hast shackled the *awful*. Eliot the revolutionary said that the next generation would be less inspired than he, a conservator of the forms which he extended, but Williams Pound and the lofty shade of Whitman, and the halleluyah ghost of Hart [48] Crane, Dylan Thomas (broken by the iamb) and the endless voice of Blake sing forever renewed inspiration.


### 7

The Beat Generation is filled with divinations, it has stiff hair, large bones, firm and robust limbs, short muscular neck, firm and erect, the head and breast high, the forehead short, hard, and peaked, with bristly hair, large feet, rather thick than broad, a harsh unequal voice, a voice of divinity, a new voice, conqueror eater voice, parasite of the old dead voice.

If you are beat, if you see death and flowers and see a person of peace beheaded, if you see one beheaded, it is terrible, you will cry, you will grow lean and shrink up, your belly will swell, a funeral will pass by, you will beat.


### 8

The poets of the Beat Generation like Jack Kerouac have entered the leperous kingdom of prose and have kissed the leper. The Beat Generation is a generation of love. Not until the sun rejects you do I reject you, this is their love. They aren't violent. To be violent is not to be beat. To be beat is to be hip. Hip means love, means indifference, means not wanting to be bugged or to bug. Hip means metropolitan cosmopolitan solitude, hip means being on a street corner bombed out of your mind.


### 9

—What do you think about the Beat Generation?—
—What point of view do you want?—
—Your point of view.—
—Oh, my point of view. Well, I was beat in a different way in my student days.—
—What do you mean?—
—I was already on the way of losing my goals when I went to College to be an English major, because it was easy.—
—You like being beat?—
—Oh, I guess I do. I belong in it half way though, the other

half is still my being a country boy in Pennsylvania around the Allegheny Mountains. I live in a little place called Greenfield which is two miles from Bethel seven miles from Frogtown about nine miles from New Wilmington five miles from West Middlesex and eight miles from the county seat.—

—When did you first become beat?—

—It was when the spade hipped me on jazz and chess.—

—Who is this negro?—

—He took off to the University of Chicago and nobody ever heard from him again.—

—I guess he didn't like being beat.—

—No, man, he was too beat.—

—And where did you take off to?—

—I stuck and got in with some screwed-up political Jewish intellectuals.—

—Oh?—

—One of them slid into radio, then TV., then movies (Hot Rod Rumble) and has been in analysis ever since 1949—guess, he still is.—

—What do you think the Beat Generation consists of?—

—Consists of? Oh, beat people with beat hip ideas who have nothing to latch on to but each other.—

—Then it's a generation of love.—

—No, man, you're nowhere. Ask me another question.—

—Don't you believe in love?—

—You're too much, man.—

### 10

The Hipster dressed in ermine in the golden halls of the Beat Generation will be the slayer of society, it is told in his enthusiastic eye. He will sack society with his sword of old prunes, climb the fortress with armies of penguins and fly away with the daughter of society. He will wed the daughter of society, and throughout all the nights of their marriage, he will drive her mad with descriptions of her father.

### 11

—Sir, would you care to comment on the general impression that the Beat Generation stands for promiscuous, even perverted, sex, and the use of narcotics, drugs which have been outlawed by the United States of America and every other civilized country in the world today?—[49]

—I would say that the Beat Generation challenges as any generation must challenge everything that has been done and acted before. We will not force ourselves into any hand-me-down-inherited straight-jacket of all cast-off moral concepts mixed with beastly superstition derived from the primitive mythology which is found in the bible—not that I have any objection to mythology in its proper place. We are human. And we are many. And we will have our voice in changing and making the laws which govern so-called civilized countries today; laws which have covered the earth with secret police, concentration camps, oppression, slavery, wars, death.—

—Is the Beat Generation a generation of outlaws? On what grounds do you presume to declare yourself exempt from your fellow humans?—

—Was the father of our country an outlaw? Yes. Was Galileo an outlaw for saying the world was round?—I say the world is round! not square! This is a fact.—

## 12

—Sir, how has your life been changed by the Beat Generation.—

—The Beat Generation, is that an established generation?—

—Yes, sir.—

—Then, my boy, the Beat Generation gets in with what's going on in history. Education in the U.S. Nowhere anyone who has anything on the ball, no education because schooly weeded down to dead level of stupidity. There are people that don't want to learn. Any moron can graduate.—

—The Beat Generation hasn't any standards.—

—The more you think about the Beat Generation the vaguer your ideas become; that's why it's so hard to write articles, you have to have a sort of neat idea, not quite true, like trying to write an article on 'Attitude of The French People'. That's why those who spent a month in a country often don't hesitate to write the best books about it.—

—Can you define the Beat Generation?—

—It consists of man, I must define man, man is a cross between a passive social monkey and an aggressive baboon. Take baboons, for instance, hard to understand how animals so vicious among themselves can also be so god damned gregarious!—

## 13

—Hey, what do you know about the Beat Generation?—
—What we are witnessing is a delicate shift of total consciousness in America—It won't be done through publicity or propaganda, articles or any form of—brainwashing persuasion—it will occur as response to altered history scene. Statue of Liberty standing surrounded by the garbage of materialism, a sea of humanity starves in the water outside her. Love puts pressure—humanity forced into the brain and Congress. New fact, Sputnik, Heisenberg, China, Soul, Angels (the image of man)—these latter apparitions of what was sensed before. The shift and new recognition can only be incarnated and commenced thru great works of Art (as Whitman rightly demanded from poets to come)—Art to stand beacon like Statue naked and courageous, individual statement of private actual, uncensored individual perception. Always assuming as did Whitman and the early democrats —that free will is not destructive. An inspiration contrary to the teachings of the evil religions. It was the atheistical enlightment which first framed the ideal democratic declaration of independence. Therefore a new art whose objectivity will be the accuracy of its introspection—the bringing forth of heretofore hidden materials, lusts, spiritual ambitions, experiences—in the new forms in which they will necessarily arrive—rather than the cringing self-consciousness of the psyche whose individuality has been so thwarted—that it masks itself and deceives others—under a guise of a received system of thought, of a system of thought at all, a received mode of feeling (which is never received but constantly occurs on its own) (when true) (when at all) or measure, stanzaic or structural, as far as its poesy is concerned. O fear of the fury of subjective revolution, death and new beat insight!—
—Now that the Beat Generation has become part of the world are you, as one of the beat, in any way concerned with world problems, politics?—[50]
—The total alteration, personal work social political poetic, emotive—demanded by alteration of consciousness—enforced by alteration of facts: the arrival on the world of the great bomb of the apocalypse, the journey from our world to others now

unknown but visionarily reachable. And in the next years, the psychic atomic bomb, already foreshadowed by advanced scientific art conceptions of the nature of matter and consciousness —Hip to Mind—: for there is now a drug which imitates schizophrenia—extract from the blood of madmen. Alteration necessitated by the new absolute insight into the possible dehumanization of man granted by our experience, we read books about, and we've been in madhouse there already anyway—the multiple destructiveness of the hideous bomb, the concentration camps of the witty and sluggish races, mass wars from China to Tanganyika, mass propaganda, mass dictatorship and brainwashing—the failures of Red Lands to accomplish mechanical civilization without essential damage to the identity of the human image.—(The Failure of America to generate the energy of Freedom—The Fall of America).

—How does the Beat Generation really see the world?—

—As a vast system of mechanical communication bestriding the world like the—of the Whore of Babylon, reducing myriad historical food fact to the lowest common denominator of—nationalistic madness—it's all over our faces, marks of weakness marks of woe—ah, constantly feeding this frightful Bane into the ear of the masses—because the juice of the individual tremble is absent—has driven them to blindness and suicide, maniacal universal selfish competition, like a great fat fairy took over the government.—

—What does the Beat Generation think about money?—

—The great American Bank must fall in Time anyway, that the bank of all the world prosper, that government Itself fall, and be replaced if at all by a new universal government reflecting the insight of the myriad individualities which populate the worlds—all those spoiled people that don't like WORK—(damned vicious psychology of sweat O brow)—the government is constituted to serve that individuality and differentiation (grassblades grassblades)—which is the only hope of that future glorious bands of angels that will be the human race when it has achieved its already many times glimpsed godhead, NOW AT HAND!—

—What have the poets to do with the Beat Generation?—

—This is the first year that a poet without folly with perfect consciousness of his pen and profound, can address his elegy to the citizens of all the worlds of the universe, knowing that if his speech makes it, if he is true to his soul, if his message is stripped to the nuts of love, and proceeds from his archtypical mind essence selfless selfhood, him, simple, poor bones,—it will inevitably reach the farthest star and most distant lone inhabitant of the strangest planets of the sky and overjoy multitudinous inhabitants of every world in creation past present and future visible and invisible—those 10 to 100 (presently statisticised) million planets unconscious wherein our brother forms in being have risen from atomic dust, left behind their message to eternity—salutation, greeting—and subsided into the dust—endless repetitions of purest spirit moving thru new forms—mind of god contemplating itself as Yorely.—[51]

# WILLIAM S. BURROUGHS

## DEPOSITION: TESTIMONY CONCERNING A SICKNESS

I awoke from The Sickness at the age of forty-five, calm and sane, and in reasonably good health except for a weakened liver and the look of borrowed flesh common to all who survive The Sickness. . . . Most survivors do not remember the delirium in detail. I apparently took detailed notes on sickness and delirium. I have no precise memory of writing the notes which have now been published under the title *Naked Lunch*. The title was suggested by Jack Kerouac. I did not understand what the title meant until my recent recovery. The title means exactly what the words say: NAKED Lunch—a frozen moment when everyone sees what is on the end of every fork.

The Sickness is drug addiction and I was an addict for fifteen years. When I say addict I mean an addict to *junk* (generic term for opium and/or derivatives including all synthetics from demerol to palfium. I have used junk in many forms: morphine, heroin, dilaudid, eukodal, pantapon, diocodid, diosane, opium, demerol, dolophine, palfium. I have smoked junk, eaten it, sniffed it, injected it in vein-skin-muscle, inserted it in rectal suppositories. The needle is not important. Whether you sniff it smoke it eat it or shove it up your ass the result is the same: addiction. When I speak of drug addiction I do not refer to keif, marijuana or any preparation of hashish, mescaline, Bannisteria Caapi, LSD6, Sacred Mushrooms or any other drug of the hallucinogen group. . . . There is no evidence that the use of any hallucinogen results in physical dependence. The action of these drugs is physiologically opposite to the action of junk. A lamentable confusion between the two classes of drugs has arisen owing to the zeal of the U.S. and other narcotic departments.

I have seen the exact manner in which the junk virus operates [15] through fifteen years of addiction. The pyramid of junk, one level eating the level below (it is no accident that junk

Reprinted from *Evergreen Review*, Vol. 4, No. 11 (January–February, 1960), pp. 15–23. Reprinted by permission of the author.

higher-ups are always fat and the addict in the street is always thin) right up to the top or tops since there are many junk pyramids feeding on peoples of the world and all built on basic principles of monopoly:

1. Never give anything away for nothing.
2. Never give more than you have to give (always catch the buyer hungry and always make him wait).
3. Always take everything back if you possibly can.

The Pusher always gets it all back. The addict needs more and more junk to maintain a human form . . . buy off the Monkey.

Junk is the mold of monopoly and possession. The addict stands by while his junk legs carry him straight in on the junk beam to relapse. Junk is quantitative and accurately measurable. The more junk you use the less you have and the more you have the more you use. All the hallucinogen drugs are considered sacred by those who use them—there are Peyote Cults and Bannisteria Cults, Hashish Cults and Mushroom Cults— "the Sacred Mushrooms of Mexico enable a man to see God"— but no one ever suggested that junk is sacred. There are no opium cults. Opium is profane and quantitative like money. I have heard that there was once a beneficent non-habit-forming junk in India. It was called *soma* and is pictured as a beautiful blue tide. If *soma* ever existed the Pusher was there to bottle it and monopolize it and sell it and it turned into plain old time JUNK.

Junk is the ideal product . . . the ultimate merchandise. No sales talk necessary. The client will crawl through a sewer and beg to buy. . . . The junk merchant does not sell his product to the consumer, he sells the consumer to his product. He does not improve and simplify his merchandise. He degrades and simplifies the client. He pays his staff in junk.

Junk yields a basic formula of "evil" virus: *The Algebra of Need.* The face of "evil" is always the face of total need. A dope fiend is a man in total need of dope. Beyond a certain frequency need knows absolutely no limit or control. In the words of total need: *"Wouldn't you?"* Yes you would. You would lie, [16] cheat, inform on your friends, steal, do *anything* to satisfy total need. Because you would be in a state of total sickness, total possession, and not in a position to act in any other way. Dope fiends are sick people who cannot act other than they do. A rabid dog cannot choose but bite. Assuming a self-righteous position is nothing to the purpose unless your purpose be to keep the junk virus in operation. And junk is a big industry. I recall talking to an American who worked for the Aftosa Commission in Mexico. Six hundred a month plus expense account: "How long will the epidemic last?" I enquired.

"As long as we can keep it going. . . . And yes . . . maybe the aftosa will break out in South America," he said dreamily.

If you wish to alter or annihilate a pyramid of numbers in a serial relation, you alter or remove the bottom number. If we wish to annihilate the junk pyramid, we must start with the bottom of the pyramid: *the Addict in the Street,* and stop tilting quixotically for the "higher ups" so called, all of whom are immediately replaceable. *The addict in the street who must have junk to live is the one irreplaceable factor in the junk equation.* When there are no more addicts to buy junk there will be no junk traffic. As long as junk need exists, someone will service it.

Addicts can be cured or quarantined—that is allowed a morphine ration under minimal supervision like typhoid carriers. When this is done, junk pyramids of the world will collapse. So far as I know, England is the only country to apply this method to the junk problem. They have about five hundred quarantined addicts in the U.K. In another generation when the quarantined addicts die off and pain killers operating on a non-junk principle are discovered, the junk virus will be like smallpox, a closed chapter—a medical curiosity.

The vaccine that can relegate the junk virus to a land-locked past is in existence. This vaccine is the Apomorphine Treatment discovered by an English doctor whose name I must withhold pending his permission to use it and to quote from his book covering thirty years of apomorphine treatment of addicts and alcoholics. The compound apomorphine is formed by boiling morphine with hydrochloric acid. It was discovered years before [17] it was used to treat addicts. For many years the only use for apomorphine which has no narcotic or pain-killing properties was as an emetic to induce vomiting in cases of poisoning. It acts directly on the vomiting center in the back brain.

I found this vaccine at the end of the junk line. I lived in one room in the Native Quarter of Tangier. I had not taken a bath in a year nor changed my clothes or removed them except to stick a needle every hour in the fibrous grey wooden flesh of terminal addiction. I never cleaned or dusted the room.

Empty ampule boxes and garbage piled to the ceiling. Light and water long since turned off for non-payment. I did absolutely nothing. I could look at the end of my shoe for eight hours. I was only roused to action when the hourglass of junk ran out. If a friend came to visit—and they rarely did since who or what was left to visit—I sat there not caring that he had entered my field of vision—a grey screen always blanker and fainter—and not caring when he walked out of it. If he had died on the spot I would have sat there looking at my shoe waiting to go through his pockets. Wouldn't you? Because I never had enough junk—no one ever does. Thirty grains of morphine a day and it still was not enough. And long waits in front of the drugstore. Delay is a rule in the junk business. The Man is never on time. This is no accident. There are no accidents in the junk world. The addict is taught again and again exactly what will happen if he does not score for his junk ration. Get up that money or else. And suddenly my habit began to jump and jump. Forty, sixty grains a day. And it still was not enough. And I could not pay.

I stood there with my last check in my hand and realized that it was my last check. I took the next plane for London.

The doctor explained to me that apomorphine acts on the back brain to regulate the metabolism and normalize the blood stream in such a way that the enzyme system of addiction is destroyed over a period of four or five days. Once the back brain is regulated apomorphine can be discontinued and only used in case of relapse. (No one would take apomorphine for kicks. *Not one case of addiction to apomorphine has ever been recorded.*) I agreed to undergo treatment and entered a nursing [18] home. For the first twenty-four hours I was literally insane and paranoid as many addicts are in severe withdrawal. This delirium was dispersed by twenty-four hours of intensive apomorphine treatment. The doctor showed me the chart. I had received minute amounts of morphine that could not possibly account for my lack of the more severe withdrawal symptoms such as leg and stomach cramps, fever and my own special symptom, The Cold Burn, like a vast hive covering the body and rubbed with menthol. Every addict has his own special symptom that cracks all control. There was a missing factor in the withdrawal equation—that factor could only be apomorphine.

I saw the apomorphine treatment really work. Eight days later I left the nursing home eating and sleeping normally. I remained completely off junk for two full years—a twelve year record. I did relapse for some months as a result of pain and illness. Another apomorphine cure has kept me off junk through this writing.

The apomorphine cure is qualitatively different from other methods of cure. I have tried them all. Short reduction, slow reduction, cortisone, antihistamines, tranquilizers, sleeping cures, tolserol, reserpine. None of these cures lasted beyond the first opportunity to relapse. I can say definitely that I was never *metabolically* cured until I took the apomorphine cure. The overwhelming relapse statistics from the Lexington Narcotic Hospital have led many doctors to say that addiction is not curable. They use a dolophine reduction cure at Lexington and have never tried apomorphine so far as I know. In fact, this method of treatment has been largely neglected. No research has been done with variations of the apomorphine formula or with synthetics. No doubt substances fifty times stronger than apomorphine could be developed and the side effect of vomiting eliminated.

Apomorphine is a metabolic and psychic regulator that can be discontinued as soon as it has done its work. The world is deluged with tranquilizers and energizers but this unique regulator has not received attention. No research has been done by any of the large pharmaceutical companies. I suggest that [19] research with variations of apomorphine and synthesis of it will open a new medical frontier extending far beyond the problem of addiction.

The smallpox vaccine was opposed by a vociferous lunatic group of anti-vaccinationists. No doubt a scream of protest will go up from interested or unbalanced individuals as the junk virus is shot out from under them. Junk is big business; there are always cranks and operators. They must not be allowed to interfere with the essential work of inoculation treatment and quarantine. *The junk virus is public health problem number one of the world today.*

Since *Naked Lunch* treats this health problem, it is necessarily brutal, obscene and disgusting. Sickness is often repulsive details not for weak stomachs.

Certain passages in the book that have been called pornographic were written as a tract against Capital Punishment in the manner of Jonathan Swift's *Modest Proposal.* These sections are intended to reveal capital punishment as the obscene, bar-

baric and disgusting anachronism that it is. As always the lunch is naked. If civilized countries want to return to Druid Hanging Rites in the Sacred Grove or to drink blood with the Aztecs and feed their Gods with blood of human sacrifice, let them see what they actually eat and drink. Let them see what is on the end of that long newspaper spoon.

I have almost completed a sequel to *Naked Lunch*. A mathematical extension of the Algebra of Need beyond the junk virus. Because there are many forms of addiction I think that they all obey basic laws. In the words of Heiderberg: "This may not be the best of all possible universes but it may well prove to be one of the simplest." If man can *see*.

### Post Script . . . Wouldn't You?

And speaking *Personally* and if a man speaks any other way we might as well start looking for his Protoplasm Daddy or Mother Cell . . . . *I Don't Want To Hear Any More Tired Old Junk Talk And Junk Con.* . . . The same things said a million [20] times and more and there is no point in saying anything because *NOTHING Ever Happens* in the junk world.

Only excuse for this tired death route is THE KICK when the junk circuit is cut off for the non-payment and the junk-skin dies of junk-lack and overdose of time and the Old Skin has forgotten the skin game simplifying a way under the junk cover the way skins will. . . . A condition of total exposure is precipitated when the Kicking Addict cannot choose but see smell and listen. . . . Watch out for the cars. . . .

It is clear that junk is a Round-the-World-Push-an-Opium-Pellet-with-Your-Nose-Route. Strictly for Scarabs—stumble bum junk heap. And as such report to disposal. Tired of seeing it around.

Junkies always beef about *The Cold* as they call it, turning up their black coat collars and clutching their withered necks . . . pure junk con. A junky does not want to be warm, he wants to be Cool-Cooler-COLD. But he wants The Cold like he wants His Junk—NOT OUTSIDE where it does him no good but INSIDE so he can sit around with a spine like a frozen hydraulic jack . . . his metabolism approaching Absolute ZERO. TERMINAL addicts often go two months without a bowel move and the intestines make with sit-down-adhesions—Wouldn't you? —requiring the intervention of an apple corer or its surgical equivalent. . . . Such is life in The Old Ice House. Why move around and waste TIME?

Room for One More Inside, Sir.

Some entities are on thermodynamic kicks. They invented thermodynamics. . . . Wouldn't you?

And some of us are on Different Kicks and that's a thing out in the open the way I like to see what I eat and visa versa mutatis mutandis as the case may be. *Bill's Naked Lunch Room.* . . . Step right up. . . . Good for young and old, man and bestial. Nothing like a little snake oil to grease the wheels and get a show on the track Jack. Which side are you on? Fro-Zen Hydraulic? Or you want to take a look around with Honest Bill?

So that's the World Health Problem I was talking about back in The Article. The Prospect Before Us Friends of MINE. Do I hear muttering about a personal razor and some bush league [21] short con artist who is known to have invented The Bill? Wouldn't You? The razor belonged to a man named Occam and he was not a scar collector. Ludwig Wittgenstein *Tractatus Logico-Philosophicus* "If a proposition is NOT NECESSARY it is MEANINGLESS and approaching MEANING ZERO."

"And what is More UNNECESSARY than junk if You Don't NEED it?"

*Answer:* "Junkies, if you are not ON JUNK."

I tell you boys, I've heard some tired conversation but no other OCCUPATION GROUP can approximate that old thermodynamic junk Slow-DOWN. Now your heroin addict does not say hardly anything and that I can stand. But your Opium "Smoker" is more active since he still has a tent and a Lamp . . . and maybe 7-9-10 lying up in there like hibernating reptiles keep the temperature up to Talking Level: How low the other junkies are "whereas We—WE have this tent and this lamp and this tent and this lamp and this tent and nice and warm in here nice and warm nice and IN HERE and nice and OUTSIDE ITS COLD. . . . ITS COLD OUTSIDE where the dross eaters and the needle boys won't last two years not six months hardly won't last stumble bum around and there is no class in them. . . . But WE SIT HERE and never increase the DOSE . . . never—never increase the dose never except TONIGHT is a SPECIAL OCCASION with all the dross eaters and needle boys out there in the cold. . . . And we never eat it never never never eat it. . . . Excuse please while I take a trip to The Source Of Living Drops they all have in pocket and opium pellets shoved up the ass in a finger stall with the Family Jewels and the other shit.

Room for one more inside, Sir.

Well when that record starts around for the billionth light year and never the tape shall change us non-junkies take drastic action and the men separate out from the Junk boys.

Only way to protect yourself against this horrid peril is come over HERE and shack up with Charybdis. . . . Treat you right kid. . . . Candy and cigarettes.

I am after fifteen years in that tent. In and out in and out in and OUT. *Over* and *Out*. So listen to Old Uncle Bill Burroughs [22] who invented the Burroughs Adding Machine Regulator Gimmick on the Hydraulic Jack Principle no matter how you jerk the handle result is always the same for given co-ordinates. Got my training early . . . wouldn't you?

Paregoric Babies of the World Unite. We have nothing to lose but Our Pushers. And THEY are NOT NECESSARY.

Look down LOOK DOWN along that junk road before you travel there and get in with the Wrong Mob. . . .

STEP RIGHT UP. . . . Only a three Dollar Bill to use BILL's telescope.

A word to the wise guy. [23]

## THE CUT UP METHOD OF BRION GYSIN

Tristan Tzara at a surrealist rally in the 1920s proposed to create a poem on the spot by pulling words out of a hat. A riot ensued wrecked the theatre. The method was grounded in/on the Freudian couch and Ma Freud's dream book.

In the summer of 1960 Brion Gysin painter and writer cut newspaper articles into sections and rearranged the sections *looking away*. Result was direct messages from write now.

Method is simple: Take a page or more or less of your own writing or from any writer living and or dead. Any written or spoken words. Cut into sections with scissors or switch blade as preferred and rearrange the sections. Looking away. Now write out result. Brion Gysin: "The cut up method places at the

Published by permission of the author.

disposal of writers the collage method used by painters for the past fifty years."

Doctor Neumann: *Theory of Games and Economic Behavior* introduced the cut up principle of random action into military and game strategy. It is now being used by Russian chess masters.

The cut up method was used in *Naked Lunch* [1] without the author's full awareness of the method he was using. The final form of *Naked Lunch* and the juxtaposition of sections was determined by the order in which material went—at random—to the printer. Subsequently I used the method with awareness scissors in *Minutes to Go* [2] and *The Exterminator*.[3]

Applications of cut up method are literally unlimited cut out from time limits. Old word lines keep you in old word slots. Cut your way out. Cut paper cut film cut tape. Scissors or switch blade as preferred. Take it to cut city.

## A NEWSPEAK PRÉCIS OF THE ARTICLE MADE IN ITS IMAGE WITH ITS MATERIALS

Heroin opium morphine palfium buys off the monkey who eats form. Result is the same. He always gets the algebra. I did not understand recovery. A lamentable confusion as the addict shrinks calm and sane in weakened liver, squares to a fraction of quantitative relief.

Self-righteous position is front room monkey under the title what is? Who must have junk to live in the structure? When there are no addicts opium in Soma. Talk exact manner in which junk virus controls words in monkey by those who purpose to keep the virus of numbers or remove the bottom number street to cover basic frequency.

Sacred non-habit-forming junk depicted as beautiful blue [12]

Reprinted from *Evergreen Review*, Vol. 4, No. 11 (January–February, 1960), pp. 12, 14. Reprinted by permission of the author.

[1] [*Naked Lunch* (Paris: Olympia Press, 1959).]

[2] [*Minutes to Go* (Paris: Two Cities Editions, 1960).]

[3] [*The Exterminator* (San Francisco: Auerhahn Press, 1960).]

sewer into plain junk. Remember? Result is the same: Total possession assuming purpose needs junk to face and body his legs.

Cold algebra called Soma before opium to grease self-righteous position. Opium to show junk around junkies. Invented junk to keep total disposal death circuit. Heroin dynamics to cover basic living habit from white time sewer monkey taking soul as title on zero around addicts.

Morphine vector total virus to grease addicts terminal time. Blue habit forming words to young cover living habit from white time sewer of World Pushers.

The razor inside, sir. Jerk the handle.

Scar collector of this needle has forgotten: Righteous position for other on track before terminal time. [14]

# Alan Ansen

## ANYONE WHO CAN PICK UP A FRYING PAN OWNS DEATH

Agatha Christie, somewhere, making fun of the plot of a hypothetical modern play, says that the young hero is actually a sort of saint: he robs, he commits mayhem, he kills and then finally he performs a miracle. She spoke better than she knew; for in the burgeoning American potlatch of yummy chloresterol, [32] high-priced protein and the infinitely extensible falsie only some sharp delinquency, whether a private needle or a public bomb, seems capable of reminding us that we live perpetually with heaven and hell.

What William S. Burroughs gives us, in his life and his writings, is the example of a deeply committed personality totally uninterested in culture as information, in a surface of "nice" people, in all those time-wasting activities with which even the most earnest hen-track makers seek to beguile the spectre.

Picture a young man brought up in Saint Louis descended

Reprinted from *Big Table* # 2, Vol. 1 (Summer, 1959), pp. 32–41, by permission of Big Table, Inc.

from the founder of one of America's great industrial enterprises. The depression reduces the family fortune but by no means completely wipes it out. At Harvard during the first New Deal administration he impresses his contemporaries with the force underlying his political intelligence, his serious studies in poetry and ethnology, his experiments with Yogi. A year or so in corrupting Europe and back to Harvard for graduate study in anthropology.

And now the break. An early traumatic experience has resulted in a rough love life and, even more important, in a loss of confidence in his family. Psychoanalysis removes fear but not a sense of isolation. Self-contrived rejection by the Army after the fall of France strengthens that sense. All of us who failed to participate in the war effort owing to one form of unclubbability or another have, I think, felt the necessity to conduct private wars of our own. Even pacifists and enemy sympathizers participate dialectically; the outsiders feel they need the danger even if they and the purpose find each other mutually dispensible. In addition Burroughs has the need for commitment, which odd jobs—exterminator, private detective, bartender—cannot give, since a small trust fund effactually excludes him from basic concern. This commitment he finds in addiction to narcotics, an addiction which swallows up his income and gives him a new grim interest in the economy. [33]

However gratifying the sense of urgency and the solidarity of weakness he finds in criminals, their stupidity gets on his nerves. After the war, establishing himself in the vicinity of Columbia University, he becomes the guide, philosopher and friend of a group of young college boys including Allen Ginsberg and Jack Kerouac, a role he has continued to play for many of us ever since with great success and to our great spiritual profit.

After a period in New Orleans Burroughs heads for Mexico with his wife and two children. There things are possible, living cheaper, dope with less trouble, boys ditto.

At the age of thirty-five, under the prodding of Ginsberg, Burroughs begins writing his first and as yet only published book, *Junkie,* an account of his life as an addict in the United States and Mexico as well as *Queer,* a further account of his Mexican adventures.

After a stay in East Texas helping to run a farm, he accompanies an anthropological expedition through Colombia and visits Peru on a quest for Yage, a drug which induces hallucinations and purportedly endows its users with telepathic powers. Out of this quest comes a series of letters to Ginsberg called *In Quest of Yage*, now part of his novel, *Naked Lunch*.

Then Tangier, his base of operations from 1954 to the beginning of 1958, when he moves to Paris in search of further psychiatric revelations. This period, given to "steeping himself in vice," to use his own words, is devoted to the composition of *Interzone*, the latest and longest section of *Naked Lunch*. The first half of this period is marked by increasing seclusion, by the horrors of long-drawn out and ineffective junk withdrawals and eventually by a cure in England. The second is distinguished by a frenzy of marijuana-stimulated composition and a progressive loosening of ties with Tangier culminating in the definitive move to Paris. Tomorrow India? Greece? Mexico again? Who knows? What we do know is that whatever the scene an incorruptible eye will enjoy its fissures and sustain its strengthlessness.

I first had the great good luck to meet Burroughs in New [34] York through Allen Ginsberg just before he sailed for Tangier. At the moment I was at a loose end, housebound out of inertia, unwilling to travel for fear of enrollment in a gaggle of jabbering queens. Meeting this totally autonomous personality gave me the courage to get up off my ass without worrying about what I was conforming or non-conforming to, and I can never thank him enough.

A tall ectomorph—in Tangier the boys called him El Hombre Invisible—his persona constituted by a magic triad of fedora, glasses and raincoat rather than by a face, his first presence is that of a con man down on his luck. But that impression soon gives way to the feeling that, whatever his luck may be, yours has been very good. A cracker accent and use of jive talk fail to conceal incisive intelligence and a frightening seriousness. "No one owns life," says Burroughs, "but anyone who can pick up a frying pan owns death."

A distinguishing feature is the mania for contacts. One sometimes feels that for him drugs and sex exist only to provide opportunities for making appointments. It is a revealing clue to his tremendous isolation.

He is an indispensable indication that it is possible to be vicious without being slack. How many addicts one knows incapable of more than a sob or a monosyllable, how many queers who seem to have no place in life except the perfume counter at Woolworth's or the economy price whorehouse. To use drugs without losing consciousness or articulateness, to love boys without turning into a mindless drab is a form of heroism. With some writers drugs take the place of the excitement of composition; with Burroughs they are rather succedanea for the beatific and malefic visions.

Burroughs' attitude toward property is most austere—living quarters tantamount to the worst hotel's worst room and no more personal possessions than what can be packed into a handbag or worn on his back plus a portable typewriter. His motives are partly prudential—one never knows when a spot of bother may render a fast departure mandatory; the less substance involuntarily [37] abandoned, the slighter the pang—and partly self-lacerating; but primarily the renunciation of possessions is the necessary consequence of his non-attachment to inessentials.

Beneath the tics and through the awareness of misery there exist a wholeness and devotedness of personality that create repose for Burroughs and instill it in others. I know of no one with whom it is such a delight to share an apartment. Not only awareness, not only psychic generosity, but a calm of spirit that can tame even the most fidgety poltergeist.

Why so much biography in the discussion of a literary figure? First, because of his importance as mentor and example in the lives and works of those writers, Ginsberg and Kerouac particularly, who are trying to recapture American poetry and prose for the total personality. Secondly, because, if, as they and I believe, writing is more than a matter of cerebrally selective craftsmanship, is in fact, the total and continuous commitment of a given history, the raw materials of that history have public importance and back up the testimony of the work. And, in the case of Burroughs, the writing is a byproduct, however, brilliant, of a force. What I am writing is not only a paean to a writer: it is also a variant of hagiography.

Seen in this light, Burroughs' closest parallel is Genet. His emergence into a sense of reality out of coddled conformity is comparable to Genet's triumph over misery and degradation through consciousness.

*Junkie* is a flat cold narrative interspersed with factual lectures. In the ecological pattern of the drug addicts the narrator is reduced to a cipher in the crowd, and the use of the first person is almost a mockery. People's actions and relations only point up the basic isolatedness of each; and the individual's sense of his own existence takes on the bleak unreality of an unloved newspaper paragraph. New York, Lexington Penitentiary, New Orleans and Mexico City pass by in a uniform chill that accurately differentiated topography and characterization somehow make chillier. It is Riesman's lonely crowd with the factitious warmth of convention replaced by the real if forbidding warmth of— junk. But that [38] isn't enough warmth to export; in fact, the sense of physiological self-sufficiency it imparts blocks all other relations. Meanwhile the tireless lecturer keeps telling us the facts in season and out, medical, legal, anthropological, with an angry impatience. The truth may make you miserable, but it is the truth.

The thirteenth and fourteenth chapters of *Junkie* overlap *Queer;* and the thirteenth, particularly, figures a new subjective approach to the theme of isolation. A sick spirit tortures its helpless body to their respective limits. If the isolation of narcotics expresses itself in an aggregate of responseless units, the isolation of homosexuality brings out a unique internality. Bare hard narrative continues in the recitation of environments, of fixes and their sexual equivalents. The conversation, however, is much less clipped than in *Junkie* and in the mouth of the narrator turns into a new form, the routine. The first routine in *Queer,* the life and times of the ideal oilman, reveals a double parentage, the lecture and the Tom Sawyer handstand meant to impress the work's *blaue Blume,* Eugene Allerton. Amidst the dust and the abjection there is a disturbing hint of the atmosphere of the Platonic dialogue told from the point of view of a dispirited Socrates rather than an admiring disciple. The other major routines in the work—a self-lacerating True Confession, the story of Reggie the British agent, the madman's history of chess and the explorer's account of his caravan—are parodies toppling over into outrageousness and are all addressed to Allerton. Only the caravan routine is spoken alone, but it is the outgrowth of an earlier routine to which Allerton refuses to go on listening, and in its description of the relations between the explorer and his hired boy menacingly announces the actual trip on which Burroughs takes Allerton in the second half of the book. They go through Panama and Ecuador formally in search of Yage, but for Burroughs it is the tantalizing but perpetually unsuccessful search for the perfectly spontaneous, perfectly responsive companion. Themes that exfoliate in *Interzone,* particularly the erotic basis of theories of political power, first appear here in a more

intimate form: it is the saddest course in *Naked Lunch*. [39]
In *Yage*, Burroughs is alone again. He recounts his travels
through the horrors of Panama and much more briefly Ecuador,
through the political noxiousness of Colombia, where, a member
of an anthropological expedition, he first tries Yage, through the
confined joys of Peru, where life is easy, and he steeps himself
in the drug. The actual discovery of the drug plays a relatively
small part in the work; at the centre are the anthropologist's field
report and Burroughs life in Yage. The formal novelty of the
work is expansion of the routines and their increasing independence of an erotic context. Only one has even an imaginary reference to Allerton, the presentation of the relation between a jealous
lover and his beloved in terms of a loan company calling on a
delinquent debtor. Two others, the death of Billy Bradshinkel,
a parody of a slick paper magazine story, and Roosevelt after
Inauguration, a violent and obscene account of the imaginary
horrors in Washington following the triumph of the New Deal,
continue at greater length the pattern of humorous exaggeration
established in the routines of *Queer* as does the Zen Routine,
in which a Mahatma devoted to what Burroughs likes to call
"fact," that is, the maximum consciousness of reality, teases and
instructs a disciple too prone to take words for things. The most
ambitious routine of all, however, Yage City, is neither parody
nor erotic philosophy but a vision of "The Composite City where
all human potentials are spread out in a vast silent market."

And that brings us to *Interzone*, the cold observer in abey-
ance, the horrid scene and the boisterous routines at the prow.
Here, to sketch a progression is pointless, since the work is conceived as a total presence. The various luckless environments
come together seeking refuge from unimaginative totalitarianisms
that their own maniacally passional selfishnesses have created.
Only the Seven Stages section of Auden's *Age of Anxiety* affords
an equal example of "their own disorder as their own punishment."

Hitherto omnipresent, "Lee," Burroughs' *nom de guerre*, is
here reduced to a sufferer in a hospital and a noncommittal witness to the evils of the County Clerk and the manias of Dr. [40]
Benway. Beyond that he fulfills his role as Tiresias, the passive
clairvoyant, by disappearing into what he sees. In fact, Lee, the
cold if concerned observer, gives way to Dr. Benway, the conscious and impassioned lecturer who shares his patients' weak-
nesses, as the author's principal mask. Interzone, the superficially

bothered resort of individuals on the lam from amalgamation, is over against Freeland, the superficially generous trap for the surrenderers of their individuality, where everything is permitted and nothing ever gets to happen.

The anthropological survey radiates out of Tangier in the Panorama and Market sections of the work. A. J.'s Annual Ball and Hassan's Rumpus Room are expanded routines trembling on the verge of such sheer free fantasy as Voices, which filter to Lee's sickchamber. Islam Inc. provides the political organization and theory that is speeding Interzone toward total calamity first through the presentation of its directorate: A. J. the large extrovert, Hassan the slinky go-between, and Clem and Jody the professionally hateful Americans; and second through a description of the parties of Interzone: the Senders, whose only interest is to exercise power with no thought of its consequences, the Liquefactionists, greedyguts who want to absorb all the richness of all other lives into themselves, the Divisionists, who create ideal responsive friends (see *Queer*) by cutting off bits of their own bodies, and the Factualists, who rejoice in the variety of existence. In this world politics derive from the data of acquaintanceship and romance: only the Factualists are living. Finally, there is Word, in which the author, all masks thrown aside, delivers a long tirade, a blend of confession, routine and fantasy ending in "a vast Moslem muttering."

And now? There are rumors of a work dealing with the night of prehistory. In his last letter to me the author says: "complete dissatisfaction with everything I have done in writing . . . Unless writing has the danger and immediate urgency of bullfighting it is nowhere to my way of thinking . . . I am tired of sitting behind the lines with an imperfect recording device receiving inaccurate bulletins . . . I must reach the Front." [41]

# Paul Bowles

## BURROUGHS IN TANGIER

I first saw Bill Burroughs in 1953, passing along a back street of Tangier in the rain. He was on H at the time, and he didn't look very fit. The next year he came to see me about some detail in his contract for *Junky*, in which he said he had been taken. I had paratyphoid and wasn't very helpful. It wasn't until the winter of 1955–56 that we became friends and started to see each other regularly. Naturally I had been told about him: how he practiced shooting in his room down in the Medina, and all the rest of the legend. When I got to know him I realized the legend existed in spite of him and not because of him: he didn't give a damn about it.

His life had no visible organization in it, but knowing he was an addictive type he had chosen that way of giving himself an automatic interior discipline which was far more rigorous than any he could have imposed on himself objectively. He lived in a damp little room whose single door opened onto the garden of the Hotel Villa Muniriya. One wall of the room, his shooting gallery, was pock-marked with bullet holes. Another wall was completely covered with snapshots, most of which he had taken on a recent trip to the headwaters of the Amazon. I liked to hear about that voyage, and always got him to talk lengthily about it.

Going there had been part of his self-imposed discipline, certainly, since the only reason he had gone was to try the effects of a local drug called Yage, a concoction made by the Indians of the region, and which must be taken on the spot since its efficacy vanishes within a few hours after it is brewed. The point about Yage is that it is, more than any other, a group drug, its particular property being the facilitation of mental telepathy and emotional empathy among those who have taken it. He insisted that with it communication was possible with the Indians, although it made him violently ill.

Reprinted from *Big Table* # 2, Vol. 1 (Summer, 1959), pp. 42–43, by permission of Big Table, Inc.

During the two years when I saw Bill regularly in Tangier, he took only kif, majoun and alcohol. But he managed to take [42] vast amounts of all three. The litter on his desk and under it, on the floor, was chaotic, but it consisted only of pages of *Naked Lunch*, at which he was constantly working. When he read aloud from it, at random (any sheet of paper he happened to grab would do) he laughed a good deal, as well he might, since it is very funny, but from reading he would suddenly (paper still in hand) go into a bitter conversational attack upon whatever aspect of life had prompted the passage he had just read. The best thing about Bill Burroughs is that he always makes sense and he is always humorous, even at his most vitriolic. At any point of the night or day you may happen to catch him, you will always find that the whole machine is going full blast, and that means that he is laughing or about to laugh.

He spends more money on food than most of us other Tangerines, I've noticed; perhaps he has more to spend—I don't know —but the fact remains that he insists on eating well, which is part of his insistence upon living just as he likes at all times. (Gertrude Stein would have called him self-indulgent; he certainly is not hampered by even a shadow of the feeling of guilt, ever.) He goes on his way enjoying even his own misfortunes. I've never heard him mention an experience that made him more than temporarily unhappy. At the Hotel Muniriya he had a Reich orgone box in which he used to sit doubled up, smoking kif. I believe he made it himself. He had a little stove in his room over which he cooked his own hashish candy, of which he was very proud, and which he distributed to anyone who was interested.

The months that Allen Ginsberg was here in Tangier, he and Bill used to sit around half the night having endless fights about literature and aesthetics. It was always Bill who attacked the intellect from all sides, which I suspect was exactly what Allen wanted to hear. Surely it was worth hearing, and worth watching too, as Bill stumbled from one side of the room to the other, shouting in his cowboy voice, stirring his drink around and around without stopping, with his index and middle finger, and with two or three kif cigarettes lighted simultaneously but lying in different ashtrays which he visited on his way around the room. [43]

# LAWRENCE FERLINGHETTI

**OVERPOPULATION**

I must have misunderstood something
in this story
There must be a misprint
in this paper
Hats off! it says here
The final war is over
Again
Here they come
Again
Parading by
the cafe terrace
I stand on my chair to see
I still can't see
the brave burned hero's face
I stand on the table
waving
my only hat
with the hole in it
I throw the hole away
into the street
after the black limousine
I don't throw my paper
I sit down with my paper
which has the explanation of everything
except there's a hole in it
Something missing in the story
where the hole is
Or I must have misunderstood something
The nations have decided
it says here
To abolish themselves at last
It's been decided at the highest level

Reprinted from *Beatitude* Magazine, No. 17, unfolioed. Reprinted by permission of the author and publisher.

and at the lowest level
to return to a primitive society
For science has conquered nature
But nature must not be conquered
So science must be abolished
And machines must go
after all their turning and turning
The automobile is a passing thing
After all
The horse is here to stay
Population has reached its limit
There's standingroom only
Nowhere
to lie down
anymore
Medicine must be abolished
so people can die
when they're supposed to
There's still room
under the surface
I keep hoping
I have misunderstood something
in this story
People still lose
and find themselves
in bed
and animals still
aren't as cruel as people
because they can't talk
but we weren't designed
to live forever and ever
And design is everything
The little enzyme they've discovered
that causes aging
must be lost in the body again
All must be begun over
in a new pastoral era
There've been too many advances
Life can't bear it
any longer
Life is not a drug
made from mushrooms

eaten by Samoyeds in Siberia
which fully retain
their intoxicating properties
when transmitted in urine
so that
an endless line of men
may get drunk over and over
on the same mushroom
a chain reaction of avid statues
with mouths at penises
I must have misunderstood something
in this story
Life is intoxicating
but can't go on and on
putting on more and more
complicated clothes
hats girdles garterbelts
uplift bras lifting higher and higher
until they fly away
and breasts fall
After all
We've got to get naked again
it says here
Though fornication's still illegal
in certain states
I must have misunderstood something
in this story
The world's no Klee mobile
And there must be an end
to all this rotation
around the goofball sun
The sun in its sic transit
barely clears the rooftops now
bumps over a Mobilgas Pegasus
and sinks behind my paper
with its hole
in which I keep hoping
I've misunderstood something
For Death is not the answer
to our problem
There must be some mistake
The editorials say

we must do something
And we cannot do anything
For something's missing
where the hole is
sitting on the terrace
of this fancy coffeehouse
on the left side of the world
where I must
have misunderstood something
As a purple blond sweeps by
and one too-high tit pops out
and falls in my plate
I return it to her
without looking too embarassed
which she takes as a good sign
She sits down
and gives me the other
wrapped in silk
I go on reading my paper
thinking I must
have misunderstood something
trying to look like
it's all happened before
It has
It's a clay mobile
with something missing
where the hole is
I look under the table and see
our legs are intertwined
Our two chairs fuze
Our arms are round each other
She's facing me
crouched in my lap
her legs around me
My white snake has entered her
Speaks of love inside of her
She moans to hear it
But
something's missing
Sex without love
wears gay deceivers
I still have one of her breasts

in my hand
The waiter comes running
Picks up my fallen paper
Hoping he's misunderstood something
None of us will ever die
As long as this goes on
The enzyme bottle
Lies open
On the table

## CONSTANTLY RISKING ABSURDITY

Constantly risking absurdity
                                and death
            whenever he performs
                        above the heads
                                of his audience
        the poet like an acrobat
                    climbs on rime
                            to a high wire of his own making
and balancing on eyebeams
                        above a sea of faces
            paces his way
                    to the other side of day
            performing entrechats
                        and sleight-of-foot tricks
        and other high theatrics

Reprinted from Lawrence Ferlinghetti, A Coney Island of the Mind (Norfolk, Conn.: New Directions, 1958), p. 30. Copyright 1955 by Lawrence Ferlinghetti. Copyright © 1958 by Lawrence Ferlinghetti. Reprinted by permission of New Directions.

and all without mistaking

any thing

for what it may not be

For he's the super realist

who must perforce perceive

taut truth

before the taking of each stance or step

in his supposed advance

toward that still higher perch

where Beauty stands and waits

with gravity

to start her death-defying leap

And he

a little charleychaplin man

who may or may not catch

her fair eternal form

spreadeagled in the empty air

of existence

## DOG

The dog trots freely in the street
and sees reality
and the things he sees
are bigger than himself

Reprinted from Lawrence Ferlinghetti, *A Coney Island of the Mind* (Norfolk, Conn.: New Directions, 1958), pp. 67–68. Copyright 1955 by Lawrence Ferlinghetti. Copyright © 1958 by Lawrence Ferlinghetti. Reprinted by permission of New Directions.

and the things he sees
are his reality
Drunks in doorways
Moons on trees
The dog trots freely thru the street
and the things he sees
are smaller than himself
Fish on newsprint
Ants in holes
Chickens in Chinatown windows
their heads a block away
The dog trots freely in the street
and the things he smells
smell something like himself
The dog trots freely in the street
past puddles and babies
cats and cigars
poolrooms and policemen
He doesn't hate cops
He merely has no use for them
and he goes past them
and past the dead cows hung up whole
in front of the San Francisco Meat Market
He would rather eat a tender cow
than a tough policeman
though either might do
And he goes past the Romeo Ravioli Factory
and past Coit's Tower
and past Congressman Doyle
He's afraid of Coit's Tower
but he's not afraid of Congressman Doyle
although what he hears is very discouraging
very depressing
very absurd
to a sad young dog like himself
to a serious dog like himself [67]
But he has his own free world to live in
His own fleas to eat
He will not be muzzled
Congressman Doyle is just another
fire hydrant
to him

The dog trots freely in the street
and has his own dog's life to live
and to think about
and to reflect upon
touching and tasting and testing everything
investigating everything
without benefit of perjury
a real realist
with a real tale to tell
and a real tail to tell it with
a real live
        barking
            democratic dog
engaged in real
           free enterprise
with something to say
           about ontology
something to say
        about reality
              and how to see it
                 and how to hear it
with his head cocked sideways
           at streetcorners
as if he is just about to have
           his picture taken
              for Victor Records
        listening for
           His Master's Voice
      and looking
          like a living questionmark
              into the
             great gramaphone
             of puzzling existence
with its wondrous hollow horn
    which always seems
   just about to spout forth
            some Victorious answer
           to everything

# NOTE ON POETRY IN SAN FRANCISCO

There are all kinds of poets here, writing very dissimilar types of poetry. . . . But I should say that the kind of poetry which has been making the most noise here is quite different from the "poetry about poetry," the poetry of technique, the poetry for poets and professors which has dominated the quarterlies and anthologies in this country for some time and which of course is also written in San Francisco. The poetry which has been making itself heard here of late is what should be called street poetry. For it amounts to getting the poet out of the inner esthetic sanctum where he has too long been contemplating his complicated navel. It amounts to getting poetry back into the street where it once was, out of the classroom, out of the speech department, and—in fact—off the printed page. The printed word has made poetry so silent. But the poetry I am talking about here is spoken poetry, poetry conceived as oral messages. It "makes it" aloud. Some of it has been read with jazz, much of it has not. A new "ashcan" school? Rock and roll? Who cares what names it's called. What is important is that this poetry is using its eyes and ears as they have not been used for a number of years. "Poetry about poetry," like much non-objective painting, has caused an atrophy of the artist's senses. He has literally forgotten (taken leave of) his senses. (I walked thru Chinatown recently with a famous academic poet, and he never saw the whole schools of fish gasping on counters, nor heard what they breathed.)

And finally, in some larger sense, it all adds up to the beginning of a very inevitable thing—the *resocialization* of poetry. But not like the Thirties.

Reprinted from the *Chicago Review*, Vol. 12, No. 1 (Spring, 1958), p. 4, by permission of the *Chicago Review*.

## HORN ON *HOWL*

Fahrenheit 451, the temperature at which books burn, has finally been determined not to be the prevailing temperature at San Francisco, though the police still would be all too happy to make it hot for you. On October 3 last, Judge Clayton Horn of Municipal Court brought in a 39-page opinion finding Shigeyoshi Murao and myself not guilty of publishing or selling obscene writings, to wit Allen Ginsberg's *Howl and Other Poems* and issue 11&12 of *The Miscellaneous Man*.

Thus ended one of the most irresponsible and callous police actions to be perpetrated west of the Rockies, not counting the treatment accorded Indians and Japanese.

When William Carlos Williams, in his Introduction to *HOWL*, said that Ginsberg had come up with "an arresting poem" he hardly knew what he was saying. The first edition of *HOWL*, Number Four in the Pocket Poets Series, was printed in England by Villiers, passed thru Customs without incident, and was published at the City Lights bookstore here in the fall of 1956. Part of a second printing was stopped by Customs on March 25, 1957, not long after an earlier issue of *The Miscellaneous Man* (published in Berkeley by William Margolis) had been seized coming from the same printer. Section 305 of the Tariff Act of 1930 was cited. The San Francisco *Chronicle* (which alone among the local press put up a real howl about censorship) reported, in part:

Collector of Customs Chester MacPhee continued his campaign yesterday to keep what he considers obscene literature away from the children of the Bay Area. He confiscated 520 copies of a paperbound volume of poetry entitled *Howl and Other Poems*. . . . "The words and the sense of the writing is obscene," MacPhee declared. "You wouldn't want your children to come across it." [145]

On April 3 the American Civil Liberties Union (to which I had submitted the manuscript of *Howl* before it went to the printer) informed Mr. MacPhee that it would contest the legality of the seizure, since it did not consider the book obscene. We an-

Reprinted from *Evergreen Review*, Vol. 1, No. 4, pp. 145–158, by permission of the author.

nounced in the meantime that an entirely new edition of *Howl* was being printed within the United States, thereby removing it from Customs jurisdiction. No changes were made in the original text, and a photo-offset edition was placed on sale at City Lights bookstore and distributed nationally while the Customs continued to sit on the copies from Britain.

On May 19, book editor William Hogan of the San Francisco *Chronicle* gave his Sunday column to an article by myself, defending *Howl* (I recommended a medal be made for Collector MacPhee, since his action was already rendering the book famous. But the police were soon to take over this advertising account and do a much better job—10,000 copies of *Howl* were in print by the time they finished with it.) In the defense of *Howl* I said I thought it to be "the most significant single long poem to be published in this country since World War II, perhaps since T. S. Eliot's *Four Quartets.*" To which many added "Alas." Fair enough, considering the barren, polished poetry and well-mannered verse which had dominated many of the major poetry publications during the past decade or so, not to mention some of the "fashionable incoherence" which has passed for poetry in many of the smaller, avant-garde magazines and little presses. *Howl* commits many poetic sins; but it was time. And it would be very interesting to hear from critics who can name another single long poem published in this country since the War which is as significant of its time and place and generation. (A reviewer in the *Atlantic Monthly* recently wrote that *Howl* may well turn out to be *The Waste Land* of the younger generation.) The central part of my article said: [146] . . . It is not the poet but what he observes which is revealed as obscene. The great obscene wastes of *Howl* are the sad wastes of the mechanized world, lost among atom bombs and insane nationalisms. . . . Ginsberg chooses to walk on the wild side of this world, along with Nelson Algren, Henry Miller, Kenneth Rexroth, Kenneth Patchen, not to mention some great American dead, mostly in the tradition of philosophical anarchism. . . . Ginsberg wrote his own best defense of *Howl* in another poem called "America." Here he asks:

What sphinx of cement and aluminum bashed open their skulls and
    ate up their brains and imagination?
Moloch! Solitude! Filth! Ugliness! Ashcans and unobtainable dollars!
    Children screaming under the stairways!
    Boys sobbing in armies! Old men weeping in the parks!

A world, in short, you wouldn't want your children to come across. . . . Thus was Goya obscene in depicting the Disasters of War, thus Whitman an exhibitionist, exhibiting man in his own strange skin.

On May 29 Customs released the books it had been holding, since the United States Attorney at San Francisco refused to institute condemnation proceedings against *Howl*.

Then the police took over and arrested us, Captain William Hanrahan of the juvenile department (well named, in this case) reporting that the books were not fit for children to read. Thus during the first week in June I found myself being booked and fingerprinted in San Francisco's Hall of Justice. The city jail occupies the upper floors of it, and a charming sight it is, a picturesque return to the early Middle Ages. And my enforced tour of it was a dandy way for the city officially to recognize the flowering of poetry in San Francisco. As one paper reported, "The Cops Don't Allow No Renaissance Here."

The ACLU posted bail. Our trial went on all summer, with a couple of weeks between each day in court. The [147] prosecution soon admitted it had no case against either Shig Murao or myself as far as the *Miscellaneous Man* was concerned, since we were not the publisher of it, in which case there was no proof we knew what was inside the magazine when it was sold at our store. And, under the California Penal Code, the willful and lewd *intent* of the accused had to be established. Thus the trial was narrowed down to *Howl*.

The so-called People's Case (I say so-called, since the People seemed mostly on our side) was presented by Deputy District Attorney Ralph McIntosh whose heart seemed not in it nor his mind on it. He was opposed by some of the most formidable legal talent to be found, in the persons of Mr. Jake ("Never Plead Guilty") Ehrlich, Lawrence Speiser (former counsel for the ACLU), and Albert Bendich (present counsel for the ACLU) —all of whom defended us without expense to us.

The critical support for *Howl* (or the protest against censorship on principle) was enormous. Here is some of what some said:

*Henry Rago, editor of* Poetry *(Chicago):*

. . . I wish only to say that the book is a thoroughly serious work of literary art. . . . There is absolutely no question in my mind or in that of any poet or critic with whom I have discussed the book

127

that it is a work of the legitimacy and validity contemplated by existing American law, as we know it in the statement of Justice Woolsey in the classic *Ulysses* case, and as we have seen it reaffirmed just recently by the Supreme Court in the Butler case. . . . I would be unworthy of the tradition of this magazine or simply of my place as a poet in the republic of letters . . . if I did not speak for the right of this book to free circulation, and against this affront not only to Allen Ginsberg and his publishers, but to the possibilities of the art of poetry in America. . . . [148]

## William Hogan of the San Francisco Chronicle:

. . . *Howl and Other Poems,* according to accepted, serious contemporary American literary standards, is a dignified, sincere and admirable work of art. . . .

## Robert Duncan and Director Ruth Witt-Diamant of the San Francisco (State College) Poetry Center:

. . . *Howl* is a significant work in American poetry, deriving both a spirit and form from Walt Whitman's *Leaves of Grass,* from Jewish religious writings. . . . It is rhapsodic, highly idealistic and inspired in cause and purpose. Like other inspired poets, Ginsberg strives to include all of life, especially the elements of suffering and dismay from which the voice of desire rises. Only by misunderstanding might these tortured outcryings for sexual and spiritual understanding be taken as salacious. The poet gives us the most painful details; he moves us toward a statement of experience that is challenging and finally noble.

## Thomas Parkinson (University of California):

. . . *Howl* is one of the most important books of poetry published in the last ten years. Its power and eloquence are obvious, and the talent of Mr. Ginsberg is of the highest order. Even people who do not like the book are compelled to testify to its force and brilliance. . . .

## James Laughlin (New Directions):

I have read the book carefully and do not myself consider it offensive to good taste, likely to lead youth astray, or be injurious to public morals. I feel, furthermore, that the book has considerable distinction as literature, being a powerful [149] and artistic expression of a meaningful philosophical attitude. . . .

*Kenneth Patchen:*

The issue here—as in every like case—is not the merit or lack of it of a book but of a Society which traditionally holds the human being to be by its very functional nature a creature of shameful, outrageous, and obscene habits. . . .

*Eugene Burdick (novelist and critic):*

The poem *HOWL* strikes me as an impressionistic, broadly gauged, almost surrealistic attempt to catch the movement, color, drama, and inevitable disappointments of life in a complex, modern society. *Howl* is a pessimistic, and indeed, almost a tragic view of life. . . . It is my impression that the total impact of the poem is far from lascivious or obscene. It is depressing, but not licentious or extravagant in its use of harsh words. . . .

*Northern California Booksellers Association:*

It may or may not be literature but it does have literary merit. . . . The proposition that adult literature must meet the standards of suitability for children is manifestly absurd. . . . To quote Supreme Court Justice Frankfurter in a similar case— ". . . the effect of this is to reduce the adult population to reading only what is fit for children . . . surely this is to burn the house down to roast the pig."

*Barney Rosset and Donald Allen, editors of the* Evergreen Review *(in which* Howl *was reprinted during the trial):*

The second issue of *Evergreen Review,* which was devoted to the work of writers in the San Francisco Bay Area, [150] attempted in large part to show the kinds of serious writing being done by the postwar generation. We published Allen Ginsberg's poem *Howl* in that issue because we believe that it is a significant modern poem, and that Allen Ginsberg's intention was to sincerely and honestly present a portion of his own experience of the life of his generation. . . . Our final considered opinion was that Allen Ginsberg's *Howl* is an achieved poem and that it deserves to be considered as such. . . .

At the trial itself, nine expert witnesses testified in behalf of *Howl.* They were eloquent witnesses, together furnishing as good a one-sided critical survey of *Howl* as could possibly be got up in any literary magazine. These witnesses were: Mark Schorer and Leo Lowenthal (of the University of California faculty), Walter Van Tilburg Clark, Herbert Blau, Arthur Foff, and Mark Linenthal (all of the San Francisco State College faculty), Kenneth Rexroth, Vincent McHugh (poet and novelist), and Luther Nichols (book editor of the San Francisco *Examiner*). A few excerpts from the trial transcript—

DR. MARK SCHORER: The theme of the poem is announced very clearly in the opening line, "I saw the best minds of my generation destroyed by madness, starving hysterical naked." Then the following lines that make up the first part attempt to create the impression of a kind of nightmare world in which people representing "the best minds of my generation," in the author's view, are wandering like damned souls in hell. That is done through a kind of series of what one might call surrealistic images, a kind of state of hallucinations. Then in the second section the mood of the poem changes and it becomes an indictment of those elements in modern society that, in the author's view, are [151] destructive of the best qualities in human nature and of the best minds. Those elements are, I would say, predominantly materialism, conformity and mechanization leading toward war. And then the third part is a personal address to a friend, real or fictional, of the poet or of the person who is speaking in the poet's voice—those are not always the same thing—who is mad and in a madhouse, and is the specific representative of what the author regards as a general condition, and with that final statement the poem ends. . . .

MR. MC INTOSH (*later in cross-examination*): I didn't quite follow your explanation to page 21, "Footnote to *Howl*." Do you call that the second phase?

MARK SCHORER: I didn't speak about "Footnote to *Howl*." I regard that as a separate poem.

MR. MC INTOSH: Oh, I'm—

MARK SCHORER: It is not one of the three parts that make up the first poem. It's a comment on, I take it, the attitude expressed in *Howl* proper, and I think what it says—if you would like my understanding of it—is that in spite of all of the depravity that *Howl* has shown, all of the despair, all of the defeat, life is essentially holy and should be so lived. In other words, the footnote gives us this state in contradistinction to the state that the poem proper has tried to present.

MR. MC INTOSH (*later*): Did you read the one in the back called

"America"? . . . What's the essence of that piece of poetry?
MARK SCHORER: I think that what the poem says is that the "I,"
the speaker, feels that he has given a piece of himself to
America and has been given nothing in return, and the poem
laments certain people who have suffered at the hands of—
well, specifically, the United States Government, men like
Tom Mooney, the Spanish Loyalists, Sacco & Vanzetti, the
Scottsboro boys and so on. [152]
MR. MC INTOSH: Is that in there?
MARK SCHORER: That's on page 33. In other words, that is the
speaker associating himself with those figures in American
history whom he regards as having been martyred. He feels
that way about himself.
MR. MC INTOSH: Well, "America" is a little bit easier to understand than *Howl,* isn't it? . . . Now [*referring to shorter poems
in the back of the book*]—you read those two? You think they
are similar, in a similar vein?
MARK SCHORER: They are very different. Those are what one
would call lyric poems and the earlier ones are hortatory poems.
MR. MC INTOSH: What?
MARK SCHORER: Poems of diatribe and indictment, the mood is
very different, hortatory.
MR. MC INTOSH: That's all.

DR. LEO LOWENTHAL: In my opinion this is a genuine work of
literature, which is very characteristic for a period of unrest
and tension such as the one we have been living through the
last decade. I was reminded by reading *Howl* of many other
literary works as they have been written after times of great
upheavals, particularly after World War One, and I found this
work very much in line with similar literary works. With regard to the specific merits of the poem *Howl,* I would say that
it is structured very well. As I see it, it consists of three parts,
the first of which is the craving of the poet for self-identification, where he roams all over the field and tries to find allies
in similar search for self-identification. He then indicts, in the
second part, the villain, so to say, which does not permit him
to find it, the Moloch of society, of the world as it is today. And
in the third part he indicates the potentiality of fulfillment by
friendship and love, although it ends on a sad and melancholic
note actually indicating that he is in search for fulfillment he
cannot find. [153]

KENNETH REXROTH: . . . The simplest term for such writing is prophetic, it is easier to call it that than anything else because we have a large body of prophetic writing to refer to. There are the prophets of the Bible, which it greatly resembles in purpose and in language and in subject matter. . . . The theme is the denunciation of evil and a pointing out of the way out, so to speak. That is prophetic literature. "Woe! Woe! Woe! The City of Jerusalem! The Syrian is about to come down or has already and you are to do such and such a thing and you must repent and do thus and so." And *Howl*, the four parts of the poem—that is including the "Footnote to *Howl*" as one additional part—do this very specifically. They take up these various specifics seriatim, one after the other. . . . And "Footnote to *Howl*," of course, again, is Biblical in reference. The reference is to the Benedicite, which says over and over again, "Blessed is the fire, Blessed is the light, Blessed are the trees, and Blessed is this and Blessed is that," and he is saying, "Everything that is human is Holy to me," and that the possibility of salvation in this terrible situation which he reveals is through love and through the love of everything Holy in man. So that, I would say, that this just about covers the field of typically prophetic poetry. . . .

HERBERT BLAU: The thing that strikes me most forcefully about *Howl* is that it is worded in what appears to be a contemporary tradition, one that did not cause me any particular consternation in reading, a tradition most evident in the modern period following the First World War, a tradition that resembles European literary tradition and is defined as "Dada," a kind of art of furious negation. By the intensity of its negation it seems to be both resurrective in quality and ultimately a sort of paean of possible hope. I wouldn't say that the chances for redemption or chances for salvation in a work of this kind are deemed to be very extensively possible but, nonetheless, the vision is not a [154] total vision of despair. It is a vision that by the salvation of despair, by the salvation of what would appear to be perversity, by the salvation of what would appear to be obscene, by the salvation of what would appear to be illicit, is ultimately a kind of redemption of the illicit, the obscene, the disillusioned and the despairing. . . .

VINCENT MC HUGH: In this case . . . we have a vision of a modern hell. Now, we have certain precedents for that, for example, the book that it makes me think of, or the work of literature that it makes me think of offhand, the work of literature which is ferociously sincere in the same way, is Mr. Pound's—some of Mr. Pound's *Cantos,* especially Canto XIV and Canto XV. These, for example, in turn derive certainly from Dante and from the famous so-called cantos in Dante, and Dante, in turn, derives from the *Odyssey,* and so on into all the mythologies of the world. . . .

The prosecution put only two "expert witnesses" on the stand —both very lame samples of academia—one from the Catholic University of San Francisco and one a private elocution teacher, a beautiful woman, who said, "You feel like you are going through the gutter when you have to read that stuff. I didn't linger on it too long, I assure you." The University of San Francisco instructor said: "The literary value of this poem is negligible. . . . This poem is apparently dedicated to a long-dead movement, Dadaism, and some late followers of Dadaism. And, therefore, the opportunity is long past for any significant literary contribution of this poem." The critically devastating things the prosecution's witnesses could have said, but didn't, remain one of the great Catholic silences of the day.

So much for the literary criticism inspired by the trial. Cross-examination by the Prosecutor was generally brilliant, as in the following bit: [155]

MR. MC INTOSH: Does Mr. Ferlinghetti attend your poetry writing ing workshop?

DR. MARK LINENTHAL: He does not.

MR. MC INTOSH: Do you attend his?

DR. LINENTHAL: I do not.

MR. MC INTOSH: You haven't been over there hearing him read poetry?

DR. LINENTHAL: No, I haven't.

(etc.)

Legally, a layman could see that an important principle was certainly in the line drawn between "hard core pornography" and writing judged to be "social speech." But more important still was the court's acceptance of the principle that if a work is determined to be "social speech" the question of obscenity may not even be raised. Or, in the words of Counsel Bendich's argument: "The first amendment to the Constitution of the United

States protecting the fundamental freedoms of speech and press prohibits the suppression of literature by the application of obscenity formulae unless the trial court first determines that the literature in question is utterly without social importance." (*Roth v. U.S.*)

. . . What is being urged here is that the majority opinion in *Roth* requires a trial court to make the constitutional determination; to decide in the first instance whether a work is utterly without redeeming social importance, *before* it permits the test of obscenity to be applied. . . .

. . . The record is clear that all of the experts for the defense identified the main theme of *Howl* as social criticism. And the prosecution concedes that it does not understand the work, much less what its dominant theme is.

Judge Horn agreed, in his opinion:

I do not believe that *Howl* is without even "the slightest redeeming social [156] importance." The first part of *Howl* presents a picture of a nightmare world; the second part is an indictment of those elements in modern society destructive of the best qualities of human nature; such elements are predominantly identified as materialism, conformity, and mechanization leading toward war. The third part presents a picture of an individual who is a specific representation of what the author conceives as a general condition. . . . "Footnote to *Howl*" seems to be a declamation that everything in the world is holy, including parts of the body by name. It ends in a plea for holy living. . . .

And the judge went on to set forth certain rules for the guidance of authorities in the future:

1. If the material has the slightest redeeming social importance it is not obscene because it is protected by the First and Fourteenth Amendments of the United States Constitution, and the California Constitution.
2. If it does not have the slightest redeeming social importance it *may* be obscene.
3. The test of obscenity in California is that the material must have a tendency to deprave or corrupt readers by exciting lascivious thoughts or arousing lustful desire to the point that it presents a clear and present danger of inciting to anti-social or immoral action.
4. The book or material must be judged as a whole by its effect on the *average adult* in the community.
5. If the material is objectionable only because of coarse and vulgar

language which is not erotic or aphrodisiac in character it is not obscene.

6. Scienter must be proved.
7. Book reviews may be received in evidence if properly authenticated.
8. Evidence of expert witnesses in the literary field is proper.
9. Comparison of the material with other similar material [157] previously adjudicated is proper.
10. The people owe a duty to themselves and to each other to preserve and protect their constitutional freedoms from any encroachment by government unless it appears that the allowable limits of such protection have been breached, and then to take only such action as will heal the breach.
11. Quoting Justice Douglas: "I have the same confidence in the ability of our people to reject noxious literature as I have in their capacity to sort out the true from the false in theology, economics, politics, or any other field."
12. In considering material claimed to be obscene it is well to remember the motto: *Honi soit qui mal y pense* (Evil to him who thinks evil).

At which the Prosecution was reliably reported to have blushed.

Under banner headlines, the *Chronicle* reported that "the Judge's decision was hailed with applause and cheers from a packed audience that offered the most fantastic collection of beards, turtle-necked shirts and Italian hair-dos ever to grace the grimy precincts of the Hall of Justice." The decision was hailed editorially as a "landmark of law." Judge Horn has since been re-elected to office, which I like to think means that the People agree it was the police who here committed an obscene action. [158]

# GARY SNYDER

## THE LATE SNOW & LUMBER STRIKE
## OF THE SUMMER OF FIFTY-FOUR

Whole towns shut down
    hitching the Coast road, only gypos
Running their beat trucks, no logs on
Gave me rides. Loggers all gone fishing
Chainsaws in a pool of cold oil
On back porches of ten thousand
Split-shake houses, quiet in summer rain.
Hitched north all of Washington
Crossing and re-crossing the passes
Blown like dust, no place to work.

Climbing the steep ridge below Shuksan
    clumps of pine
      float out the fog
No place to think or work
    drifting.

On Mt. Baker, alone
In a gully of blazing snow:
Cities down the long valleys west
Thinking of work, but here,
Burning in sun-glare
Below a wet cliff, above a frozen lake,
The whole Northwest on strike
Black burners cold, [6]
The green-chain still,
I must turn and go back:
    caught on a snowpeak
      between heaven and earth
And stand in lines in Seattle.
Looking for work. [7]

Reprinted from Gary Snyder, *Riprap* (Ashland, Mass.: Origin Press, 1959), pp. 6–7, by permission of the author.

## MILTON BY FIRELIGHT

*Piute Creek, August 1955*

"O hell, what do mine eyes
            with grief behold?"
Working with an old
Singlejack miner, who can sense
The vein and cleavage
In the very guts of rock, can
Blast granite, build
Switchbacks that last for years
Under the beat of snow, thaw, mule-hooves.
What use, Milton, a silly story
Of our lost general parents,
            eaters of fruit?

The Indian, the chainsaw boy,
And a string of six mules
Came riding down to camp
Hungry for tomatoes and green apples.
Sleeping in saddle-blankets
Under a bright night-sky
Han River slantwise by morning.
Jays squall
Coffee boils

In ten thousand years the Sierras
Will be dry and dead, home of the scorpion.
Ice-scratched slabs and bent trees. [10]
No paradise, no fall,
Only the weathering land
The wheeling sky,
Man, with his Satan
Scouring the chaos of the mind.
Oh Hell!

Reprinted from Gary Snyder, *Riprap* (Ashland, Mass.: Origin Press, 1959),
pp. 10–11, by permission of the author.

Fire down
Too dark to read, miles from a road
The bell-mare clangs in the meadow
That packed dirt for a fill-in
Scrambling through loose rocks
On an old trail
All of a summer's day. [11]


## COLD MOUNTAIN POEMS


In the Japanese art exhibit that came to America in 1953 was a small
sumi sketch of a robe-tattered wind-swept long-haired laughing man
holding a scroll, standing on a cliff in the mountains. This was Kanzan,
or Han-shan, "Cold Mountain"—his name taken from where he lived.
He is a mountain madman in an old Chinese line of ragged hermits.
When he talks about Cold Mountain he means himself, his home, his
state of mind. He lived in the T'ang dynasty—traditionally A.D. 627–
650, although Hu Shih dates him 700–780. This makes him roughly
contemporary with Tu Fu, Li Po, Wang Wei, and Po Chü-i. His poems,
of which three hundred survive, are written in T'ang colloquial: rough
and fresh. The ideas are Taoist, Buddhist, Zen. He and his sidekick
Shih-te (Jittoku in Japanese) became great favorites with Zen painters of later days—the scroll, the broom, the wild hair and laughter.
They became Immortals and you sometimes run onto them today in
the skidrows, orchards, hobo jungles, and logging camps of America.
G.S.


*Preface to the Poems of Han-shan by*
*Lu Ch'iu-Yin, Governor of T'ai Prefecture*

No one knows just what sort of man Han-shan was. There are
old people who knew him: they say he was a poor man, a crazy
character. He lived alone seventy li west of the T'ang-hsing
district of T'ien-t'ai at a place called Cold Mountain. He often
went down to the Kuo-ch'ing Temple. At the temple lived Shih-
te, who ran the dining hall. He sometimes saved leftovers for
Han-shan, hiding them in a bamboo tube. Han-shan would come

Reprinted from *Evergreen Review,* Vol. 2, No. 6, pp. 69–80, by permission
of the author.

and carry it away; walking the long veranda, calling and shouting happily, talking and laughing to himself. Once the monks followed him, caught him, and made fun of him. He stopped, clapped his hands, and laughed greatly—Ha Ha!—for a spell, then left. [69]

He looked like a tramp. His body and face were old and beat. Yet in every word he breathed was a meaning in line with the subtle principles of things, if only you thought of it deeply. Everything he said had a feeling of the Tao in it, profound and arcane secrets. His hat was made of birch bark, his clothes were ragged and worn out, and his shoes were wood. Thus men who have made it hide their tracks: unifying categories and interpenetrating things. On that long veranda calling and singing, in his words of reply Ha Ha!—the three worlds revolve. Sometimes at the villages and farms he laughed and sang with cowherds. Sometimes intractable, sometimes agreeable, his nature was happy of itself. But how could a person without wisdom recognize him?

I once received a position as a petty official at Tan-ch'iu. The day I was to depart, I had a bad headache. I called a doctor, but he couldn't cure me and it turned worse. Then I met a Buddhist Master named Feng-kan, who said he came from the Kuo-ch'ing Temple of T'ien-t'ai especially to visit me. I asked him to rescue me from my illness. He smiled and said, "The four realms are within the body; sickness comes from illusion. If you want to do away with it, you need pure water." Someone brought water to the Master, who spat it on me. In a moment the disease was rooted out. He then said, "There are miasmas in T'ai prefecture, when you get there take care of yourself." I asked him, "Are there any wise men in your area I could look on as Master?" He replied, "When you see him you don't recognize him, when you recognize him you don't see him. If you want to see him, you can't rely on appearances. Then you can see him. Han-shan is a Manjusri hiding at Kuo-ch'ing. Shih-te is a Samantabhadra. They look like poor fellows and act like madmen. Sometimes they go and sometimes they come. They work in the kitchen of the Kuo-ch'ing dining hall, tending the fire." When he was done talking he left.

I proceeded on my journey to my job at T'ai-chou, not forgetting this affair. I arrived three days later, immediately went [70] to a temple, and questioned an old monk. It seemed the Master had been truthful, so I gave orders to see if T'ang-hsing really contained a Han-shan and Shih-te. The District Magistrate reported to me: "In this district, seventy li west, is a mountain. People used to see a poor man heading from the cliffs to stay awhile at Kuo-ch'ing. At the temple dining hall is a similar man named Shih-te." I made a bow, and went to Kuo-ch'ing. I asked some people around the temple, "There used to be a Master named Feng-kan here. Where is his place? And where can Han-shan and Shih-te be seen?" A monk named Tao-ch'iao spoke up: "Feng-kan the Master lived in back of the library. Nowadays nobody lives there; a tiger often comes and roars. Han-shan and Shih-te are in the kitchen." The monk led me to Feng-kan's yard. Then he opened the gate: all we saw was tiger tracks. I asked the monks Tao-ch'iao and Pao-te, "When Feng-kan was here, what was his job?" The monks said, "He pounded and hulled rice. At night he sang songs to amuse himself." Then we went to the kitchen, before the stoves. Two men were facing the fire, laughing loudly. I made a bow. The two shouted HO! at me. They struck their hands together—Ha Ha!—great laughter. They shouted. Then they said, "Feng-kan—loose-tongued, loose-tongued. You don't recognize Amitabha, why be courteous to us?" The monks gathered round, surprise going through them. "Why has a big official bowed to a pair of clowns?" The two men grabbed hands and ran out of the temple. I cried, "Catch them"—but they quickly ran away. Han-shan returned to Cold Mountain. I asked the monks, "Would those two men be willing to settle down at this temple?" I ordered them to find a house, and to ask Han-shan and Shih-te to return and live at the temple.

I returned to my district and had two sets of clean clothes made, got some incense and such, and sent it to the temple —but the two men didn't return. So I had it carried up to Cold Mountain. The packer saw Han-shan, who called in a loud voice, "Thief! Thief!" and retreated into a mountain cave. He shouted, "I tell you man, strive hard!"—entered the cave and [71] was gone. The cave closed of itself and they weren't able to follow. Shih-te's tracks disappeared completely.

I ordered Tao-ch'iao and the other monks to find out how they had lived, to hunt up the poems written on bamboo, wood, stones, and cliffs—and also to collect those written on the walls of peoples' houses. There were more than three hundred. On the wall of the Earth-shrine Shih-te had written some *gatha*. It was all brought together and made into a book.

I hold to the principle of the Buddha-mind. It is fortunate to meet with men of Tao, so I have made this eulogy.

*Twenty-four Poems by Han-shan*

### 1

The path to Han-shan's place is laughable,
A path, but no sign of cart or horse.
Converging gorges—hard to trace their twists
Jumbled cliffs—unbelievably rugged.
A thousand grasses bend with dew,
A hill of pines hums in the wind.
And now I've lost the shortcut home,
Body asking shadow, how do you keep up?

### 2

In a tangle of cliffs I chose a place—
Bird-paths, but no trails for men.
What's beyond the yard?
White clouds clinging to vague rocks.
Now I've lived here—how many years—
Again and again, spring and winter pass.
Go tell families with silverware and cars
"What's the use of all that noise and money?"

### 3

In the mountains it's cold.
Always been cold, not just this year.
Jagged scarps forever snowed in
Woods in the dark ravines spitting mist.
Grass is still sprouting at the end of June,
Leaves begin to fall in early August.
And here am I, high on mountains,
Peering and peering, but I can't even see the sky.

### 4

I spur my horse through the wrecked town,
The wrecked town sinks my spirit.
High, low, old parapet-walls
Big, small, the aging tombs.

I waggle my shadow, all alone;
Not even the crack of a shrinking coffin is heard.
I pity all these ordinary bones,
In the books of the Immortals they are nameless.


## 5

I wanted a good place to settle:
Cold Mountain would be safe.
Light wind in a hidden pine—
Listen close—the sound gets better.
Under it a gray-haired man
Mumbles along reading Huang and Lao.
For ten years I haven't gone back home
I've even forgotten the way by which I came. [73]


## 6

Men ask the way to Cold Mountain
Cold Mountain: there's no through trail.
In summer, ice doesn't melt
The rising sun blurs in swirling fog.
How did I make it?
My heart's not the same as yours.
If your heart was like mine
You'd get it and be right here.


## 7

I settled at Cold Mountain long ago,
Already it seems like years and years.
Freely drifting, I prowl the woods and streams
And linger watching things themselves.
Men don't get this far into the mountains,
White clouds gather and billow.
Thin grass does for a mattress,
The blue sky makes a good quilt.
Happy with a stone underhead
Let heaven and earth go about their changes.

### 8

Clambering up the Cold Mountain path,
The Cold Mountain trail goes on and on:
The long gorge choked with scree and boulders,
The wide creek, the mist-blurred grass.
The moss is slippery, though there's been no rain
The pine sings, but there's no wind.
Who can leap the world's ties
And sit with me among the white clouds? [74]


### 9

Rough and dark—the Cold Mountain trail,
Sharp cobbles—the icy creek bank.
Yammering, chirping—always birds
Bleak, alone, not even a lone hiker.
Whip, whip—the wind slaps my face
Whirled and tumbled—snow piles on my back.
Morning after morning I don't see the sun
Year after year, not a sign of spring.


### 10

I have lived at Cold Mountain
These thirty long years.
Yesterday I called on friends and family:
More than half had gone to the Yellow Springs.
Slowly consumed, like fire down a candle;
Forever flowing, like a passing river.
Now, morning, I face my lone shadow:
Suddenly my eyes are bleared with tears.


### 11

Spring-water in the green creek is clear
Moonlight on Cold Mountain is white
Silent knowledge—the spirit is enlightened of itself
Contemplate the void: this world exceeds stillness. [75]

GARY SNYDER

### 12

In my first thirty years of life
I roamed hundreds and thousands of miles.
Walked by rivers through deep green grass
Entered cities of boiling red dust.
Tried drugs, but couldn't make Immortal;
Read books and wrote poems on history.
Today I'm back at Cold Mountain:
I'll sleep by the creek and purify my ears.

### 13

I can't stand these bird-songs
Now I'll go rest in my straw shack.
The cherry flowers out scarlet
The willow shoots up feathery.
Morning sun drives over blue peaks
Bright clouds wash green ponds.
Who knows that I'm out of the dusty world
Climbing the southern slope of Cold Mountain?

### 14

Cold Mountain has many hidden wonders,
People who climb here are always getting scared.
When the moon shines, water sparkles clear
When wind blows, grass swishes and rattles.
On the bare plum, flowers of snow
On the dead stump, leaves of mist.
At the touch of rain it all turns fresh and live
At the wrong season you can't ford the creeks. [76]

### 15

There's a naked bug at Cold Mountain
With a white body and a black head.
His hand holds two book-scrolls,
One the Way and one its Power.
His shack's got no pots or oven,
He goes for a walk with his shirt and pants askew.
But he always carries the sword of wisdom:
He means to cut down senseless craving.

144

### 16

Cold Mountain is a house
Without beams or walls.
The six doors left and right are open
The hall is blue sky.
The rooms all vacant and vague
The east wall beats on the west wall
At the center nothing.

Borrowers don't bother me
In the cold I build a little fire
When I'm hungry I boil up some greens.
I've got no use for the kulak
With his big barn and pasture—
He just sets up a prison for himself.
Once in he can't get out.
Think it over—
You know it might happen to you. [77]

### 17

If I hide out at Cold Mountain
Living off mountain plants and berries—
All my lifetime, why worry?
One follows his karma through.
Days and months slip by like water,
Time is like sparks knocked off flint.
Go ahead and let the world change—
I'm happy to sit among these cliffs.

### 18

Most T'ien-t'ai men
Don't know Han-shan
Don't know his real thought
& call it silly talk.

### 19

Once at Cold Mountain, troubles cease—
No more tangled, hung-up mind.
I idly scribble poems on the rock cliff,
Taking whatever comes, like a drifting boat.

## 20

Some critic tried to put me down—
"Your poems lack the Basic Truth of Tao"
And I recall the old-timers
Who were poor and didn't care.
I have to laugh at him,
He misses the point entirely,
Men like that
Ought to stick to making money. [78]

## 21

I've lived at Cold Mountain—how many autumns.
Alone, I hum a song—utterly without regret.
Hungry, I eat one grain of Immortal-medicine
Mind solid and sharp; leaning on a stone.

## 22

On top of Cold Mountain the lone round moon
Lights the whole clear cloudless sky.
Honor this priceless natural treasure
Concealed in five shadows, sunk deep in the flesh.

## 23

My home was at Cold Mountain from the start,
Rambling among the hills, far from trouble.
Gone, and a million things leave no trace
Loosed, and it flows through the galaxies
A fountain of light, into the very mind—
Not a thing, and yet it appears before me:
Now I know the pearl of the Buddha-nature
Know its use: a boundless perfect sphere.

## 24

When men see Han-shan
They all say he's crazy
And not much to look at—
Dressed in rags and hides.

They don't get what I say
& I don't talk their language.
All I can say to those I meet:
"Try and make it to Cold Mountain." [79]

Notes

THE PREFACE:

Feng-kan is reckoned in the traditional line of Zen Masters, but in mid-T'ang the Zen people did not yet constitute a separate Buddhist sect. They were rather a "meditation-group" living in the mountains or the monasteries of the T'ien-t'ai (Japanese Tendai) sect, and the Vinaya (displine) sect.

Manjusri is the Bodhisattva of wisdom, Samantabhadra the Bodhisattva of love, Amitabha the Bodhisattva of boundless compassion.

A *gatha* is a short Buddhist poem.

A doggerel eulogistic poem, also by Lu Ch'iu-yin, follows the biography. I have not translated it.

THE POEMS:

4—a rare example of a poem in the literary manner. Han-shan usually writes in the colloquial, as very few Chinese poets have done.

5—the gray-haired man is Han-shan himself. Huang is "The Book of the Yellow Emperor" and Lao is Lao-tzu, the *Tao Te Ching*.

15—the Way and its Power, i.e., the *Tao Te Ching*.

22, 23—the full moon, the pearl. Symbols of the Buddha-nature inherent in all beings.

Most of Han-shan's poems are written in the "old-song" (*ku-shih*) style, with five or seven characters to a line. [80]

## SPRING *SESSHIN* AT SHOKOKU-JI

Shokoku Temple is in northern Kyoto, on level ground, with a Christian college just south of it and many blocks of crowded little houses and stone-edged dirt roads north. It is the mother-temple of many branch temples scattered throughout Japan, and one of the several great temple-systems of the Rinzai Sect of Zen.

Reprinted from the *Chicago Review*, Vol. 12, No. 1 (Spring, 1958), pp. 41–49, by permission of the *Chicago Review* and the author.

Shokoku-ji is actually a compound: behind the big wood gate and tile-topped crumbling old mud walls are a number of temples each with its own gate and walls, gardens, and acres of wild bamboo grove. In the center of the compound is the soaring double-gabled Lecture Hall, silent and airy, an enormous dragon painted on the high ceiling, his eye burning down on the very center of the cut-slate floor. Except at infrequent rituals the hall is unused, and the gold-gilt Buddha sits on its high platform at the rear untroubled by drums and chanting. In front of the Lecture Hall is a long grove of fine young pines and a large square lotus-pond. To the east is a wooden belltower and the unpretentious gate of the *Sodo,* the training school for Zen monks, or *Unsui.*[1] [41] They will become priests of Shokoku-ji temples. A few, after years of *zazen* (meditation), *koan* study,[2] and final mastery of the *Avatamsaka* (*Kegon*) philosophy, become *Roshi*[3] (Zen Masters), qualified to head Sodos, teach lay groups, or do what they will. Laymen are also permitted to join the Unsui in evening *Zendo* (meditation hall) sessions, and some, like the Unsui, are given a *koan* by the Roshi and receive regular *sanzen*

[1] *Unsui.* The term is literally "cloud, water"—taken from a line of an old Chinese poem, "To drift like clouds and flow like water." It is strictly a Zen term. The Japanese word for Buddhist monks and priests of all sects is *bozu* (bonze). One takes no formal vows upon becoming an Unsui, although the head is shaved and a long Chinese-style robe called *koromo* is worn within Sodo walls. Unsui are free to quit the Zen community at any time. During the six months of the year in which the Sodo is in session (spring and fall) they eat no meat, but during the summer and winter off-periods they eat, drink, and wear what they will. After becoming temple priests (*Osho,* Chinese *Ho-shang*) the great majority of Zen monks marry and raise families. The present generation of young Unsui is largely from temple families.

[2] *Koans* are usually short anecdotes concerning the incomprehensible and illogical behavior and language of certain key Chinese Zen Masters of the T'ang dynasty. The *koan* assigned to the student is the subject of his meditation, and his understanding of it is the subject of *sanzen,* an interview with the Zen Master. Very advanced students are also required to relate *koan*-understanding to the intellectual concepts of Buddhist philosophy.

[3] *Roshi.* Literally, "old master"—Chinese *Lao-shih.* A Roshi is not simply a person who "understands" Zen, but specifically a person who has received the seal of approval from his own Zen Master and is his "Dharma heir." A person may comprehend Zen to the point that his Roshi will say he has no more to teach him, but if the Roshi does not feel the student is intellectually and scholastically equipped to transmit Zen as well, he will not permit him to be his heir. Most Roshi are Zen monks, but laymen and women have also achieved this title.

—the fierce face-to-face moment where you spit forth truth or perish—from him. Thus being driven, through time and much *zazen*, to the very end of the problem.

In the routine of Sodo life, there are special weeks during the year in which gardening, carpentry, reading, and such, are suspended, and the time given over almost entirely to *zazen*. During these weeks, called *sesshin*, "concentrating the mind"—*sanzen* is received two to four times a day and hours of *zazen* in the Zendo are much extended. Laymen who will observe the customs of Sodo life and are able to sit still are allowed to join in the *sesshin*. At Shokoku-ji, the spring *sesshin* is held the first week of May.

The *sesshin* starts in the evening. The participants single-file circle into the mat-floored Central Hall of the Sodo and sit in a double row in dim light. The Roshi silently enters, sits at the head, and everyone drinks tea, each fishing his own teacup out of the deep-sleeved black robe. Then the *Jikijitsu*—head Unsui of the Zendo (a position which revolves among the older men, changing every six months)—reads in formal voice the rules of [42] Zendo and *sesshin*, written in archaic medieval Japanese. The Roshi says you all must work very hard; all bow and go out, returning to the Zendo for short meditation and early sleep.

At three A.M. the *Fusu* (another older Zenbo who is in charge of food, finances and meeting people) appears in the Zendo ringing a hand-bell. Lights go on—ten-watt things tacked under the beams of a building lit for centuries by oil lamps—and everyone wordlessly and swiftly rolls up his single quilt and stuffs it in a small cupboard at the rear of his mat, leaps off the raised platform that rings the hall, to the stone floor, and scuffs out in straw sandals to dash icy water on the face from a stone bowl. They come back quickly and sit crosslegged on their *zazen* cushions, on the same mat used for sleeping. The Jikijitsu stalks in and sits at his place, lighting a stick of incense and beginning the day with the rifleshot crack of a pair of hardwood blocks whacked together and a ding on a small bronze bell. Several minutes of silence, and another whack is heard from the Central Hall. Standing up and slipping on the sandals, the group files out of the Zendo trailing the Jikijitsu—who hits his bell as he walks—and goes down the roofed stone path, fifty yards long, that joins the Zendo and the Central Hall. Forming two lines and sitting on the mats, they begin to chant sutras. The choppy Sino-Japanese words follow the rhythm of a fish-shaped wooden drum and a

deep-throated bell. They roar loud and chant fast. The Roshi
enters and between the two lines makes deep bows to the Buddha-
image before him, lights incense, and retires. The hard-thumping
drum and *sutra*-songs last an hour, then suddenly stop and all
return to the Zendo. Each man standing before his place, they
chant the *Prajña-paramita-hridaya Sutra,* the Jikijitsu going so
fast now no one can follow him. Then hoisting themselves onto
the mats they meditate. After half an hour a harsh bell-clang
is heard from the Roshi's quarters. The Jikijitsu bellows "Get-
out!" and the Zenbos dash out racing, feet slapping the cold
stones and robes flying, to kneel in line whatever order they make
it before the *sanzen* room. A ring of the bell marks each new
entrance before the Roshi. All one [43] hears from outside is an
occasional growl and sometimes the whack of a stick. The men
return singly and subdued from *sanzen* to their places.

Not all return. Some go to the kitchen, to light brushwood
fires in the brick stoves and cook rice in giant black pots. When
they are ready they signal with a clack of wood blocks, and those
in the Zendo answer by a ring on the bell. Carrying little nested
sets of bowls and extra-large chopsticks, they come down the
covered walk. It is getting light, and at this time of year the
camellia are blooming. The moss-floored garden on both sides of
the walk is thick with them, banks under pine and maple, white
flowers glowing through mist. Even the meal, nothing but salty
radish pickles and thin rice gruel, is begun and ended by whacks
of wood and chanting of short verses. After breakfast the Zenbos
scatter: some to wash pots, others to mop the long wood verandas
of the central hall and sweep and mop the Roshi's rooms or rake
leaves and paths in the garden. The younger Unsui and the outsiders dust, sweep, and mop the Zendo.

The Shokoku-ji Zendo is one of the largest and finest in Japan.
It is on a raised terrace of stone and encircled by a stone walk.
Outside a long overhang roof and dark unpainted wood—inside
round log posts set on granite footings—it is always cool and
dark and very still. The floor is square slate laid diagonal. The
raised wood platform that runs around the edge has mats for
forty men. Sitting in a three-walled box that hangs from the
center of the ceiling, like an overhead crane operator, is a life-
size wood statue of the Buddha's disciple Kasyapa, his eyes real
and piercing anyone who enters the main door. In an attached
room to the rear of the Zendo is a shrine to the founder of Shokoku-ji, his statue in wood, eyes peering out of a dark alcove.

By seven A.M. the routine chores are done and the Jikijitsu invites those cleaning up the Zendo into his room for tea. The Jikijitsu and the Fusu both have private quarters, the Fusu lodging in the Central Hall and the Jikijitsu in a small building adjoining the Zendo. The chill is leaving the air, and he slides open the [44] paper screens, opening a wall of his room to the outside. Sitting on mats and drinking tea they relax and smoke and quietly kid a little, and the Jikijitsu—a tigerish terror during the *zazen* sessions—is very gentle. "You'll be a Roshi one of these days" a medical student staying the week said to him. "Not me, I can't grasp *koans*," he laughs, rubbing his shaved head where the Roshi has knocked him recently. Then they talk of work to be done around the Sodo. During *sesshin* periods work is kept to a minimum, but some must be done. Taking off robes and putting on ragged old dungarees everyone spreads out, some to the endless task of weeding grass from the moss garden, others to the vegetable plots. The Jikijitsu takes a big mattock and heads for the bamboo-grove to chop out a few bamboo shoots for the kitchen. Nobody works very hard, and several times during the morning they find a warm place in the sun and smoke.

At ten-thirty they quit work and straggle to the kitchen for lunch, the main meal. *Miso*-soup full of vegetables, plenty of rice, and several sorts of pickles. The crunch of bicycles and shouts of children playing around the bell-tower can be heard just beyond the wall. After lunch the laymen and younger Unsui return to the Zendo. More experienced men have the greater responsibilities of running the Sodo, and they keep busy at accounts, shopping, and looking after the needs of the Roshi. Afternoon sitting in the Zendo is informal—newcomers take plenty of time getting comfortable, and occasionally go out to walk and smoke a bit. Conversation is not actually forbidden, but no one wants to talk.

Shortly before three, things tighten up and the Jikijitsu comes in. When everyone is gathered, and a bell heard from the Central-Hall, they march out for afternoon sutra-chanting. The sutras re- cited vary from day to day, and as the leader announces new titles some men produce books from their sleeves to read by, for not all have yet memorized them completely. Returning to the Zendo, they again recite the *Prajña-paramita-hridaya Sutra,* and the Jikijitsu chants a piece alone, his voice filling the hall, head [45] tilted up to the statue of Kasyapa, hand cupped to his mouth as though calling across miles.

After sitting a few minutes the signal is heard for evening meal, and all file into the kitchen, stand, chant, sit, and lay out their bowls. No one speaks. Food is served with a gesture of "giving" and one stops the server with a gesture of "enough." At the end of the meal—rice and pickles—a pot of hot water is passed and each man pours some into his bowls, swashes it around and drinks it, wipes out his bowls with a little cloth. Then they are nested again, wrapped in their cover, and everyone stands and leaves.

It is dusk and the Zendo is getting dark inside. All the Zenbos begin to assemble now, some with their cushions tucked under arm, each bowing before Kasyapa as he enters. Each man, right hand held up before the chest flat like a knife and cutting the air, walks straight to his place, bows toward the center of the room, arranges the cushions, and assumes the crosslegged "half-lotus" posture. Others arrive too—teachers, several college professors, and half a dozen university students wearing the black uniforms that serve for classrooms, bars, and temples equally well—being all they own. Some enter uncertainly and bow with hesitation, afraid of making mistakes, curious to try zazen and overwhelmed by the historical weight of Zen, something very "Japanese" and very "high class." One student, most threadbare of all, had a head shaved like an Unsui and entered with knowledge and precision every night, sitting perfectly still on his cushions and acknowledging no one. By seven-thirty the hall is half-full—a sizeable number of people for present-day Zen sessions—and the great bell in the bell-tower booms. As it booms the man ringing it, swinging a long wood beam ram, sings out a sutra over the shops and homes of the neighborhood. When he has finished, the faint lights in the Zendo go on and evening zazen has begun.

The Jikijitsu sits at the head of the hall, marking the half-hour periods with wood clackers and bell. He keeps a stick of incense burning beside him, atop a small wood box that says "not yet" on it in Chinese. At the end of the first half-hour he claps the [46] blocks once and grunts "kinhin." This is "walking zazen," and the group stands—the Unsui tying up sleeves and tucking up robes—and at another signal they start marching single file around the inside of the hall. They walk fast and unconsciously in step, the Jikijitsu leading with a long samurai stride. They circle and circle, through shadow and under the light, ducking below Kasyapa's roost, until suddenly the Jikijitsu claps his blocks and yells "Get-out!"—the circle broken and everyone dashing for the door. Night *sanzen*. Through the next twenty minutes they return to resume meditation—not preparing an answer now, but considering the Roshi's response.

*Zazen* is a very tight thing. The whole room feels it. The Jikijitsu gets up, grasps a long flat stick and begins to slowly prowl the hall, stick on shoulder, walking before the rows of sitting men, each motionless with eyes half-closed and looking straight ahead downward. An inexperienced man sitting out of balance will be lightly tapped and prodded into easier posture. An Unsui sitting poorly will be without warning roughly knocked off his cushions. He gets up and sits down again. Nothing is said. Anyone showing signs of drowsiness will feel a light tap of the stick on the shoulder. He and the Jikijitsu then bow to each other, and the man leans forward to receive four blows on each side of his back. These are not particularly painful—though the loud whack of them can be terrifying to a newcomer—and serve to wake one well. One's legs may hurt during long sitting, but there is no relief until the Jikijitsu rings his bell. The mind must simply be placed elsewhere. At the end of an hour the bell does ring and the second *kinhin* begins—a welcome twenty minutes of silent rhythmic walking. The walking ends abruptly and anyone not seated and settled when the Jikijitsu whips around the hall is knocked off his cushion. Zen aims at freedom but its practice is disciplined.

Several Unsui slip out during *kinhin*. At ten they return—they can be heard coming, running full speed down the walk. They enter carrying big trays of hot noodles, *udon*, in large lacquer bowls. They bow to the Jikijitsu and circle the room setting a [47] bowl before each man; giving two or even three bowls to those who want them. Each man bows, takes up chopsticks, and eats the noodles as fast as he can. Zenbos are famous for fast noodle-eating and no one wants to be last done. As the empty bowls are set down they are gathered up and one server follows, wiping the beam that fronts the mats with a rag, at a run. At the door the servers stop and bow to the group. It bows in return. Then one server announces the person—usually a friend or patron of the Sodo—who footed the bill for the *sesshin* noodles that night. The group bows again. Meditation is resumed. At ten-thirty there is another rest period and men gather to smoke and

153

chat a little in back. "Are there really some Americans interested in Zen?" they ask with astonishment—for their own countrymen pay them scant attention.

At eleven bells ring and wood clacks, and final sutras are chanted. The hall is suddenly filled with huge voices. The evening visitors take their cushions and leave, each bowing to the Jiki-jitsu and Kasyapa as he goes. The others flip themselves into their sleeping quilts immediately and lie dead still. The Jikijitsu pads once around, says "Take counsel of your pillow" and walks out. The hall goes black. But this is not the end, for as soon as the lights go out, everyone gets up again and takes his sitting cushion, slips outside, and practices *zazen* alone wherever he likes for another two hours. The next day begins at three A.M.

This is the daily schedule of the *sesshin*. On several mornings during the week, the Roshi gives a lecture (*teisho*) based on some anecdote in the Zen textbooks—usually from *Mumonkan* or *Hekiganroku*. As the group sits in the Central Hall awaiting his entrance, one Zenbo stands twirling a stick around the edge-tacks of a big drum, filling the air with a deep reverberation. The Roshi sits crosslegged on a very high chair, receives a cup of tea, and delivers lectures that might drive some mad—for he tells these poor souls beating their brains out night after night that "The Perfect Way is without difficulty" and he means it and they know he's right. [48]

In the middle of the week everyone gets a bath and a new head-shave. There is a Zen saying that "while studying *koans* you should not relax even in the bath" but this one is never heeded. The bath-house contains two deep iron tubs, heated by brush-wood fires stoked below from outside. The blue smoke and sweet smell of crackling *hinoki* and *sugi* twigs, stuffed in by a fire-tender, and the men taking a long time and getting really clean. Even in the bath-house you bow—to a small shrine high on the wall—both before and after bathing. The Jikijitsu whets up his razor and shaves heads, but shaves his own alone and without mirror. He never nicks himself any more.

On the day after bath they go begging (*takahatsu*). It rained this day, but putting on oiled-paper slickers over their robes and wearing straw sandals they splashed out. The face of the begging Zenbo can scarcely be seen, for he wears a deep bowl-shaped woven straw hat. They walk slowly, paced far apart, making a weird wailing sound as they go, never stopping. Sometimes they walk for miles, crisscrossing the little lanes and streets of Kyoto.

They came back soaked, chanting a sutra as they entered the Sodo gate, and added up a meagre take. The rain sluiced down all that afternoon, making a green twilight inside the Zendo and a rush of sound.

The next morning during tea with the Jikijitsu, a college professor who rents rooms in one of the Sodo buildings came in and talked of *koans*. "When you understand Zen, you know that the tree is really *there*."—The only time anyone said anything of Zen philosophy or experience the whole week. Zenbos never discuss *koans* or *sanzen* experience with each other.

The *sesshin* ends at dawn on the eighth day. All who have participated gather in the Jikijitsu's room and drink powdered green tea and eat cakes. They talk easily, it's over. The Jikijitsu, who has whacked or knocked them all during the week, is their great friend now—compassion takes many forms. [49]

## NOTE ON THE RELIGIOUS TENDENCIES

This religiosity is primarily one of practice and personal experience, rather than theory. The statement commonly heard in some circles, "All religions lead to the same goal" is the result of fantastically sloppy thinking and no practice. It is good to remember that all religions are nine-tenths fraud and are responsible for numerous social evils.

Within the beat generation you find three things going on:

*1. Vision and illumination-seeking.* This is most easily done by systematic experimentation with narcotics. Marijuana is a daily standby and peyote is the real eye-opener. These are sometimes supplemented by dips into yoga technique, alcohol, and Subud. Although a good deal of personal insight can be obtained by the intelligent use of drugs, being high all the time leads nowhere because it lacks intellect, will, and compassion; and a personal drug kick is of no use to anyone else in the world.

*2. Love, respect for life, abandon, Whitman, pacifism, anarchism, etc.* This comes out of various traditions including Quakers, Shinshu Buddhism, Sufism. And from a loving and

Reprinted from *Liberation*, Vol. 4, No. 4 (June, 1959), p. 11. By permission.

open heart. At its best this state of mind has led people to actively resist war, start communities, and try to love one another. It is also partly responsible for the mystique of "angels," the glorification of skidroad and hitch-hiking, and a kind of mindless enthusiasm. If it respects life, it fails to respect heartless wisdom and death; and this is a shortcoming.

3. *Discipline, aesthetics, and tradition.* This was going on well before the beat generation got into print. It differs from the "All is one" stance in that its practitioners settle on one traditional religion, try to absorb the feel of its art and history, and carry out whatever ascesis is required. One should become an Aimu bear-dancer or a Yurok shaman as well as a Trappist monk, if he put himself to it. What this bit often lacks is what 2 and 3 have, i.e. real commitment to the stewpot of the world and real insight into the vision-lands of the unconscious.

The unstartling conclusion is that if a person cannot comprehend all three of these aspects—contemplation (and not by use of drugs), morality (which usually means social protest to me), and wisdom—in his beat life, he just won't make it. But even so he may get pretty far out, and that's probably better than moping around classrooms or writing books on Buddhism and Happiness for the masses, as the squares (who will shortly have succeeded in putting us all down) do.

# PHILIP WHALEN

## EXCERPT: SOURDOUGH MOUNTAIN LOOKOUT

*from a poem for Kenneth Rexroth*

From Sauk Lookout two years before
Some of the view was down the Skagit
To Puget Sound
From above the lower ranges deep in forest
Lighthouses on clear nights.

This rock is a spur from the main range
Cuts the valley in two and is broken
By the river
Ross Dam repairs the break
Makes trolley-buses run
Through dim Seattle far away . . .

I'm surrounded by mountains here
    A circle of 108 beads (originally seeds
    of *ficus religiosa,* Bo-tree)
A circle continuous
    with one odd bead larger than the rest,
    bearing a tassel
    hair-tuft (the man who sat under the tree)
In the center of the circle a
Void     an empty figure containing [29]
All that's multiplied
Each bead a repetition a world
Of ignorance and sleep.

Today is the day the goose gets cooked
Day of liberation for the crumbling flower
Knobcone pinecone in the flames
Brandy in the sun

                which as I said will disappear
Anyway it'll be invisible soon

Reprinted from the *Chicago Review,* Vol. 12, No. 1, pp. 29–30, by permission of the *Chicago Review.*

Exchanging places with the stars now in my head
To be growing rice in China through the night
   Magnetic storms across the solar plains
   Make aurora borealis shimmy bright
   Beyond the mountains to the north.

Closing the lookout in the morning
Thick ice on the shutters
Coyote almost whistling on a nearby ridge

   The mountain is there between two lakes
   I brought back a piece of its rock
   Heavy      dark-honey-color
   With a seam of crystal, some of the quartz
   Stained by its matrix
   Practically indestructible . . .
   A shift from opacity to brilliance
   (Zenbos say, "Lightning flash and flint-spark")
   Like the mountains where it was made.

What we see of the world is the mind's
Invention and the mind
   . . . . .
Can shift instantly [30]


## A DIM VIEW OF BERKELEY IN THE SPRING


A graduated row of children, the biggest
Old enough to feel the boredom
Leading the rest, tearing up flowers in the driveway

The boredom, the tension

Fraternity men crowded into the wire cage—
A volley-ball court—jumping, hollering, laughing
      ( only one is headed down the hill with his books to the
               campus, smoothing his crewed-down hair )
Too loud,

This poem originally appeared in *Ark III* (Winter, 1957), pp. 17–18, and is reprinted here by permission of the author.

TENSION: The flying ball an indeterminate
Future, the Army? The Navy? Marriage before
Or later?

Leap, shout, a pattern of release that actually comes
Much later in some parked car
Trying to make out with some chick who
WON'T, she wants a home of her own to do it in
  (Who can blame her?)
Then going back to the house with a stone-ache
Or gooey underwear, the tension
Relieved so they can sleep or built high enough
To be dreamed off or jacked away in the shower at 3 A.M.

Where's the action? What's going on?

The Suez is not at home to anyone.
Mr. Dullness says, 'War is no longer profitable.'
Daddy Warbucks in the White House says
'Everything is going to be just dandy.'

What are we going to do? [17]

In Hungary they had a good idea
They all got together to kill the government
But the government mowed them down . . . who cares
About revolutions, the old corpses in the street routine?
Who cares?

Several hundred of us crowded in to watch a student
Gassed to death at Q
Later, a lot of other students went to peek at the body
Preserved in the basement of the University
      THE MURDERER ON ICE
So we all saved the trouble and expense of a trip
To Central Europe

Charley Olson told me, ' "Intolerable" is all right, a very
Dramatic word, but that isn't it at all.'
What I mean is, nobody
Can stand it, the tension, the boredom, whatever . . .
Mama and Papa scream at each other about the new deep-freeze,

          ('. . . and sometimes I just turn the TV off & go do
                    something else, I get so tired of it.'—that

159

Was the egg-lady speaking) and
The children continue destroying the flowers,
Being too young to go to the show at night alone. [18]


## FOR C


I wanted to bring you this Jap iris
Orchid-white with yellow blazons
But I couldn't face carrying it down the street
Afraid everyone would laugh
And now they're dying of my cowardice.

Abstract beauty in the garden,
In my hand, in the street it is a sign
A whole procession of ithyphallic satyrs
Through a town whose people like to believe:
"I was made like Jesus, out of Love; my daddy was a spook."

The upright flower would scare them. "What's shot,"
They think, "from the big flesh cannon will decay."
Not being there I can't say that being born is a chance
To learn, to love and to save each other from ourselves:
Live ignorance rots us worse than any grave.

And lacking the courage to tell you, "I'm here,
Such as I am; I need you and you need me"
Planning to give you this flower instead—
Intending it to mean "This is really I, tall, slender,
Perfectly formed"—is uglier than their holy fantasies,

Worse to look at than my own gross shape.
After all this fuss about flowers I walked out,
Just to walk, not going to see you (I had nothing to bring—
This poem wasn't finished, didn't say
What was on my mind; I'd given up)

Reprinted from Philip Whalen, *Like I Say* (Totem Press in association with Corinth Books, 32 West 8th Street, New York 11, New York, 1960), p. 28. Copyright 1960 by Philip Whalen and reprinted by permission of the author. This poem originally appeared in *Evergreen Review*, Vol. 1, No. 5, pp. 58–59.

I saw bushes of crimson rhododendron, sparkling wet,
Beside the hospital walk—I had to see you.
If you were out, I'd leave these flowers.
Even if I couldn't write or speak
At least I broke and stole that branch with love.


## MARTYRDOM OF TWO PAGANS


Out on a limb and frantically sawing
The saw teeth go dull and at last
Wear smooth
Leaving us here, still throned in the air
    Like the sage in the basket
    And the one in the jar
Either branch or tree will fall
Or we'll both drop, sleeping
A heavenly meal for the animal saints
Who march continuously round the bole

A distinction or a difference, I said
Either one a horn on Io's head
A giddy heifer chased by bees
All are immortal
Laugh and lie down

Discriminate or perish, he replied
    While all with one voice (about
    the space of two hours) cried out
    Great is Diana of the Ephesians!
Stay awake, he said, sleep is confusion
    My eyelids have grown tea-leaves for the pot
Brew it strong
Defy illusion
The weakened branch snaps off
We join the company of saints

Reprinted from *Ark II, Moby I*, p. 38, by permission of the author. Copyright 1960 by Philip Whalen.

Remaining conscious—
though dismembered
To the last.

The sacred beasts all ate
And marched and sang:
    'Love is better than hate
    Love is better than hate
Love is better than hate
    and stronger than hell'
For we took our shoes off
As we fell.

# MICHAEL MC CLURE

## POINT LOBOS: ANIMISM

It is possible my friend,
If I have had a fat belly
That the wolf lives on fat
Gnawing slowly
Through a visceral night of rancor.
It is possible that the absence of pain
May be so great
That the possibility of care
May be impossible.

Perhaps to know pain.
Anxiety, rather than the fear
Of the fear of anxiety.
This talk of miracles!

Of Animism:
I have been in a spot so full of spirits
That even the most joyful animist
Brooded
When all in sight was less to be cared about
Than death
And there was no noise in the ears
That mattered.
(I knelt in the shade
By a cold salt pool
And felt the entrance of hate
On many legs,
The soul like a clambering
Water vascular system. [4]

No scuttling could matter
Yet I formed in my mind

Reprinted from Michael McClure, *Hymns to St. Geryon and Other Poems*
(San Francisco, Calif.: The Auerhahn Press, 1959), pp. 4–5, by permission
of the publisher.

The most beautiful
Of maxims.
How could I care
For your illness or mine?)
This talk of bodies!

It is impossible to speak
Of lupine or tulips
When one may read
His name
Spelled by the mold on the stumps
When the forest moves about one.

Heel. Nostril.
Light. Light! Light!
This is the bird's song
You may tell it
To your children. [5]


## PEYOTE POEM


Clear—the senses bright—sitting in the black chair—Rocker—
the white walls reflecting the color of clouds
moving over the sun. Intimacies! The rooms

not important—but like divisions of all space
of all hideousness and beauty. I hear
the music of myself and write it down

for no one to read. I pass fantasies as they
sing to me with Circe-Voices. I visit
among the peoples of myself and know all
I need to know.
I KNOW EVERYTHING! I PASS INTO THE ROOM

there is a golden bed radiating all light

the air is full of silver hangings and sheathes

Reprinted from Michael McClure, *Hymns to St. Geryon and Other Poems* (San Francisco, Calif.: The Auerhahn Press, 1959), pp. 39–50, by permission of the publisher.

I smile to myself. I know
all that there is to know. I see all there
is to feel. I am friendly with the ache
in my belly. The answer

to love is my voice. There is no Time!
No answers. The answer to feeling is my feeling.

The answer to joy is joy without feeling.

The room is a multicolored cherub
of air and bright colors. The pain in my stomach [39]
is warm and tender. I am smiling. The pain
is many pointed, without anguish.

Light changes the room from yellows to violet!

The dark brown space behind the door is precious
intimate, silent and still. The birthplace
of Brahms. I know

all that I need to know. There is no hurry.

I read the meanings of scratched walls and cracked ceilings.

I am separate. I close my eyes in divinity and pain.

I blink in solemnity and unsolemn joy.

I smile at myself in my movements. Walking
I step higher in carefulness. I fill

space with myself. I see the secret and distinct
patterns of smoke from my mouth

I am without care part of all. Distinct.
I am separate from gloom and beauty. I see all.

---

(SPACIOUSNESS

And grim intensity—close within myself. No longer
a cloud
but flesh real as rock. Like Herakles [40]

of primordial substance and vitality.
And not even afraid of the thing shorn of glamor

but accepting.
The beautiful things are not of ourselves

but I watch them. Among them.

---

And the Indian thing. It is true!
Here in my Apartment I think tribal thoughts.)

---

STOMACHE!!!

There is no time. I am visited by a man
who is the god of foxes
there is dirt under the nails of his paw
fresh from his den.
We smile at one another in recognition.

I am free from Time. I accept it without triumph

—a fact.

Closing my eyes there are flashes of light.

My eyes won't focus but leap. I see that I have three feet.
I see seven places at once!
The floor slants—the room slopes
things melt
into each other. Flashes
of light [41]

and meldings. I wait.

seeing the physical thing pass.

I am on a mesa of time and space.

!STOM—ACHE!

Writing the music of life
in words.
Hearing the round sounds of the guitar
as colors.
Feeling the touch of flesh.

Seeing the loose chaos of words
on the page.
(ultimate grace)
(Sweet Yeats and his ball of hashish.)

---

My belly and I are two individuals
joined together
in life.

---

THIS IS THE POWERFUL KNOWLEDGE

we smile with it.

---

At the window I look into the blue-gray
gloom of dreariness.
I am war. Into the dragon of space.
I stare into clouds seeing
their misty convolutions. [42]

The whirls of vapor

I will small clouds out of existence.

They become fish devouring each other.

And change like Dante's holy spirits

becoming an osprey frozen skyhigh

to challenge me. [43]

2

The huge bird with bug eyes. Caught in dynamic profile.
Feet stretched out forward
glaring at me.
Feathery cloudtips of feathers
dark gray on gray against blue.

---

From the cliff of the park—the city—a twilight
foggy vista. Green grass over the stone,
pink auras of neon. The spires lean

into the clouds. I remember the window, wonder.

Out over the rooftops from the window.

I am at the top of the park. I look

for the clouds in the calm sky.

Tendrils and wisps. I see 180 degrees.

MY STOMACH IS SWOLLEN AND NUMB!

I have entered the essential-barrenness
there is no beauty the exotic has come to an end I face the facts
of emptiness, I recognize that time is a measurement is arbitrary,
I look for the glamor of metamorphosis, for the color of transmu-
[tation,
I wait to become the flask of a wonder to see diamonds, there is no
purpose. Pain without anguish space without loveliness. The pure
facts of vision are here there is the City! There is the wonder
as far as the eye can see the close buildings I see them so close.
[44]
Oh and I am so glad to see them. This is the change

that I do not care but know.

THE GIANT, COMIC, FIERCE, BIRD FROM MY WINDOW!
The spirits, souls rising to form it need no explanation
in the world.
Vast expanse without interest—undrab.
Here is the light full of grains and color
the pink auras and flesh orange. The rasping sounds,

hideous buildings leaning into emptiness.

The fact of my division is simple I am a spirit
of flesh in the cold air. I need no answer

I do not lean on others. I am separate, distinct.

There is nothing to drag me down.

Back at the window again I look for the Osprey

I remember the flow of blood, the heat
and the cold almost-fear beneath it. There is nothing

in the night but fast clouds. No stars. Smokey gray
and black the rooms are the color of blue Mexican glass
and white. I see to the undercoats of paint

to the green and brown. I am caught in reveries of love.

The tassles of the shag rug are lace.

I am in the Park above all and cold. [45]

I am in the room in light Hell and warm Heaven.

I am lost in memories. I move feeling the pleasant bulk
  of my body. I am pleased with my warm pain

  I think of its cessation with pleasure.

  I know it will not change. I know I am here, beyond all

  in myself.

The passage—my eyes ache with joy in the warmth.

'The edge of the cloth like tassles—a shag rug

white—the loops lace over your shoulder—

the white wall behind—green showing through
lace again a sweet memory in the gloom.

The smells clear in my head over your shoulder.
Your brown arm on the tick cloth. Blue stripes

on white the smell of smoke and the smell of bodies.

Oh and the void again with space and no Time.
Our breath moving in the corners of the room! [46]


3

I AM MOVING IN THE YELLOW KITCHEN
  high never to come down—the ceiling brown.

  I am looking at the face of the red clock—
    meaningless.

  I know of the sky from my window and I do not turn
    to look, I am
  motionless forever standing unmoving—
  a body of flesh in the empty air.

  I am in the barren warm universe of no Time.
    The ache in my belly is a solid thing.
    There is no joy or tremor, I smoke a cigarette in the small
  room elbow to the stove seeing what is new—
  barren as my cigarette and hand in the air hearing the whir of
                                                    [unheard
    sounds, seeing the place of new things to the air. In
  no relation, feeling the solid blankness of all things having

169

my stomach solid and aching, I am aloof
- and we are one,
in the bare room my stomach and I held together by dry
warmth in space.
There is no reason for this! There is nothing but forms
in emptiness—unugly
and without beauty. It is that.

I AM STANDING HERE MYSELF BY THE STOVE
without reason or time.
I am the warmth and it is within me. [47]

---

BELLY BELLY BELLY! UNENDING AND BLANK.

---

I am in the instant of space, I see all I am aware of all
I am curious but knowing that there is no more than this—the
[happenings
of the world continue about me there are worls and wisps
[of smoke
there are the sounds of late afternoon and early evening
with forever between them I see it passing between them
I cannot be surprised—there is no news to me it has always
[been
this way—going into a memory would be to go into a long
black tunnel. The room is huge and spacious without
PATTERN OR REASON. IT HAS ALWAYS BEEN THIS
[WAY. THERE ARE THE COLORS
of early evening as they have always been. I am as I shall
always be. Standing feeling myself in the inert.

I raise my head with the beauty of final knowledge
I step high in pride benevolence and awareness. The
[pain
is part of me. The pain in my belly. The clouds
are passing and I will not stop them.

COLOR IS REALITY! THE EYE IS A MATCHFLAME!

The pain is a solid lump—all of the anguish
I am freed from.

The answer to joy is joy without feeling. The answer to
[love

is my voice.

The room is a solid of objects and air.

I KNOW EVERYTHING, I AM FILLED WITH WEARINESS
[48]

I close my eyes in divinity and pain.

I blink in solemnity and unsolemn joy.

I am free of the instant there is no Time!

I have lived out the phases of life from patterned opu-
[lence
to stark and unheeding.

My stomach is gentle love, gentle love.

I AM AT THE POINT OF ALL HUGENESS AND MEANING

---

The pain of my stomach has entered my chest
throat and head.

---

The enormous leap! I look from the precipice

of my window.
I watch from my warmth, feeling.

THERE ARE NO CATEGORIES!!!

---

(OH WONDER, WONDER, IN DREARINESS AND BEAUTY
aloof in perpetual unamazed astonishment
[warm
as stone in the emptiness of vast space
seeing the small and limitless scale
of vastness. My hand before me. Seeing

all reachable and real. The answer to love
is my voice.
I am sure. This is the ultimate [49]
about me. My feelings real to me. Solid

as walls.—I see the meaning
of walls—divisions of space,
backgrounds of color. )

HEAVEN AND HELL THIS IS REACHABLE I AM SICK IN
[LACK OF JOY

and joyful in lack of joy and sick
in sickness of joy. Oh dry
stomach! And not ecstatic in knowledge.

I KNOW ALL THAT THERE IS TO KNOW,

feel all that there is to feel.

Piteously clear air. Radiance without glow.

Perfection.

———————————————————

I hear all that there is to hear.
There is no noise but a lack of sound.
I am on the plain of Space.

There are no spirits but spirits.

The room is empty of all but visible things.

THERE ARE NO CATEGORIES! OR JUSTIFICATIONS!

I am sure of my movements I am a bulk
in the air. [50]

# JOHN WIENERS

## A POEM FOR PAINTERS

      Our age bereft of nobility
How can our faces show it?
I look for love.
    My lips stand out
dry and cracked with want
         of it.
         Oh it is well.

Again we go driven by forces
we have no control over. Only
           in the poem
comes an image—that we rule
     the line by the pen
in the painter's hand one foot
         away from me.
Drawing the face
     and its torture.
That is why no one dares tackle it.
Held as they are in the hands
      of forces they
    cannot understand.
         That despair
is on my face and shall show
in the fine lines of any man.

I had love once in the palm of my hand.
    See the lines there.
         How we played
its game, are playing now
in the bounds of white and heartless fields.
    Fall down on my head,

Reprinted from John Wieners, The *Hotel Wentley Poems* (San Francisco, Calif.: The Auerhahn Press, 1958), pp. 5–10. Reprinted by permission of the author and the publisher.

173

love, drench my flesh in the streams
                of fine sprays. Like
                        French perfume
        so that I light up as
                        morning glorys and
I am showered by the scent
        of the finished line. [5]

                No circles
but that two parallels do cross
And carry our souls and
bodies together as the planets
        Showing light on the surface
                        of our skin, knowing
        that so much flows through
                the veins underneath.
The cheeks puffed with it.
        Our pockets full.


        2

Pushed on by the incompletion
        of what goes before me
I hesitate before this paper
        scratching for the right words.
Paul Klee scratched for seven years
        on smoked glass to develop
        his line, Lavigne says: Look
at his face! he who has spent
        all night drawing mine.

The sun
also rises on the rooftops
        beginning with violet.
I begin in blue knowing what's cool.


        3

My middle name is Joseph and I
walk beside an ass on the way to
what Bethlehem, where a new babe is born.
        Not the second hand of Yeats but
first prints on a cloudy windowpane. [7]

4

America, you boil over

The cauldron scalds.
Flesh is scarred.
Eyes shot.

The street aswarm with
vipers and heavy armed bandits.
There are bandages on the wounds
but blood flows unabated.
                    Oh stop
               up the drains.
          We are run over.


5

Let us stay with what we know.
That love is my strength, that
I am overpowered by it:
                    Desire
                         that too
is on the face: gone stale.
When green was the bed my love
and I laid down upon.
Such it is, heart's complaint,
You hear upon a day in June.
And I see no end in view
when summer goes, as it will,
upon the roads, like singing
companions across the land.

South of Mission, Seattle,
over the Sierra Mountains,
the Middle West and Michigan,
moving east again, easy
coming into Chicago and
the cattle country, calling
to each other over canyons, [8]
careful not to be caught
at night, they are still out,
the destroyers, and down

into the South, familiar land,
lush places, blue mountains
of Carolina, into Black Mountain
and you can sleep out, or
straight across into states

I cannot think of their names
this nation is so large, like
our hands, our love it lives
with no lover, looking only
for the beloved, back home
into the heart, New York,
New England, Vermont, green
mountains and Massachusetts
my city, Boston and the sea
again to smell what this calm
ocean cannot tell us. The seasons.
Only the heart remembers
and records in the words


### 6

At last. I come to the last defense.

> My poems contain no
> wilde beestes, no
> lady of the lake, music
> of the spheres, or organ chants.

> Only the score of a man's
> struggle to stay with
> what is his own, what
> lies within him to do.

> Without which is nothing.
> And I come to this
> knowing the waste, [9]
> leaving the rest up to love
> and its twisted faces,
> my hands claw out at
> only to draw back from the
> blood already running there. [10]

CRITICISM AND COMMENTARY

# Kenneth Rexroth

## DISENGAGEMENT: THE ART OF THE BEAT GENERATION

Literature generally, but literary criticism in particular, has always been an area in which social forces assume symbolic guise, and work out—or at least exemplify—conflicts taking place in the contemporary, or rather, usually the just-past wider arena of society. Recognition of this does not imply the acceptance of any general theory of social or economic determinism. It is a simple, empirical fact. Because of the pervasiveness of consent in American society generally, that democratic leveling up or down so often bewailed since de Tocqueville, American literature, especially literary criticism, has usually been ruled by a "line." The fact that it was spontaneously evolved and enforced only by widespread consent has never detracted from its rigor —but rather the opposite. It is only human to kick against the prodding of an Erich Auerbach or an Andrey Zhdanov. An invisible, all-enveloping compulsion is not likely to be recognized, let alone protested against.

After World War I there was an official line for general consumption: "Back to Normalcy." Day by day in every way, we are getting better and better. This produced a literature which tirelessly pointed out that there was nothing whatsoever normal about us. The measure of decay in thirty [28] years is the degree of acceptance of the official myth today—from the most obscure hack on a provincial newspaper to the loftiest metaphysicians of the literary quarterlies. The line goes: "The generation of experimentation and revolt is over." This is an etherealized corollary of the general line: "The bull market will never end."

I do not wish to argue about the bull market, but in the arts nothing could be less true. The youngest generation is in a state of revolt so absolute that its elders cannot even recognize it. The

Reprinted from *New World Writing No. 11* (New York: The New American Library, 1957), pp. 28–41. Reprinted by permission of The New American Library and Kenneth Rexroth.

disaffiliation, alienation, and rejection of the young has, as far as their elders are concerned, moved out of the visible spectrum altogether. Critically invisible, modern revolt, like X-rays and radioactivity, is perceived only by its effects at more materialistic social levels, where it is called delinquency.

"Disaffiliation," by the way, is the term used by the critic and poet, Lawrence Lipton, who has written several articles on this subject, the first of which, in the *Nation*, quoted as epigraph, "We disaffiliate . . ."—John L. Lewis.

Like the pillars of Hercules, like two ruined Titans guarding the entrance to one of Dante's circles, stand two great dead juvenile delinquents—the heroes of the post-war generation: the great saxophonist, Charlie Parker, and Dylan Thomas. If the word deliberate means anything, both of them certainly deliberately destroyed themselves.

Both of them were overcome by the horror of the world in which they found themselves, because at last they could no longer overcome that world with the weapon of a purely lyrical art. Both of them were my friends. Living in San Francisco I saw them seldom enough to see them with a perspective which was not distorted by exasperation or fatigue. So as the years passed, I saw them each time in the light of an accelerated personal conflagration.

The last time I saw Bird, at Jimbo's Bob City, he was so gone —so blind to the world—that he literally sat down on me before he realized I was there. "What happened, man?" I said, referring to the pretentious "Jazz Concert." "Evil, man, evil," he said, and that's all he said for the rest of the night. About dawn he got up to blow. The rowdy crowd chilled into stillness and the fluent melody spiraled through it.

The last time I saw Dylan, his self-destruction had not just passed the limits of rationality. It had assumed the terrifying inertia of inanimate matter. Being with him was like being swept away by a torrent of falling stones.

Now Dylan Thomas and Charlie Parker have a great deal more in common than the same disastrous end. As artists, they were very similar. They were both very fluent. But this fluent, enchanting utterance had, compared with important artists of [29] the past, relatively little content. Neither of them got very far beyond a sort of entranced rapture at his own creativity. The principal theme of Thomas's poetry was the ambivalence of birth and death—the pain of blood-stained creation. Music, of course, is not so explicit an art, but anybody who knew Charlie Parker knows that he felt much the same way about his own gift. Both of them did communicate one central theme: Against the ruin of the world, there is only one defense—the creative act. This, of course, is the theme of much art—perhaps most poetry. It is the theme of Horace, who certainly otherwise bears little resemblance to Parker or Thomas. The difference is that Horace accepted his theme with a kind of silken assurance. To Dylan and Bird it was an agony and terror. I do not believe that this is due to anything especially frightful about their relationship to their own creativity. I believe rather that it is due to the catastrophic world in which that creativity seemed to be the sole value. Horace's column of imperishable verse shines quietly enough in the lucid air of Augustan Rome. Art may have been for him the most enduring, orderly, and noble activity of man. But the other activities of his life partook of these values. They did not actively negate them. Dylan Thomas's verse had to find endurance in a world of burning cities and burning Jews. He was able to find meaning in his art as long as it was the answer to air raids and gas ovens. As the world began to take on the guise of an immense air raid or gas oven, I believe his art became meaningless to him. I think all this could apply to Parker just as well, although, because of the nature of music, it is not demonstrable—at least not conclusively.

Thomas and Parker have more in common than theme, attitude, life pattern. In the practice of their art, there is an obvious technical resemblance. Contrary to popular belief, they were not great technical innovators. Their effects are only superficially startling. Thomas is a regression from the technical originality and ingenuity of writers like Pierre Reverdy or Apollinaire. Similarly, the innovations of bop, and of Parker particularly, have been vastly overrated by people unfamiliar with music, especially by that ignoramus, the intellectual jitterbug, the jazz aficionado. The tonal novelties consist in the introduction of a few chords used in classical music for centuries. And there is less rhythmic difference between progressive jazz, no matter how progressive, and Dixieland, than there is between two movements of many conventional symphonies.

What Parker and his contemporaries—Gillespie, Davis, Monk, Roach (Tristano is an anomaly), etc.—did was to absorb the musical ornamentation of the older jazz into the basic [30] structure, of which it then became an integral part, and with which it then

181

developed. This is true of the melodic line which could be put together from selected passages of almost anybody—Benny Carter, Johnny Hodges. It is true of the rhythmic pattern in which the beat shifts continuously, or at least is continuously sprung, so that it becomes ambiguous enough to allow the pattern to be dominated by the long pulsations of the phrase or strophe. This is exactly what happened in the transition from baroque to rococo music. It is the difference between Bach and Mozart.

It is not a farfetched analogy to say that this is what Thomas did to poetry. The special syntactical effects of a Rimbaud or an Edith Sitwell—actually ornaments—become the main concern. The metaphysical conceits, which fascinate the Reactionary Generation still dominant in backwater American colleges, were embroideries. Thomas's ellipses and ambiguities are ends in themselves. The immediate theme, if it exists, is incidental, and his main theme—the terror of birth—is simply reiterated.

This is one difference between Bird and Dylan which should be pointed out. Again, contrary to popular belief, there is nothing crazy or frantic about Parker either musically or emotionally. His sinuous melody is a sort of naïve transcendence of all experience. Emotionally it does not resemble Berlioz or Wagner; it resembles Mozart. This is true also of a painter like Jackson Pollock. He may have been eccentric in his behavior, but his paintings are as impassive as Persian tiles. Partly this difference is due to the nature of verbal communication. The insistent talk-aboutiveness of the general environment obtrudes into even the most idyllic poetry. It is much more a personal difference. Thomas certainly wanted to tell people about the ruin and disorder of the world. Parker and Pollock wanted to substitute a work of art for the world.

Technique pure and simple, rendition, is not of major importance, but it is interesting that Parker, following Lester Young, was one of the leaders of the so-called saxophone revolution. In modern jazz, the saxophone is treated as a woodwind and played with conventional embouchure. Metrically, Thomas's verse was extremely conventional, as was, incidentally, the verse of that other tragic enragé, Hart Crane.

I want to make clear what I consider the one technical development in the first wave of significant post-war arts. Ornament is confabulation in the interstices of structure. A poem by Dylan Thomas, a saxophone solo by Charles Parker, a painting by Jackson Pollock—these are pure confabulations as ends in themselves. Confabulation has come to determine structure. Uninhibited lyricism should be distinguished from [31] its exact opposite—the sterile, extraneous invention of the corn-belt metaphysicals, or present blight of poetic professors.

Just as Hart Crane had little influence on anyone except very reactionary writers—like Allen Tate, for instance, to whom Valéry was the last word in modern poetry and the felicities of an Apollinaire, let alone a Paul Éluard were nonsense—so Dylan Thomas's influence has been slight indeed. In fact, his only disciple—the only person to imitate his style—was W. S. Graham, who seems to have imitated him without much understanding, and who has since moved on to other methods. Thomas's principal influence lay in the communication of an attitude—that of the now extinct British romantic school of the New Apocalypse—Henry Treece, J. F. Hendry, and others—all of whom were quite conventional poets.

Parker certainly had much more of an influence. At one time it was the ambition of every saxophone player in every high school band in America to blow like Bird. Even before his death this influence had begun to ebb. In fact, the whole generation of the founding fathers of bop—Gillespie, Monk, Davis, Blakey, and the rest—are just now at a considerable discount. The main line of development today goes back to Lester Young and bypasses them.

The point is that many of the most impressive developments in the arts nowadays are aberrant, idiosyncratic. There is no longer any sense of continuing development of the sort that can be traced from Baudelaire to Éluard, or for that matter, from Hawthorne through Henry James to Gertrude Stein. The cubist generation before World War I, and, on a lower level, the surrealists of the period between the wars, both assumed an accepted universe of discourse, in which, to quote André Breton, it was possible to make definite advances, exactly as in the sciences. I doubt if anyone holds such ideas today. Continuity exits, but like the neo-swing music developed from Lester Young, it is a continuity sustained by popular demand.

In the plastic arts, a very similar situation exists. Surrealists like Hans Arp and Max Ernst might talk of creation by hazard —of composing pictures by walking on them with painted soles, or by tossing bits of paper up in the air. But it is obvious that they were self-deluded. Nothing looks anything like an Ernst or an Arp but another Ernst or Arp. Nothing looks less like their work than the happenings of random occasion. Many of the post-World War II abstract expressionists, apostles of the discipline of spontaneity and hazard, look alike, and do look like accidents. The aesthetic appeal of pure paint laid on at random may exist, but it is a very impoverished appeal. Once again what has happened is an all-consuming [32] confabulation of the incidentals, the accidents of painting. It is curious that at its best, the work of this school of painting—Mark Rothko, Jackson Pollock, Clyfford Still, Robert Motherwell, Willem de-Kooning, and the rest—resembles nothing so much as the passage painting of quite unimpressive painters: the mother-of-pearl shimmer in the background of a Henry McFee, itself a formula derived from Renoir; the splashes of light and black which fake drapery in the fashionable imitators of Hals and Sargent. Often work of this sort is presented as calligraphy—the pure utterance of the brush stroke seeking only absolute painteresque values. You have only to compare such painting with the work of, say, Sesshu, to realize that someone is using words and brushes carelessly.

At its best the abstract expressionists achieve a simple rococo decorative surface. Its poverty shows up immediately when compared with Tiepolo, where the rococo rises to painting of extraordinary profundity and power. A Tiepolo painting, however confabulated, is a universe of tensions in vast depths. A Pollock is an object of art—bijouterie—disguised only by its great size. In fact, once the size is big enough to cover a whole wall, it turns into nothing more than extremely expensive wallpaper. Now there is nothing wrong with complicated wallpaper. There is just more to Tiepolo. The great Ashikaga brush painters painted wallpapers, too—at least portable ones, screens.

A process of elimination which leaves the artist with nothing but the play of his materials themselves cannot sustain interest in either artist or public for very long. So, in the last couple of years, abstract expressionism has tended toward romantic suggestion—indications of landscape or living figures. This approaches the work of the Northwest school—Clayton Price, Mark Tobey, Kenneth Callahan, Morris Graves—who have of all recent painters come nearest to conquering a territory which painting could occupy with some degree of security. The Northwest school, of course, admittedly is influenced by the ink painters of the Far East, and by Tintoretto and Tiepolo. The dominant school of post-World War II American painting has really been a long detour into plastic nihilism. I should add that painters like Ernie Briggs seem to be opening up new areas of considerable scope within the main traditional abstract expressionism —but with remarkable convergence to Tobey or Tintoretto, as you prefer.

Today American painting is just beginning to emerge with a transvaluation of values. From the mid-nineteenth century on, all ruling standards in the plastic arts were subject to continual attack. They were attacked because each on-coming generation had new standards of their own to put in their [33] place. Unfortunately, after one hundred years of this, there grew up a generation ignorant of the reasons for the revolt of their elders, and without any standards whatever. It has been necessary to create standards anew out of chaos. This is what modern education purports to do with finger painting in nursery schools. This is why the Northwest school has enjoyed such an advantage over the abstract expressionists. Learning by doing, by trial and error, is learning by the hardest way. If you want to overthrow the cubist tradition of architectural painting, it is much easier to seek out its opposites in the history of culture and study them carefully. At least it saves a great deal of time.

One thing can be said of painting in recent years—its revolt, its rejection of the classic modernism of the first half of the century, has been more absolute than in any other art. The only ancestor of abstract expressionism is the early Kandinsky—a style rejected even by Kandinsky himself. The only painter in a hundred years who bears the slightest resemblance to Tobey or Graves is Odilon Redon (perhaps Gustave Moreau a little), whose stock was certainly not very high with painters raised in the cubist tradition.

The ready market for prose fiction—there is almost no market at all for modern painting, and very much less for poetry—has had a decisive influence on its development. Sidemen with Kenton or Herman may make a good if somewhat hectic living, but any novelist who can write home to mother, or even spell his own name, has a chance to become another Brubeck. The deliberately and painfully intellectual fiction which appears in the literary quarterlies is a by-product of certain classrooms. The only significant fiction in America is popular fiction. Nobody realizes this better than the French. To them our late-born imitators of Henry James and E. M. Forster are just *chiens qui fument*, and arithmetical horses and bicycling seals. And there is no more perishable commodity than the middle-brow novel. No one today reads Ethel L. Voynich or Joseph Hergesheimer, just as no one in the future will read the writers' workshop pupils and teachers who fill the literary quarterlies. Very few people, except themselves, read them now.

On the other hand, the connection between the genuine highbrow writer and the genuinely popular is very close. Hemingway had hardly started to write before his style had been reduced to a formula in *Black Mask*, the first hard-boiled detective magazine. In no time at all he had produced two first-class popular writers, Raymond Chandler and Dashiell Hammett. Van Vechten, their middle-brow contemporary, is forgotten. It is from Chandler and Hammett and Hemingway [34] that the best modern fiction derives; although most of it comes out in hard covers, it is always thought of as written for a typical pocket book audience. Once it gets into pocketbooks it is sometimes difficult to draw the line between it and its most ephemeral imitators. Even the most *précieux* French critics, a few years ago, considered Horace McCoy America's greatest contemporary novelist. There is not only something to be said for their point of view; the only thing to be said against it is that they don't read English.

Much of the best popular fiction deals with the world of the utterly disaffiliated. Burlesque and carnival people, hipsters, handicappers and hop heads, wanted men on the lam, an expendable squad of soldiers being expended, anyone who by definition is divorced from society and cannot afford to believe even an iota of the social lie—these are the favorite characters of modern post-war fiction, from Norman Mailer to the latest ephemerid called *Caught*, or *Hung Up*, or *The Needle*, its bright cover winking invitingly in the drugstore. The first, and still the greatest, novelist of total disengagement is not a young man at all, but an elderly former I.W.W. of German ancestry, B. Traven, the author of *The Death Ship* and *The Treasure of Sierra Madre*.

It is impossible for an artist to remain true to himself as a man, let alone an artist, and work within the context of this society. Contemporary mimics of Jane Austen or Anthony Trollope are not only beneath contempt. They are literally unreadable. It is impossible to keep your eyes focused on the page. Writers as far apart as J. F. Powers and Nelson Algren agree in one thing— their diagnosis of an absolute corruption.

The refusal to accept the mythology of press and pulpit as a medium for artistic creation, or even enjoyable reading matter, is one explanation for the popularity of escapist literature. Westerns, detective stories and science fiction are all situated beyond the pale of normal living. The slick magazines are only too well aware of this, and in these three fields especially exert steady pressure on their authors to accentuate the up-beat. The most shocking example of this forced perversion is the homey science fiction story, usually written by a woman, in which a one-to-one correlation has been made for the commodity-ridden tale of domestic whimsey, the stand-by of magazines given away in the chain groceries. In writers like Judith Merrill the space pilot and his bride bat the badinage back and forth while the robot maid makes breakfast in the jet-propelled lucite orange squeezer and the electronic bacon rotobroiler, dropping pearls of dry assembly plant wisdom (like plantation wisdom but drier), the whilst. Still, few yield to these pressures, for the obvious reason that fiction [35] indistinguishable from the advertising columns on either side of the page defeats its own purpose, which is to get the reader to turn over the pages when he is told "continued on p. 47."

Simenon is still an incomparably better artist and psychologist than the psychological Jean Stafford. Ward Moore is a better artist than Eudora Welty, and Ernest Haycox than William Faulkner, just as, long ago, H. G. Wells was a better artist, as artist, than E. M. Forster, as well as being a lot more interesting. At its best, popular literature of this sort, coming up, meets highbrow literature coming down. It has been apparent novel by novel that Nelson Algren is rising qualitatively in this way. In his latest novel, thoroughly popular in its materials, *A Walk on the Wild Side*, he meets and absorbs influences coming down from the top, from the small handful of bona fide highbrow writers working today—Céline, Jean Genêt, Samuel Beckett, Henry Miller. In Algren's case this has been a slow growth, and he has carried his audience with him. Whatever the merits of his subject matter or his thesis—"It is better to be out than in. It is better to be on the lam than on the cover of *Time* Magazine"—his style started out as a distressing mixture of James Farrell and Kenneth Fearing. Only recently has he achieved an idiom of his own.

There is only one thing wrong with this picture, and that is that the high-brow stimulus still has to be imported. Algren, who is coming to write more and more like Céline, has no difficulty selling his fiction. On the other hand, an author like Jack Kerouac, who is in his small way the peer of Céline, Destouches or Beckett, is the most famous "unpublished" author in America. Every publisher's reader and adviser of any moment has read him and is enthusiastic about him. In other words, anybody emerging from the popular field has every advantage. It is still extremely difficult to enter American fiction from the top down.

The important point about modern fiction is that it is salable, and therefore viable in our society, and therefore successful in the best sense of the word. When a novelist has something to say, he knows people will listen. Only the jazz musician, but to a much lesser degree, shares this confidence in his audience. It is of the greatest social significance that the novelists who say, "I am proud to be delinquent" are nevertheless sold in editions of hundreds of thousands.

Nobody much buys poetry. I know. I am one of the country's most successful poets. My books actually sell out—in editions of two thousand. Many a poet, the prestige ornament of a publisher's list, has more charges against his royalty account [36] than credits for books sold. The problem of poetry is the problem of communication itself. All art is a symbolic criticism of values, but poetry is specifically and almost exclusively that. A painting decorates the wall. A novel is a story. Music . . . soothes a savage breast. But poetry you have to take straight. In addition, the entire educational system is in a conspiracy to make poetry as unpalatable as possible. From the seventh grade teacher who rolls her eyes and chants H.D. to the seven types of ambiguity factories, grinding out little Donnes and Hopkinses with hayseeds in their hair, everybody is out to de-poetize forever the youth of the land. Again, bad and spurious painting, music, and fiction are not really well-organized, except on obvious commercial levels, where they can be avoided. But in poetry Gresham's Law is supported by the full weight of the powers that be. From about 1930 on, a conspiracy of bad poetry has been as carefully organized as the Communist Party, and today controls most channels of publication except the littlest of the little magazines. In all other departments of American culture, English influence has been at a steadily declining minimum since the middle of the nineteenth century. In 1929, this was still true of American poetry. Amy Lowell, Sandburg, H.D., Pound, Marianne Moore, William Carlos Williams, Wallace Stevens—all of the major poets of the first quarter of the century owed far more to Apollinaire or Francis Jammes than they did to the whole body of the English tradition. In fact, the new poetry was essentially an anti-English, pro-French movement—a provincial but clear echo of the French revolt against the symbolists. On the other hand, Jules Laforgue and his English disciples. Ernest Dowson and Arthur Symons, were the major influence on T. S. Eliot. Unfortunately Mr. Eliot's poetic practice and his thoroughly snobbish critical essays which owed their great cogency to their assumption, usually correct, that his readers had never heard of the authors he discussed— Webster, Crashaw, or Lancelot Andrewes—lent themselves all too easily to the construction of an academy and the production of an infinite number of provincial academicians—policemen entrusted with the enforcement of Gresham's Law.

Behind the façade of this literary Potemkin village, the main stream of American poetry, with its sources in Baudelaire, Lautréamont, Rimbaud, Apollinaire, Jammes, Reverdy, Salmon, and later Breton and Éluard, has flowed on unperturbed, though visible only at rare intervals between the interstices of the academic hoax. Today the class magazines and the quarterlies are filled with poets as alike as two bad pennies. It is my opinion that these people do not really exist. Most of them are androids designed by Ransom, Tate, and Co., and animated [37] by Randall Jarrell. They are not just counterfeit; they are not even real counterfeits, but counterfeits of counterfeits. On these blurred and clumsy coins the lineaments of Mr. Eliot and I. A. Richards dimly can be discerned, like the barbarized Greek letters which nobody could read on Scythian money.

This is the world in which over every door is written the slogan: "The generation of experiment and revolt is over. Bohemia died in the twenties. There are no more little magazines." Actually there have never been so many little magazines. In spite of the fantastic costs of printing, more people than ever are bringing out little sheets of free verse and making up the losses out of their own pockets. This world has its own major writers, its own discoveries, its own old masters, its own tradition and continuity. Its sources are practically exclusively French, and they are all post-symbolist, even anti-symbolist. It is the Reactionary Generation who are influenced by Laforgue, the symbolists, and Valéry. Nothing is more impressive than the strength, or at least the cohesion, of this underground movement. Poets whom the quarterlies pretend never existed, like Louis Zukovsky and Jack Wheelwright, are still searched out in large libraries or obscure bookshops and copied into notebooks by young writers. I myself have a complete typewritten collection of the pre-reactionary verse of Yvor Winters. And I know several similar collections of "forgotten modernists" in the libraries of my younger friends. People are always turning up who say something like, "I just discovered a second-hand copy of Parker Tyler's *The Granite Butterfly* in a Village bookshop. It's great, man." On the other hand, I seriously doubt whether *The Hudson Review* would ever consider for a moment publishing a line of Parker Tyler's verse. And he is certainly not held up as an example in the Iowa Writers' Workshop. There are others who have disappeared entirely—Charles Snider, Sherry Mangan, R. E. F. Larsson, the early Winters, the last poems of Ford Madox Ford. They get back into circulation, as far as I know, only when I read them to somebody at home or on the air, and then I am always asked for a copy. Some of the old avant garde seem to have written themselves out, for instance, Mina Loy. There are a few established old masters, outstanding of whom are, of course, Ezra Pound and William Carlos Williams. I am not a passionate devotee of Pound myself. In fact, I think his influence is largely pernicious. But no one could deny its extent and power amongst young people today. As for Williams, more and more people, even some of the Reactionary Generation, have come to think of him as our greatest living poet. Even Randall Jarrell and R. P. Blackmur have good words to say for him. [38]

Then there is a middle generation which includes Kenneth Patchen, Jean Garrigue, myself, and a few others—notably Richard Eberhart, who looks superficially as if he belonged with the Tates and Blackmurs but who is redeemed by his directness, simplicity, and honesty, and Robert Fitzgerald and Dudley Fitts. Curiously enough, in the taste of the young, Kenneth Fearing is not included in this group, possibly because his verse is too easy. It does include the major work, for example, *Ajanta*, of Muriel Rukeyser.

I should say that the most influential poets of the youngest established generation of the avant garde are Denise Levertov, Robert Creeley, Charles Olson, Robert Duncan, and Philip Lamantia. The most influential avant garde editor is perhaps Cid Corman, with his magazine *Origin*. Richard Emerson's *Golden Goose* and Robert Creeley's *Black Mountain Review* seem to have suspended publication temporarily. Jonathan Williams, himself a fine poet, publishes the Jargon Press.

All of this youngest group have a good deal in common. They are all more or less influenced by French poetry, and by Céline,

Beckett, Artaud, Genêt, to varying degrees. They are also influenced by William Carlos Williams, D. H. Lawrence, Whitman, Pound. They are all interested in Far Eastern art and religion; some even call themselves Buddhists. Politically they are all strong disbelievers in the State, war, and the values of commercial civilization. Most of them would no longer call themselves anarchists, but just because adopting such a label would imply adherence to a "movement." Anything in the way of an explicit ideology is suspect. Contrary to gossip of a few years back, I have never met anybody in this circle who was a devotee of the dubious notions of the psychologist, Wilhelm Reich; in fact, few of them have ever read him, and those who have consider him a charlatan.

Although there is wide diversity—Olson is very like Pound; Creeley resembles Mallarmé; Denise Levertov in England was a leading New Romantic, in America she has come under the influence of William Carlos Williams; Robert Duncan has assimilated ancestors as unlike as Gertrude Stein and Éluard, and so on—although this diversity is very marked, there is a strong bond of aesthetic unity too. No avant garde American poet accepts the I. A. Richards–Valéry thesis that a poem is an end in itself, an anonymous machine for providing aesthetic experiences. All believe in poetry as communication, statement from one person to another. So they all avoid the studied ambiguities and metaphysical word play of the Reactionary Generation and seek clarity of image and simplicity of language.

In the years since the war, it would seem as though more [39] and more of what is left of the avant garde has migrated to Northern California. John Berryman once referred to the Lawrence cult of "mindless California," and Henry Miller and I have received other unfavorable publicity which has served only to attract people to this area. Mr. Karl Shapiro, for instance, once referred to San Francisco as "the last refuge of the Bohemian remnant"—a description he thought of as invidious. Nevertheless it is true that San Francisco is today the seat of an intense literary activity not unlike Chicago of the first quarter of the century. A whole school of poets has grown up—almost all of them migrated here from somewhere else. Some of them have national reputations, at least in limited circles. For example, Philip Lamantia among the surrealists; William Everson (Br. Antoninus, O.P)— perhaps the best Catholic poet. Others have come up recently, like Lawrence Ferlinghetti, Allen Ginsberg, Gary Snyder, Philip

Whalen, James Harmon, Michael McClure, and still have largely local reputations. But the strength of these reputations should not be underestimated. The Poetry Center of San Francisco State College, directed by Ruth Witt-Diamant, gives a reading to a large audience at least twice a month. And there are other readings equally well attended every week in various galleries and private homes.

This means that poetry has become an actual social force—something which has always sounded hitherto like a Utopian dream of the William Morris sort. It is a very thrilling experience to hear an audience of more than three hundred people stand and cheer and clap, as they invariably do at a reading by Allen Ginsberg, certainly a poet of revolt if there ever was one.

There is no question but that the San Francisco renaissance is radically different from what is going on elsewhere. There are hand presses, poetry readings, young writers elsewhere—but nowhere else is there a whole younger generation culture pattern characterized by total rejection of the official high-brow culture—where critics like John Crowe Ransom or Lionel Trilling, magazines like the *Kenyon, Hudson* and *Partisan* reviews, are looked on as "The Enemy"—the other side of the barricades.

There is only one trouble about the renaissance in San Francisco. It is too far away from the literary market place. That, of course, is the reason why the Bohemian remnant, the avant garde have migrated here. It is possible to hear the story about what so-and-so said to someone else at a cocktail party twenty years ago just one too many times. You grab a plane or get on your thumb and hitchhike to the other side of the continent for good and all. Each generation, the great [40] Latin poets came from farther and farther from Rome. Eventually, they ceased to even go there except to see the sights.

Distance from New York City does, however, make it harder to get things, if not published, at least nationally circulated. I recently formed a collection for one of the foundations of avant garde poetry printed in San Francisco. There were a great many items. The poetry was all at least readable, and the hand printing and binding were in most cases very fine indeed. None of these books were available in bookstores elsewhere in the country, and only a few of them had been reviewed in newspapers or magazines with national circulation.

Anyway, as an old war horse of the revolution of the word, things have never looked better from where I sit. The avant garde has not only not ceased to exist. It's jumping all over the place. Something's happening, man.

The disengagement of the creator, who, as creator, is necessarily judge, is one thing, but the utter nihilism of the emptied-out hipster is another. What is going to come of an attitude like this? It is impossible to go on indefinitely saying: "I am proud to be a delinquent," without destroying all civilized values. Between such persons no true enduring interpersonal relationships can be built, and of course, nothing resembling a true "culture" —an at-homeness of men with each other, their work, their loves, their environment. The end result must be the desperation of shipwreck—the despair, the orgies, ultimately the cannibalism of a lost lifeboat. I believe that most of an entire generation will go to ruin—the ruin of Céline, Artaud, Rimbaud, voluntarily, even enthusiastically. What will happen afterwards I don't know, but for the next ten years or so we are going to have to cope with the youth we, my generation, put through the atom smasher. Social disengagement, artistic integrity, voluntary poverty—these are powerful virtues and may pull them through, but they are not the virtues we tried to inculcate—rather they are the exact opposite. [41]

# John P. Sisk

## BEATNIKS AND TRADITION

The beat generation writers have had a very good press if one uses as a standard the extent to which public curiosity has been focused on them, but they have had an indifferent to poor press if the function of a good press is to clarify. The bulk of what has been written about them has taken their delinquent conduct and assertions of disengagement at face value, with the result that they are condemned as lacking any serious connection with American culture and as being as much outside society as they themselves contend they are.

This is a convenient position to take but not a very useful one, even if the whole tru:<sup>th</sup> about them were their adolescent alienation from society. Beat literature may turn out to be an ephemeral oddity that fifty years from now exists only for desperate Ph.D. candidates, or it may prove to have been the nighttown madness out of which one or two authentic writers were born, but that is another matter. In the meantime, the important and easily-overlooked fact is that it is in the American grain, and that however we react to it we are reacting to part of ourselves.

The Beat generation writers are in what may be called the subversive tradition in American literature—"subversive" because writers in this tradition so often appear as destructive forces to the middle class from which they come. To the writers of the subversive tradition organized society tends to be the Enemy. The Enemy is corrupt; hamstrung by convention; hypocritical, smug, selfish, superficial; ruled by fear, cliché and sentimentality; suspicious of the individual and creative originality; afraid to let itself go, to trust what Keats calls the holiness of the heart's affections; passionately addicted to that great American document, the dollar bill. Obviously, the Enemy does not always recognize itself in this description.

Reprinted from *The Commonweal*, 70 (April 17, 1959), 74–77. Reprinted by permission of the author and *The Commonweal*, the weekly journal of opinion edited by Catholic laymen.

The seeds of this tradition arrived with the first settlers and quickly flowered in such people as Thomas Morton, Roger Williams and Anne Hutchinson, that antinomian daughter of the inner light who today might be quite at home in a San Francisco pad. But the shape of this tradition is clearer for us if we begin [74] with Emerson and Thoreau and the reformist turmoil of the 1840's, when, as Emerson reported to Carlyle, "Not a reading man but has a draft of a new community in his pocket." If the Beats are "way out" the transcendentalists were there ahead of them, less licentiously but not less flamboyantly.

Thoreau (an important figure for the Beats) is the ideal subversive. He not only writes but acts out in hyperbolic terms his criticism of the Enemy's corruption; he both states and is civil disobedience. Then there is Hawthorne, a disputed figure, admittedly, but even by D. H. Lawrence's reading a subversive in disguise; Melville, ambiguous but more certainly a subversive; Whitman, the spiritual father who all but overwhelms Allen Ginsberg, and the Twain of *The Adventures of Huckleberry Finn,* the fatherhood of Kerouac's *On the Road.* The Enemy's reaction to Twain's masterpiece, long ago expressed in the *Boston Transcript,* has a familiar ring today: the Public Library committee decided to exclude the book because it was "rough, coarse and inelegant, dealing with a series of experiences not elevating . . . being more suited to the slums than to intelligent, respectable people."

But it is in our own century that the subversive tradition has proliferated. For nearly two generations now the American writer has been distinguished by his dissatisfaction with the shape and aims of society. This is apparent enough in London, Dreiser, Anderson, O'Neill, Odets, Eliot, Wolfe, Dos Passos, Fitzgerald, Nathan and Mencken, many of whom society has already admitted into the family library. The dissatisfaction—or subversiveness—is even more marked, because in contexts more immediate to us, in writers like Hemingway, Steinbeck, Miller, West, Mailer, Salinger, Wright, Algren, Vidal, Bowles and Saroyan. At present, all writers of value, says Kenneth Rexroth in an apologia for the Beat generation writers, agree on the "diagnosis of an absolute corruption." The statement is defensible only if we allow Mr. Rexroth to pick the valued writers, but at least it puts the emphasis where it belongs.

The fact is that the writer is by nature the critic of the society of "intelligent and respectable people." He [75] and that society are locked in a dialectic. The dialectic sometimes proceeds on moderate terms, particularly when there is no question of the writer's important position within society or when he speaks for a socially valued elite. But in America, and especially in the twentieth century, this dialectic has been carried on in hyperbolic terms: the extreme positions that society takes have been countered by the writer's extreme positions.

Thus Dreiser's remorseless realism counters the daydream of an acquisitive paradise; Mencken's irreverent mockery counters the stultification that comes from worshipping false gods; Wolfe's restless, romantic search for the meaning of America counters the naive and dangerous clarity with which a business society tries to define America; Hemingway's tight-lipped heroics counter the attempt to end heroism by organization; Salinger's and Capote's sentimental sympathy for the misfit and the outcast counters the callousness that goes with conformity and respectability; e. e. cummings' anarchism counters the growing conviction (to reverse Emerson's phrase) of the insufficiency of the private man; and Miller's and Kerouac's irrationalism counters the positivism of a society huddled desperately around its nuclear experts.

To recognize this is not necessarily to accept as infallible the diagnosis of society's evils expressed or implied in these writers. Nor is it to demand of them, as a criterion of value, a workable social program, which, if you could find it at all, might only reflect a political, economic and social virginity. The point is that such direction and order as society has depends upon all the dialectic tensions within it, and so far as this argument between the writer and society is concerned the important thing is neither position taken separately but the two together. Each is with respect to the other a control (though by no means a Hegelian guarantee) against potentially destructive excesses.

Thus, for instance, the corruption of society drove Twain to attack it, but his awareness of society's opposition (which was also a demand) freed him from the fear of a nihilistic strain in his own personality which could have been destructive to his artistic effort. One can even say (contra Van Wyck Brooks) that the pressure of society forced Twain to measure it by its own professed Christian standards more severely than he would otherwise have been inclined to, which was exactly what his book and society needed. Completely liberated from the tension of this conflict between Twain and society, *Huck Finn* would have little value, morally, socially or artistically.

The trouble is that in proportion as the terms of this dialectic have become extreme, the word "society" in literary circles has come to mean that part of society that is insensitive or hostile to the values of the writer; and the writer, taking his synecdoche literally, has often imagined himself as a thorough-going outsider. This throws an emphasis on the heroic adventure of writing and makes it possible for beginners and second-stringers, who do not pay enough attention to their proper business, to do a good deal of swaggering and posing as they equate literature with opposition to orthodoxy. It also makes it possible to forget the point Twain's great story dramatizes: that the important moral and social function of writers in the subversive tradition has been to counter the corruption of the whole of which they are articulate parts. That, like Twain and Fitzgerald, they have so often found the corruption to be within themselves only gives their statement of it authenticity and drama.

All of this is true of the Beat generation writers. No matter how completely they try to cut themselves off, they remain a critically engaged part of society, though the directness and value of their engagement may be less than that of many of their subversive predecessors. One cannot read Holmes, Kerouac, Corso, Ferlinghetti or Ginsberg without realizing that their interest, even to themselves, is always in relation to the society that contains them. They depend upon the city, the physical symbol of society, to exacerbate in them the pearl of beatness.

The inarticulate hipster who feels that a violent attachment to the values of society is square dramatizes by the attitudes he assumes a rebuke of society. But the articulate hipster with his fundamental assumption of society's corruption is even more plainly engaged. Even stylistically he depends upon the literature of the square world, the rhythms and patterns of which he cannot get out of his head. Kerouac's spontaneous prose depends for its effect upon traditional prose, just as Wordsworth's "language really used by men" depended for its effect upon the poetic diction he was trying hard not to write. To recognize this is not necessarily to invalidate Kerouac's prose or Wordsworth's verse, but simply to recognize that in matters of style, as in all other matters, no man is an island.

The Beat writers have an at least functional awareness that

they are a part of society that is countered and to an extent controlled by another part. Like Twain they have a kind of subconscious expectation that the rest of society will ultimately keep them from [76] destructive excess, even though they may as individuals destroy themselves. On the other hand, society has a similar expectation: that critics of this sort—ideally, granted, more responsible critics than these—will protect it from its excesses. For all the indignation the Beat writers have aroused, I think it must be admitted that the general reading public is remarkably permissive towards them, as it has learned to be towards all writers in the subversive tradition—as if it is a part of a developing national awareness of that tradition's function as the hyper-sensitive, if often quite fantastic, conscience of America. This is indicated in the number of twentieth century writers now generally accepted as part of the mainstream of American literature, who when they first appeared seemed shockingly outside it.

In a pluralist society such as ours there are, of course, all sorts of tensions: regional, racial, economic, political and religious. The potential for turmoil is tremendous. What stands against it is whatever we hold in common as Americans, and much of this we are not aware of, since it is expressed in patterns of conduct that have become habitual. We are very little aware, for instance, of the extent to which we have protected ourselves by a general, if mainly implicit, agreement not to court turmoil by divisive action. The result is that the very considerable degree of harmony we live in has as its base a dangerously negative and apprehensive element, and that a great deal of the dialectical interchange that is necessary for the health of society is suppressed.

This fear of dissension helps to explain the dearth of popular satire (why, for instance, T.V. loads up on horse opera and retires Sid Caesar to the guest-star pool), but it also helps to explain the extreme attitudes of subversive writers like the Beatniks, who are in a sense forced to bear more than their fair share of the dialectic burden. Society, possibly because of its uneasy conscience, fails to engage itself effectively with such opposition; perhaps it is best to say that it dares not for fear of coming face to face with its deviation from the American Dream.

It would follow, I think, that until society releases its normal interplay of criticism the subversive tradition in literature will continue to take up (will be even forced by society to take up) the extreme positions of such works as Miller's *The Air Conditioned Nightmare*, West's *Miss Lonelyhearts*, Algren's *A Walk on the Wild Side* or Salinger's *The Catcher in the Rye*. The solution for society is not to take subversive writers to its bosom, hoping that they will settle down to contented sequels of *Executive Suite*. The solution is to engage seriously with them in the act of criticism.

Such an engagement would assume that the Beat writers merit no preferred treatment simply because of their tradition-sanctioned subversiveness; and it would assume that they must prove themselves as writers and not expect to get by on novelty, shock-effect or sublime intentions. As a matter of fact, Beat writing suffers as literature because of its unhappy conviction that it is impossible to "make," in the traditional artist's sense, without corrupting. Hence the Beat writers' violent and surrealist dislike of the New Critics and the university poets. The poet is defined as prophet or visionary; he is a seer more than a maker; the sign of his authentic vision is the quality of unchecked outpour, of rhapsodic, jazz-inspired improvisation in his utterance. He is the poet as inspired madman. Hence the importance of Kerouac's hero, Dean Moriarty, whose chaotic, rhapsodic life is itself a Beat poem.

The appeal of the Beat writers is, however, bound up with their visionary, rhapsodic concept of the poet. In their enthusiastic acceptance of the visionary and spiritual element in life, in their indiscriminate assertion that all is holy—that we are all, as Kerouac says, angels even if we do not know it, in their passionate concern with the individual and their rejection of all that inhibits his free development, in their unqualified commitment to experience, they underline traditionally sacred American patterns of thought and action.

But at the same time, by isolating and dramatizing to the hilt these patterns, they can force us to reexamine some familiar subversive themes at a moment in our history when we most need to. We are at a point when we can least afford to be uncertain about the role of intellect, about the right relation of the individual to society, about the nature of man, about the extent of our involvement with all men everywhere. Ginsberg's "Howl" is a very American poem and Kerouac's *On the Road* is a very American novel. By this I do not mean that they are for that reason either good or bad as literature, but simply that they give us back as in a distorting mirror the anarchism and antinomianism, the dream of utopian freedom and innocence to be found in a commitment to instinct and feeling, that have always been elements in American culture; and which, if they are not consciously confronted and controlled, will, as they have often in the past, muddle our efforts to live effectively as a society in a complex world.

Dean Moriarty may strike one as the silliest holy fool in all literature. Nevertheless, he is a recognizable caricature of an image in the American heart as he rushes madly about the country, shirking all social obligations, trying passionately to dig everyone and everything, convinced that if he goes fast enough and has enough violent experiences the great ultimate secret will be laid bare to him. Kerouac's subversive service is to hold up that image while we measure ourselves against it. [77]

# Norman Podhoretz

## THE KNOW-NOTHING BOHEMIANS

Allen Ginsberg's little volume of poems, *Howl,* which got the
San Francisco renaissance off to a screaming start a year or so
ago, was dedicated to Jack Kerouac ("new Buddha of American
prose, who spit forth intelligence into eleven books written in
half the number of years . . . creating a spontaneous bop prosody and original classic literature"), William Seward Burroughs
("author of *Naked Lunch,* an endless novel which will drive
everybody mad"), and Neal Cassady ("author of *The First Third,*
an autobiography . . . which enlightened Buddha"). So far,
everybody's sanity has been spared by the inability of *Naked
Lunch* to find a publisher,* and we may never get the chance
to discover what Buddha learned from Neal Cassady's autobiography, but thanks to the Viking and Grove Presses, two of
Kerouac's original classics, *On the Road* and *The Subterraneans,*
have now been revealed to the world. When *On the Road* appeared last year, Gilbert Milstein commemorated the event in
the New York *Times* by declaring it to be "a historic occasion"
comparable to the publication of *The Sun Also Rises* in the
1920's. But even before the novel was actually published, the
word got around that Kerouac was the spokesman of a new
group of rebels and Bohemians who called themselves the Beat
Generation, and soon his photogenic countenance (unshaven, of
course, and topped by an unruly crop of rich black hair falling
over his forehead) was showing up in various mass-circulation
magazines, he was being interviewed earnestly on television,
and he was being featured in a Greenwich Village nightclub
where, in San Francisco fashion, he read specimens of his spontaneous bop prosody against a background of jazz music.

Though the nightclub act reportedly flopped, *On the Road*

Reprinted from *Partisan Review,* Vol. XXV, No. 2 (Spring, 1958), pp. 305–
311, 313–316, 318. Reprinted by permission of the author.
* [It has been published by the Olympia Press in Paris.]

sold well enough to hit the best-seller lists for several weeks, and it isn't hard to understand why. Americans love nothing so much as representative documents, and what could be more interesting in this Age of Sociology than a novel that speaks for the "young generation?" (The fact that Kerouac is thirty-five or thereabouts was generously not held against him.) Beyond that, however, I think that the unveiling of the Beat Generation was greeted with a certain relief by many people who [305] had been disturbed by the notorious respectability and "maturity" of postwar writing. This was more like it—restless, rebellious, confused youth living it up, instead of thin, balding, buttoned-down instructors of English composing ironic verses with one hand while changing the baby's diapers with the other. Bohemianism is not particularly fashionable nowadays, but the image of Bohemia still exerts a powerful fascination—nowhere more so than in the suburbs, which are filled to overflowing with men and women who uneasily think of themselves as conformists and of Bohemianism as the heroic road. The whole point of *Marjorie Morningstar* was to assure the young marrieds of Mamaroneck that they were better off than the apparently glamorous *luftmenschen* of Greenwich Village, and the fact that Wouk had to work so hard at making this idea seem convincing is a good indication of the strength of prevailing doubt on the matter.

On the surface, at least, the Bohemianism of *On the Road* is very attractive. Here is a group of high-spirited young men running back and forth across the country (mostly hitch-hiking, sometimes in their own second-hand cars), going to "wild" parties in New York and Denver and San Francisco, living on a shoe-string (GI educational benefits, an occasional fifty bucks from a kindly aunt, an odd job as a typist, a fruit-picker, a parking-lot attendant), talking intensely about love and God and salvation, getting high on marijuana (but never heroin or cocaine), listening feverishly to jazz in crowded little joints, and sleeping freely with beautiful girls. Now and again there is a reference to gloom and melancholy, but the characteristic note struck by Kerouac is exuberance:

We stopped along the road for a bite to eat. The cowboy went off to have a spare tire patched, and Eddie and I sat down in a kind of homemade diner. I heard a great laugh, the greatest laugh in the world, and here came this rawhide oldtimes Nebraska farmer with a bunch of other boys into the diner; you could hear his raspy cries clear across the plains, across the whole gray world of them that day.

Everybody else laughed with him. He didn't have a care in the world and had the hugest regard for everybody. I said to myself, Wham, listen to that man laugh. That's the West, here I am in the West. He came booming into the diner, calling Maw's name, and she made the sweetest cherry pie in Nebraska, and I had some with a mountainous scoop of ice cream on top. "Maw, rustle me up some grub afore I have to start eatin myself or some damn silly idee like that." And he threw himself on a stool and went hyaw hyaw hyaw hyaw. "And throw some beans in it." It was the spirit of the West sitting right next to me. I wished I knew his whole raw life and what the hell he'd been doing all these years besides laughing and yelling like that. Whooee, I told my soul, and the cowboy came back and off we went to Grand Island. [306]

Kerouac's enthusiasm for the Nebraska farmer is part of his general readiness to find the source of all vitality and virtue in simple rural types and in the dispossessed urban groups (Negroes, bums, whores). His idea of life in New York is "millions and millions hustling forever for a buck among themselves . . . grabbing, taking, giving, sighing, dying, just so they could be buried in those awful cemetery cities beyond Long Island City," whereas the rest of America is populated almost exclusively by the true of heart. There are intimations here of a kind of know-nothing populist sentiment, but in other ways this attitude resembles Nelson Algren's belief that bums and whores and junkies are more interesting than white-collar workers or civil servants. The difference is that Algren hates middle-class respectability for moral and political reasons—the middle class exploits and persecutes—while Kerouac, who is thoroughly unpolitical, seems to feel that respectability is a sign not of moral corruption but of spiritual death. "The only people for me," says Sal Paradise, the narrator of *On the Road*, "are the mad ones, the ones who are mad to live, mad to talk, mad to be saved, desirous of everything at the same time, the ones who never yawn or say a commonplace thing, but burn, burn, burn like fabulous yellow roman candles exploding like spiders across the stars. . . ." This tremendous emphasis on emotional intensity, this notion that to be hopped-up is the most desirable of all human conditions, lies at the heart of the Beat Generation ethos and distinguishes it radically from the Bohemianism of the past.

The Bohemianism of the 1920's represented a repudiation of the provinciality, philistinism, and moral hypocrisy of American life—a life, incidentally, which was still essentially small-town and rural in tone. Bohemia, in other words, was a movement created in the name of civilization: its ideals were intelligence, cultivation, spiritual refinement. The typical literary figure of the 1920's was a midwesterner (Hemingway, Fitzgerald, Sinclair Lewis, Eliot, Pound) who had fled from his home town to New York or Paris in search of a freer, more expansive, more enlightened way of life than was possible in Ohio or Minnesota or Michigan. The political radicalism that supplied the characteristic coloring of Bohemianism in the 1930's did nothing to alter the urban, cosmopolitan bias of the 1920's. At its best, the radicalism of the 1930's was marked by deep intellectual seriousness and aimed at a state of society in which the fruits of civilization would be more widely available—and ultimately available to all.

The Bohemianism of the 1950's is another kettle of fish altogether. It is hostile to civilization; it worships primitivism, instinct, energy, [307] "blood." To the extent that it has intellectual interests at all, they run to mystical doctrines, irrationalist philosophies, and left-wing Reichianism. The only art the new Bohemians have any use for is jazz, mainly of the cool variety. Their predilection for bop language is a way of demonstrating solidarity with the primitive vitality and spontaneity they find in jazz and of expressing contempt for coherent, rational discourse which, being a product of the mind, is in their view a form of death. To be articulate is to admit that you have no feelings (for how can real feelings be expressed in syntactical language?), that you can't respond to anything (Kerouac responds to everything by saying "Wow!"), and that you are probably impotent.

At the one end of the spectrum, this ethos shades off into violence and criminality, main-line drug addiction and madness. Allen Ginsberg's poetry, with its lurid apocalyptic celebration of "angel-headed hipsters," speaks for the darker side of the new Bohemianism. Kerouac is milder. He shows little taste for violence, and the criminality he admires is the harmless kind. The hero of *On the Road*, Dean Moriarty, has a record: "From the age of eleven to seventeen he was usually in reform school. His specialty was stealing cars, gunning for girls coming out of high school in the afternoon, driving them out to the mountains, making them, and coming back to sleep in any available hotel bathtub in town." But Dean's criminality, we are told, "was not something that sulked and sneered; it was a wild yea-saying overburst of American joy; it was Western, the west wind, an ode from the Plains, something new, long prophesied, long a-coming (he only stole cars for joy rides)." And, in fact, the species of Bohemian that Kerouac writes about is on the whole rather law-abiding. In *The Subterraneans,* a bunch of drunken boys steal a pushcart in the middle of the night, and when they leave it in front of a friend's apartment building, he denounces them angrily for "screwing up the security of my pad." When Sal Paradise (in *On the Road*) steals some groceries from the canteen of an itinerant workers' camp in which he has taken a temporary job as a barracks guard, he comments, "I suddenly began to realize that everybody in America is a natural-born thief"—which, of course, is a way of turning his own stealing into a bit of boyish prankishness. Nevertheless, Kerouac is attracted to criminality, and that in itself is more significant than the fact that he personally feels constrained to put the brakes on his own destructive empulses.

Sex has always played a very important role in Bohemianism: sleeping around was the Bohemian's most dramatic demonstration of his freedom from conventional moral standards, and a defiant denial [308] of the idea that sex was permissible only in marriage and then only for the sake of a family. At the same time, to be "promiscuous" was to assert the validity of sexual experience in and for itself. The "meaning" of Bohemian sex, then, was at once social and personal, a crucial element in the Bohemian's ideal of civilization. Here again the contrast with Beat Generation Bohemianism is sharp. On the one hand, there is a fair amount of sexual activity in *On the Road* and *The Subterraneans.* Dean Moriarity is a "new kind of American saint" at least partly because of his amazing sexual power: he can keep three women satisfied simultaneously and he can make love any time, anywhere (once he mounts a girl in the back seat of a car while poor Sal Paradise is trying to sleep in front). Sal, too, is always on the make, and though he isn't as successful as the great Dean, he does pretty well: offhand I can remember a girl in Denver, one on a bus, and another in New York, but a little research would certainly unearth a few more. The heroine of *The Subterraneans,* a Negro girl named Mardou Fox, seems to have switched from one to another member of the same gang and back again ("This has been an incestuous group in its time"), and we are given to understand that there is nothing unusual about such an arrangement. But the point of all this hustle and bustle is not freedom from ordinary social restrictions or defiance of convention (except in relation to homosexuality, which is Ginsberg's preserve: among "the best minds" of Ginsberg's gen-

eration who were destroyed by America are those "who let themselves be ——— in the ——— by saintly motorcyclists, and
screamed with joy, / who blew and were blown by those human
seraphim, the sailors, caresses of Atlantic and Caribbean love").
The sex in Kerouac's book goes hand in hand with a great deal
of talk about forming permanent relationships ("although I have
a hot feeling sexually and all that for her," says the poet Adam
Moorad in *The Subterraneans*, "I really don't want to get any
further into her not only for these reasons but finally, the big
one, if I'm going to get involved with a girl now I want to be
permanent like permanent and serious and long termed and I can't
do that with her"), and a habit of getting married and then
duly divorced and re-married when another girl comes along.
In fact, there are as many marriages and divorces in *On the Road*
as in the Hollywood movie colony (must be that California cli-
mate): "All those years I was looking for the woman I wanted
to marry," Sal Paradise tells us. "I couldn't meet a girl without
saying to myself, What kind of wife would she make?" Even
more revealing is Kerouac's refusal to admit that any of his characters ever make love wantonly or lecherously—no matter how
casual the encounter it must [309] always entail sweet feelings
toward the girl. Sal, for example, is fixed up with Rita Betten-
court in Denver, whom he has never met before. "I got her in
my bedroom after a long talk in the dark of the front room. She
was a nice little girl, simple and true [naturally], and tremendously frightened of sex. I told her it was beautiful. I wanted to
prove this to her. She let me prove it, but I was too impatient
and proved nothing. She sighed in the dark. 'What do you want
out of life?' I asked, and I used to ask that all the time of girls."
This is rather touching, but only because the narrator is really
just as frightened of sex as that nice little girl was. He is frightened of failure and he worries about his performance. For *performance* is the point—performance and "good orgasms," which
are the first duty of man and the only duty of woman. What
seems to be involved here, in short, is sexual anxiety of enormous
proportions—an anxiety that comes out very clearly in *The Subterraneans*, which is about a love affair between the young writer,
Leo Percepied, and the Negro girl, Mardou Fox. Despite its
protestations, the book is one long agony of fear and trembling
over sex:

I spend long nights and many hours making her, finally I have her,
I pray for it to come, I can hear her breathing harder, I hope against

hope it's time, a noise in the hall (or whoop of drunkards next door) takes her mind off and she can't make it and laughs—but when she does make it I hear her crying, whimpering, the shuddering electrical female orgasm makes her sound like a little girl crying, moaning in the night, it lasts a good twenty seconds and when it's over she moans, "O why can't it last longer," and "O when will I when you do?"— "Soon now I bet," I said, "you're getting closer and closer"—

Very primitive, very spontaneous, very elemental, very beat.

For the new Bohemians interracial friendships and love affairs apparently play the same role of social defiance that sex used to play in older Bohemian circles. Negroes and whites associate freely on a basis of complete equality and without a trace of racial hostility. But putting it that way understates the case, for not only is there no racial hostility, there is positive adulation for the "happy, true-hearted, ecstatic Negroes of America."

At lilac evening I walked with every muscle aching among the lights of 27th and Welton in the Denver colored section, wishing I were a Negro, feeling that the best the white world had offered was not enough ecstasy for me, not enough life, joy, kicks, darkness, music, not enough night. . . . I wished I were a Denver Mexican, or even a poor overworked Jap, anything but what I was so drearily, a "white man" disillusioned. All my life I'd had white ambitions. . . . I passed the dark porches of Mexican and Negro homes; soft voices were there, [310] occasionally the dusky knee of some mysterious sensuous gal; and dark faces of the men behind rose arbors. Little children sat like sages in ancient rocking chairs.

It will be news to the Negroes to learn that they are so happy and ecstatic; I doubt if a more idyllic picture of Negro life has been painted since certain Southern ideologues tried to convince the world that things were just as fine as fine could be for the slaves on the old plantation. Be that as it may, Kerouac's love for Negroes and other dark-skinned groups is tied up with his worship of primitivism, not with any radical social attitudes. Ironically enough, in fact, to see the Negro as more elemental than the white man, as Ned Polsky has acutely remarked, is "an inverted form of keeping the nigger in his place." But even if it were true that American Negroes, by virtue of their position in our culture, have been able to retain a degree of primitive spontaneity, the last place you would expect to find evidence of this is among Bohemian Negroes. Bohemianism, after all, is for the Negro a means of entry into the world of the whites, and no Negro Bohemian is going to cooperate [311] in the attempt to identify him with Harlem or Dixieland. The only major Negro character in either of Kerouac's two novels is Mardou Fox, and she is about as primitive as Wilhelm Reich himself.

The plain truth is that the primitivism of the Beat Generation serves first of all as a cover for an anti-intellectualism so bitter that it makes the ordinary American's hatred of eggheads seem positively benign. Kerouac and his friends like to think of themselves as intellectuals ("they are intellectual as hell and know all about Pound without being pretentious or talking too much about it"), but this is only a form of newspeak. Here is an example of what Kerouac considers intelligent discourse—"formal and shining and complete, without the tedious intellectualness":

We passed a little kid who was throwing stones at the cars in the road. "Think of it," said Dean. "One day he'll put a stone through a man's windshield and the man will crash and die—all on account of that little kid. You see what I mean? God exists without qualms. As we roll along this way I am positive beyond doubt that everything will be taken care of for us—that even you, as you drive, fearful of the wheel . . . the thing will go along of itself and you won't go off the road and I can sleep. Furthermore we know America, we're at home; I can go anywhere in America and get what I want because it's the same in every corner, I know the people, I know what they do. We give and take and go in the incredibly complicated sweetness zigzagging every side."

You see what he means? Formal and shining and complete. No tedious intellectualness. Completely unpretentious. "There was nothing clear about the things he said but what he meant to say was somehow made pure and clear." *Somehow.* Of course. If what he wanted to say had been carefully thought out and precisely articulated, that would have been tedious and pretentious and, no doubt, *somehow* unclear and clearly impure. But so long as he utters these banalities with his tongue tied and with no comprehension of their meaning, so long as he makes noises that came out of his soul (since they couldn't possibly have come out of his mind), he passes the test of true intellectuality.

Which brings us to Kerouac's spontaneous bop prosody. This "prosody" is not to be confused with bop language itself, which has such a limited vocabulary (Basic English is a verbal treasure-house by comparison) that you couldn't write a note to the milkman in it, much less a novel. Kerouac, however, manages to remain true to the spirit of hipster slang while making forays into enemy territory (i.e., the English language) by his simple inability to express anything in words. The only method he has of describing an object is to summon up the same half-dozen adjectives over and over again: "greatest," "tremendous," [313] "crazy," "mad," "wild," and perhaps one or two others. When it's more than just mad or crazy or wild, it becomes "really mad" or "really crazy" or "really wild." (All quantities in excess of three, incidentally, are subsumed under the rubric "innumerable," a word used innumerable times in *On the Road* but not so innumerably in *The Subterraneans*.) The same poverty of resources is apparent in those passages where Kerouac tries to handle a situation involving even slightly complicated feelings. His usual tactic is to run for cover behind cliché and vague signals to the reader. For instance: "I looked at him; my eyes were watering with embarrassment and tears. Still he stared at me. Now his eyes were blank and looking through me. . . . Something clicked in both of us. In me it was suddenly concern for a man who was years younger than I, five years, and whose fate was wound with mine across the passage of the recent years; in him it was a matter that I can ascertain only from what he did afterward." If you can ascertain what this is all about, either beforehand, during, or afterward, you are surely no square.

In keeping with its populistic bias, the style of *On the Road* is folksy and lyrical. The prose of *The Subterraneans*, on the other hand, sounds like an inept parody of Faulkner at his worst, the main difference being that Faulkner usually produces bad writing out of an impulse to inflate the commonplace while Kerouac gets into trouble by pursuing "spontaneity." Strictly speaking, spontaneity is a quality of feeling, not of writing: when we call a piece of writing spontaneous, we are registering our impression that the author hit upon the right words without sweating, that no "art" and no calculation entered into the picture, that his feelings seem to have spoken themselves, seem to have sprouted a tongue at the moment of composition. Kerouac apparently thinks that spontaneity is a matter of saying whatever comes into your head, in any order you happen to feel like saying it. It isn't the *right* words he wants (even if he knows what they might be), but the first words, or at any rate the words that most obviously announce themselves as deriving from emotion rather than cerebration, as coming from "life" rather than "literature," from the guts rather than the brain. (The brain, remember, is the angel of death.) But writing that springs easily and "spontaneously" out of strong feelings is *never* vague; it always has a quality of sharpness and precision because it is in the nature of strong feelings to be aroused by specific objects. The notion that a diffuse, generalized, and unrelenting enthusiasm is the mark of great sensitivity and responsiveness is utterly fantastic, an idea that comes from taking drunkenness or drug-addition as the state of perfect emotional vigor. The effect of such enthusiasm is actually to wipe out the world [314] altogether, for if a filling station will serve as well as the Rocky Mountains to arouse a sense of awe and wonder, then both the filling station and the mountains are robbed of their reality. Kerouac's conception of feeling is one that only a solipsist could believe in—and a solipsist, be it noted, is a man who does not relate to anything outside himself.

Solipsism is precisely what characterizes Kerouac's fiction. *On the Road* and *The Subterraneans* are so patently autobiographical in content that they become almost impossible to discuss as novels; if spontaneity were indeed a matter of destroying the distinction between life and literature, these books would unquestionably be It. "As we were going out to the car Babe slipped and fell flat on her face. Poor girl was overwrought. Her brother Tim and I helped her up. We got in the car; Major and Betty joined us. The sad ride back to Denver began." Babe is a girl who is mentioned a few times in the course of *On the Road;* we don't know why she is overwrought on this occasion, and even if we did it wouldn't matter, since there is no reason for her presence in the book at all. But Kerouac tells us that she fell flat on her face while walking toward a car. It is impossible to believe that Kerouac made this detail up, that his imagination was creating a world real enough to include wholly gratuitous elements; if that were the case, Babe would have come alive as a human being. But she is only a name; Kerouac never even describes her. She is in the book because the sister of one of Kerouac's friends was there when he took a trip to Central City, Colorado, and she slips in *On the Road* because she slipped that day on the way to the car. What is true of Babe who fell flat on her face is true of virtually every incident in *On the Road* and *The Subterraneans.* Nothing that happens has any dramatic reason for happening. Sal Paradise meets such-and-such people on the road whom he likes or (rarely) dislikes; they exchange a few words, they have a few beers together, they part. It is all very unremarkable and commonplace, but for Kerouac it is always the greatest, the wildest, the most. What you get in these two books is a man proclaiming that he is *alive* and offering every trivial experience he has ever had in evidence. Once I did this, once I did that (he is saying) and by God, it *meant* something! Because I *responded!* But if it meant something, and you responded so powerfully, why can't you explain what it meant, and why do you have to insist so?

I think it is legitimate to say, then, that the Beat Generation's worship of primitivism and spontaneity is more than a cover for hostility to intelligence; it arises from a pathetic poverty of feeling as well. The hipsters and hipster-lovers of the Beat Generation are rebels, all right, but not against anything so sociological and historical as the [315] middle class or capitalism or even respectability. This is the revolt of the spiritually underprivileged and the crippled of soul—young men who can't think straight and so hate anyone who can; young men who can't get outside the morass of self and so construct definitions of feeling that exclude all human beings who manage to live, even miserably, in a world of objects; young men who are burdened unto death with the specially poignant sexual anxiety that America—in its eternal promise of erotic glory and its spiteful withholding of actual erotic possibility—seems bent on breeding, and who therefore dream of the unattainable perfect orgasm, which excuses all sexual failures in the real world. Not long ago, Norman Mailer suggested that the rise of the hipster may represent "the first wind of a second revolution in this century, moving not forward toward action and more rational equitable distribution, but backward toward being and the secrets of human energy." To tell the truth, whenever I hear anyone talking about instinct and being and the secrets of human energy, I get nervous; next thing you know he'll be saying that violence is just fine, and then I begin wondering whether he really thinks that kicking someone in the teeth or sticking a knife between his ribs are deeds to be admired. History, after all—and especially the history of modern times—teaches that there is a close [316] connection between ideologies of primitivistic vitalism and a willingness to look upon cruelty and blood-letting with complacency, if not downright enthusiasm. The reason I bring this up is that the spirit of hipsterism and the Beat Generation strikes me as the same spirit which animates the young savages in leather jackets who have been running amuck in the last few years with their switch-blades and zip guns. What does Mailer think of those wretched kids, I wonder? What does he think of the gang that stoned a nine-year-old boy to death in Central Park in broad daylight a few months ago, or the one that set fire to an old man drowsing on a bench near the Brooklyn waterfront one summer's day, or the one that pounced on a crippled child and orgiastically stabbed him over and over and over again even after he was good and dead? Is that what he means by the liberation of instinct and the mysteries of being? Maybe so. At least he says somewhere in his article that two eighteen-year-old hoodlums who bash in the brains of a candy-store keeper are murdering an institution, committing an act that "violates private property"—which is one of the most morally gruesome ideas I have ever come across, and which indicates where the ideology of hipsterism can lead. I happen to believe that there is a direct connection between the flabbiness of American middle-class life and the spread of juvenile crime in the 1950's, but I also believe that juvenile crime can be explained partly in terms of the same resentment against normal feeling and the attempt to cope with the world through intelligence that lies behind Kerouac and Ginsberg. Even the relatively mild ethos of Kerouac's books can spill over easily into brutality, for there is a suppressed cry in those books: Kill the intellectuals who can talk coherently, kill the people who can sit still for five minutes at a time, kill those incomprehensible characters who are capable of getting seriously involved with a woman, a job, a cause. How can anyone in his right mind pretend that this has anything to do with private property or the middle class? No. Being for or against what the Beat Generation stands for has to do with denying that incoherence is superior to precision; that ignorance is superior to knowledge; that the exercise of mind and discrimination is a form of death. It has to do with fighting the notion that sordid acts of violence are justifiable so long as they are committed in the name of "instinct." It even has to do with fighting the poisonous glorification of the adolescent in American popular culture. It has to do, in other words, with being for or against intelligence itself. [318]

# Dorothy Van Ghent

## COMMENT

The distinguishing characteristic of the Beat Generation is, it seems to me, the fact that they have a myth. The myth follows authentic archaic lines, and goes something like this. The hero is the "angelheaded hipster." He comes of anonymous parentage, parents whom he denies in correct mythological fashion. He has received a mysterious call—to the road, the freights, the jazz-dens, the "negro streets." This is the night journey or journey underground (Kerouac's title, *The Subterraneans*, is pertinent). Where he goes is hell, the realm of death, ruled by the H- or Hades-Bomb. The hero is differentiated from the mass of the population of hell by his angelic awareness: he knows where he is. He knows that in hell it is silly to act as if you were in heaven, so he acts like a damned soul. His tortures—the heroic "ordeals" of myth—send him into ecstasy and he bursts into song, song filled with metaphors of destruction, an ironic, invertedly apocalyptic Mollie Bloom paean of assent. The familiar end of myth is some form of transcendence—capture of the golden fleece or the golden apples, marriage with the princess, discovery of the "real" parents, who are royal—representing the achievement of a higher wisdom or higher form of being gained by the hero's disciplined technique in encountering evil. The Beats say they are a religious movement, and the Beat literature constantly indicates the far and visionary goal of the hero's quest—the return to the Kingdom, the transcendent kingdom of love and brotherhood and life: "authenticity," one of the Beats has called it. This can come about only by the regeneration of the whole world. [27]

The imagery of Beat literature is demonic, appropriate to myth in an age of irony. Both in the prose and the poetry, the

Reprinted from *The Wagner Literary Magazine* (Spring, 1959), pp. 27–28. Reprinted by permission of *The Wagner* [College] *Literary Magazine* and its Faculty Advisor, Willard Maas.

structure tends to be additive (for where is one going?) and the cadences to be cumulative, flowing the gathering, passionate pulsation, and explosion of breath. This is the cadence of lyrical prophecy and apocalyptic vision. Hebraic literature, Whitman, Blake, and Christopher Smart come to mind. Witness the similarity of movement between Ginsberg's *Howl*—

I saw the best minds of my generation destroyed by madness, starving hysterical naked
dragging themselves through the negro streets at dawn looking for an angry fix,
angelheaded hipsters burning for the ancient heavenly connection to the starry dynamo in the machinery of night . . .

and Smart's *Jubilate Agno*—

Rejoice in God, O ye Tongues; give the glory to the Lord, and the Lamb.
Nations, and languages, and every Creature, in which is the breath of Life . . .
Let Noah and his company approach the throne of Grace, and do homage to the Ark of their Salvation . . .

The moral predicament of the Beats is not new. For the past seventeen years, the bulk of my students have been of the Desist Generation (I am taking this name from Stan Brakhage's film *Desist*). The Desists were in the same moral predicament, but they were numbed by it; their mode of behavior was "to desist" from feeling anything at all. Without myth, passion has no focus and dies; action and voice are impossible. In the Beat literature we are observing the development of an articulate myth of swift growth and in the very process of its formation. That the Beats have a collective passion and a collective voice is, in itself, an important and exciting phenomenon. [28]

# Warren Tallman

## KEROUAC'S SOUND

It is always an implicit and frequently an explicit assumption of the Beat writers that we live, if we do at all, in something like the ruins of our civilization. When the Second World War was bombed out of existence in that long-ago '45 summer, two cities were in literal fact demolished. But psychically, all cities fell. And what the eye sees as intact is a lesser truth than what the psyche knows is actually in ruins. The psyche knows that the only sensible way to enter a modern city is Gregory Corso's way, very tentatively, "two suitcases filled with despair." This assumption that the cities which live in the psyche have all gone smash is one starting point of Beat.

But if our cities are in something like ruins, there have been survivors. Those have survived who had the least to lose, those whose psychic stance in face of modern experience had already been reduced to minimum needs: the angry Negro, the pathological delinquent, the hopeless addict. These outcasts had already fought and *lost* the battle each of us makes to establish his psyche within the social continuum. The Negro who feels that integration offers worse defeats than those already suffered at hands of the segregation to which he has long-since adjusted; the delinquent who realizes that continued irresponsibility is the only effective physician to the ills which previous irresponsibilities have brought upon him; the addict who knows that the extent to which he is hooked by his habit is as nothing alongside the extent to which he is hooked by the social purgatory he must endure in order to feed that habit—these advanced types of the social outcast have long since had to forego the psychic luxuries available to those of us who are not outcasts. Crucially, they have had to give up that main staple of psychic continuity, Ego. Here,

Reprinted from *Evergreen Review*, Vol. 4, No. 11, pp. 153–169. This article originally appeared in *The Tamarack Review* (Spring, 1959), pp. 58–74, and is reprinted here by permission of the author.

from Clellon Holmes's novel *Go,* is an addict evaluating the reaction of fellow passengers on a bus: [153]

they knew I was completely saturated with narcotics and had this disgusting skin disease and everything . . . I realize they think I'm revolting, abhorrent . . . but not only that, I know *why* they think that . . . and more important, I *accept* the fact that they do . . . They're disgusted because they've got to save their own egos, you see. But I haven't got one, I mean I don't care about all that anymore, so it doesn't matter to me . . . I just accept it so as not to get hung up.

The outcast knows that ego, which demands self-regard, is the enemy that can trap him into kinds of social commitment which his psyche cannot afford. Ego is for the squares. Let them be trapped. To be released from the claims of ego is to be released from the claims of others, a very necessary condition for survival if you happen to be an outcast. But the consequences can be devastating. For when ego vanishes, the continuity of one's existence is likely to vanish with it.

A most vivid instance of what can happen to a man when the continuity of his life is suddenly disrupted comes not from the Beat writers but from Conrad, in *Nostromo*. Decoud, isolated by circumstances, "dreaded the sleepless nights in which the silence, remaining unbroken in the shape of a cord to which he hung with both hands, vibrated with senseless phrases." The "senseless phrases" happen to be the names of the woman he loves, of the man with whom he is conspiring, and of the man against whom they conspire. Just because the most meaningful continuity in his life has been reduced by solitude to "senseless phrases," he begins to wish that the cord of silence to which he clings will snap; as, with his suicide, it does. The kinds of solitude from which the city-bred outcasts suffer are not as severe as Decoud's, doubtless, and the loss of continuity which follows from the abandonment of ego not as total. But what Decoud suffers in a total way is known in less intense but still devastating ways to all those outcasts who waken, without ego, to the consequent draft of their aimless day.

It is an axiom of the human spirit that whosoever wanders into purgatory will attempt to escape. With luck, with courage, with ingenuity, some succeed. The solution of the outcast who has given up a large part of his ego has been to fall back not [154] upon the mercy of society—for society has long since been committed to the merciless proposition that only certain men are brothers—but upon, or rather into the moment. The moment becomes the outcast's island, his barricade, his citadel. Having lost his life in the social continuum, cast out and cyphered, he finds it again within the moment. But when the social outcast takes over the moment as his province, he is faced with yet another problem. He must make it habitable. How unsuccessful most such outcast efforts have been can best be seen in any skid-road district, where men come to their vacant pauses within what Ginsberg describes as "the drear light of Zoo." However, some of the animals in the skid road and slum zoos have long since rebelled. Up from the rhythms and intensities which animate the Negro, the delinquent, and the addict have risen the voices that dig and swing on the Beat streets in the North American night, a music and a language, Jazz and Hip.

First the language. Strictly speaking, a hipster is an addict and hip talk is the addict's private language. But it has become much more. Granting many exceptions in which addiction is incurred accidentally, it is almost axiomatic that the addict is an outcast first and acquires his habit in an effort to escape from the psychic ordeal of being brotherless, unable to exert claims upon anybody's love. But once hooked, he is necessarily a man living from moment to moment, from fix to fix. The intervals between become a kind of purgatorial school in which one learns to care about less and less: not surroundings, not status, not appearance, not physical condition, not even crimes, but only for the golden island ahead where one can score, then fix, then swing. To swing is to enter into full alliance with the moment and to do this is to triumph over the squares who otherwise run the world. For to enter the moment, you must yield to the moment. The square person can never get the camel caravan of his ego-commitments through the eye of the needle which opens out upon hipster heaven. Excluded from the moment and consequently seeking it out ahead in a future which never has been and never will be, all that the square person can dig is his own grave. The hip person knows that the only [155] promised land is Now and that the only way to make the journey is to dig everything and go until you make it and can swing.

Hip talk, then, is Basic English which charts the phases, the psychology, even the philosophy of those outcasts who live for, with, and—when they can—within the moment. It is in fact less a language than a language art in which spontaneity is every-

217

thing. The words are compact, mostly monosyllabic, athletic: dig, go, make it, man, cat, chick, flip, goof, cool, crazy, swing. In his very suggestive essay, "The White Negro," Norman Mailer argues that the basic words of hip form a nucleus which charts and organizes the energies of the hipster into maximum mobility for his contentions with the squares, as indeed with other hipsters, for the sweets of this world. Mailer's emphasis upon the endless battle between hip and square is true, I think, but not true enough because less vital than is the hipster's even deeper need to establish a new continuity for his life. The most severe ordeal of his constantly emphasized isolation is not loss of the social sweets but loss of the moment. It is against this fate that he has evolved his cryptic language art. The talented hipster is as sensitive to the nuances and possibilities of his language as he necessarily is to the nuances and possibilities of his always threatened moment. Which is why the real hip cat who can dig and swing with the other cats in hipland has such close affinities with the aristocrat among such outcasts, the jazzman.

Jazz swings in and with the moment. The universal name for a good group is "a swinging group," one in which each individual is attuned to all of the others so that improvisation can answer improvisation without loss of group harmony. Baby Dodds, who drummed with Louis Armstrong in the early jazz days, describes this process very clearly:

Louis would make something on his horn, in an afterbeat, or make it so fast that he figured I couldn't make it that fast, or he'd make it in syncopation or in Charleston time, or anything like that for a trick. And I would come back with something on the snare drums and with an afterbeat on the bass drum or a roll [156] or something. But I had to keep the bass drum going straight for the band. I couldn't throw the band . . . at all times I heard every instrument distinctly.

Jazz played in this way can be a spontaneous, swinging poem in which the group first creates the shape, the musical metrics of the given moment. Then individuals begin to improvise in the way Dodds describes or the talented soloist to move his sound out into the possibilities of the moment. When this happens the jazzman and the hip person who can swing with him experience release into the moment that is being created, as Kerouac notes, "so he said it and sang it and blew it through to the stars and on out." Since such release is the hip person's deepest need and desire, the jazzman becomes the hipster hero who has moved among the mountains of the moment and in so doing has conquered the most vindictive of their enemies, time. In jazz the moment prevails.

But sounds die out. And are replaced by other sounds. Where jazz was factory whistles will be when Daddio Time turns on tic toc dawn to light the hipman and the jazzman home. And the square eye of morning tells both what each had been trying to forget, that when you fall out of the moment and happen to be an outcast you are back among the ruins in a world where only certain men are brothers. At which point the Beat writers appear on the scene, chanting Holy, Holy, Holy—but with a Bop beat.

BOP: In a conventional tune the melody moves along not quite like but something like an escalator, steadily and as the feet would expect, so that the good children of this world can keep their eyes fixed upward for the sign that says: TOYS. But the restless outcast children in the department store of this world know that the journey is NOW. As their jazz escalator goes at a syncopated beat from level to level, the outcast children dip into the toy shop of the moment and come up with little hops, skips, and jumps that are answered back by other hops, skips, and jumps, until, by the time the syncopated escalator reaches the top level, everybody is hopping and jumping about, together and as individuals, and this of course is improvisation—the life [157] of jazz. However, this dual progression in which the syncopated beat of the melody escalator carries the spontaneous action of the improvisations from level to level has given way, with the advent of Bop, to a music which seems to travel from level to level on the improvisations alone. That is, the melody (the escalator) has been assimilated into the pattern of improvisations (hop, skip, jump) and the improvisations—always the life impulse of jazz—have dominated in this merger. At best Bop has freed jazz from the tedium of banal melodies. It has also given emphasis to a principle of spontaneous creative freedom which has been taken over by the Beat writers in ways likely to have a strong influence upon North American poetry and fiction.

In conventional fiction the narrative continuity is always clearly discernible. But it is impossible to create an absorbing narrative without at the same time enriching it with images, asides, themes and variations—impulses from within. It is evident that in much recent fiction—Joyce, Kafka, Virginia Woolf, and Faulkner are obvious examples—the narrative line has tended to weaken, merge with, and be dominated by the sum of variations. Each narrative step in Faulkner's work is likely to provoke many side-winding pages before a next narrative step is taken. More, a lot of Faulkner's power is to be found in the sidewindings. In brief, what happens in jazz when the melody merges with the improvisations and the improvisations dominate, has been happening in fiction for some time now.

However, the improvisations of jazz are incomparably more fluent than have been the variations of fiction. The jazzman is free to move his sound, which is simply himself, where and as the moment prompts, "one mountain, two mountains, ten clouds, no clouds." But the fiction man has always had to move his style, which also is himself, into the present-day deviousness, the "messy imprecision" of words. The fiction man encounters deviousness and imprecision in our language because an evident fragmentation has overtaken meanings in our time. Empson's *Seven Types of Ambiguity,* the first work to *exploit* the plight of meanings in our time, may well turn out to have been the handwriting on the wall announcing the breakup of our camp, the only camp that truly signifies: the human one. For it [158] is not, as Empson supposed, our language that is ambiguous. It is our relations with one another. Trust lacking, meanings become ambiguous. And when meanings become ambiguous language becomes imprecise, difficult, devious.

There have been a number of attempts, heroic in their single-mindedness, to confront with language the increasing ambiguity of meanings, notably those of Joyce and Eliot. But the result has been a fiction and poetry so circuitously difficult as to require years-long efforts of creation and explication—which is to communicate the slow way. The outcome for most persons has been a distinct breakdown of any vital connection with our best literature. To the fact of this breakdown the Beat writers bring a new solution.

Their solution is to be Beat. To be Beat is to let your life come tumbling down into a humpty-dumpty heap, and with it, into the same heap, the humpty-dumpty meanings which language attempts to sustain. There are fewer things beneath heaven and earth than our present-day multiple-meaning philosophers would have us believe. From the ruin of yourself pick up yourself (if you can) but let old meanings lie. Now cross on over to the outcast side of the street to where the hip folk and the jazz folk live, for the way your life is now is the way their lives have been for years. Step right in through the Open Door to where the tenor man is crouching with the bell mouth of his horn down in the basement near his feet, reaching for the waters of life that come rocking up through the debris of the day that dawned over Hiroshima everywhere long 1945 ago. The sound you hear is life, "the pit and prune juice of poor beat life itself in the god-awful streets of man." And life is Holy. And this is the meaning of words. Life is holy, and the journey is Now. Say it with a Bop beat.

## Kerouac's Sound

Kerouac's sound starts up in his first novel, *The Town and the City*, and anyone who grew up with or remembers the sentimental music of the 1930s will recognize what he is doing. The New England nights and days of his childhood and youth are [159] orchestrated with slow violins, to which sound the children whose lives he chronicles are stirred into awareness as the stars dip down and slow breezes sweep along diminishing strings towards soft music on a farther shore. It is the considerable achievement of the novel that Kerouac is able to sustain the note of profound sentimentality his style conveys even as he is tracing, with remorseless intelligence, the downfall of the New England family, the Martins, who try to sustain their lives on this tone. The sound bodies forth their myth—soft music on a farther shore—while the action brings both myth and sound down in ruins.

The protagonist is George Martin, one version and a good one of the mythical American—big, outgoing, direct—who sustains his life, his certainties, his soul on the music Kerouac builds in around him: at the rim of all things, violins. He rises at dawn, splashing, coughing, spluttering, and plunges into the day like a playful porpoise, rolling in the life element. But his cough is cancer, and the novel concerns the downfall of this man. His career carries from the town, where he was known to every man, to New York City where he has no acquaintances at all. He ends his life on a mean Brooklyn street in a mean apartment with only a direct if ravaged love for his dispersed and tormented children to see him through disease into silence.

A main sign of Kerouac's control over the melody he projects is to be seen in the variety of fates to which he sends the Martin children. One son goes via books to success at Harvard and then on into the books and the sterility of a quasi-homosexual existence. Another son heads for adventure on the big trucks that whirr across the North American night only to discover that the whirring of trucks is a nothing song for a nowhere journey. Another son ends at Okinawa. The principal son goes via a football scholarship to Pennsylvania and early stardom. But just as he is about to become Saturday's hero and thus confirm his father's belief in the rightness of his myth, the son rebels in order to destroy the myth; and so helps destroy his father's life; and so his own. One daughter elopes with a jazzman and ends divorced in bohemian New York, singing at a second-rate bar. Another daughter disperses to Los Angeles. Another to [160] Seattle. All of the children plunge like the playful porpoises their father had taught them to be into the swaying waters of the myth he created, soft music on a farther shore. All drown. The football-playing son who manages to break the myth, and with it his own life, swims for love of the father back to shore. He is seen at the last on a rainy roadway, hitch-hiking west and known to no man— but with no more violins.

I think it is evident that in creating this testimonial to a gone childhood, Kerouac is also breaking with the mood of that era. How decisively he does break becomes plain in his second published novel, On the Road, where the sounds become BIFF, BOFF, BLIP, BLEEP, BOP, BEEP, CLINCK, ZOWIE! Sounds break up. And are replaced by other sounds. The journey is NOW. The narrative is a humpty-dumpty heap. Such is the condition of NOW. The ruins extend from New York City, down to New Orleans, on down to Mexico City, back up to Denver, out to San Francisco, over to Chicago, back to New York—six cities at the end points of a cockeyed star. The hero who passed from star-point to star-point is Dean Moriarty, the mad Hamlet of the moment, shambled after by Sal Paradise, who tells the story. And all that Sal can say is, "Yes, he's mad," and "Yes, he's my brother." Moriarty is the hero-prince of all Beat people, a "madman angel and bum" out to con the North American nightmare of a chance for his soul to live. Nothing that his tormented hands reach for will come into his hands except the holiness which comes rocking up direct from the waters of life upon the jazz rhythms with which Kerouac pitches his cockeyed star of wonder about.

Moriarty is a Denver jailkid who does not have to wait for his life to come down in ruins. It begins that way. His mother "died when Dean was a child" and his wino father is so indistinguishable from all the other winos in all the skid-road districts where Dean thinks he may find him that "I never know whether to ask." Kerouac provides only enough details about "all the bitterness and madness" of Dean's Denver childhood to make it clear that the social forms to which all good children go for their bread of life (or so they think) were made forbidden areas for Dean by reason of rejection, guilt, shame, rage, hatred—the dreadful emotions likely to orchestrate the secret lives of [161] children who one day wake up Beat. Hence the car-stealing frenzies in which he turns himself into a car so that his thwarted energies can come "blasting out of his system like daggers." On the maddest night of the novel he climaxes one such (five-car) binge by stealing a police detective's auto (inviting punishment) which he abandons in front of the house where he then passes out in peace and calm of mind—drunk—all passion spent.

An even more definite sign of Moriarty's inability to live within existing social forms consists in the insane doubling-up of those relationships from which he does seek satisfaction, brotherhood, love. No sooner does he dig Sal Paradise the very most than he must rush into an even more intense relationship with Paradise's friend, Carlo Marx. No sooner does he set up housekeeping with his first wife, Marylou, than he must arrange an elaborate time-schedule in order to set up parallel housekeeping with his second, interchangeable wife, Camille. The Denver bohemia must be matched by bohemian San Francisco. His life on the west coast is a process of creating the complications which will be resolved by flight to the east coast. Tormented by almost complete inability to live within even the relaxed bohemian life-forms, Moriarty turns again and again to the one form in which his energies find something like release and fulfilment—the road.

In a car on the road, surrounded by darkness, the existing forms vanish and with them vanishes the distraught, guilt-tormented self. Speed, strangeness and space, dark forests, heavy-shouldered mountains and open prairies bring new transient forms, semi-forms, even formless forms, rushing into place. All of these are fleetingly familiar, for all of these are life. And because life is holy, the soul moves in behind the wheel and "every moment is precious" as the mad city Hamlet gives way to a road-going Quixote who cares only for the soul's journey, the one sweet dreadful childhood could not steal from him. Thus "It was remarkable," Sal Paradise tells us, "how Dean could go mad and then continue with his soul . . . calmly and sanely as though nothing had happened." The mad self blends into the speeding car as the sane soul continues down the one road of life on the only journey which "must eventually lead to [162] the whole world."

An apotheosis of sorts is achieved briefly in Mexico on the strangest yet most strangely familiar of all the roads Moriarty and Paradise take, on a womb-like jungle night, "hot as the inside of a baker's oven." Here the travellers are taken over by "billions of insects" until "the dead bugs mingled with my blood." Time, self, and history are temporarily annihilated and there is only the "rank, hot and rotten jungle" from which a prophetic white horse, "immense and phosphorescent," emerges to pace majestically, mysteriously past Moriarty's for-once sleeping head. When they waken from this dream of annihilation and rebirth it is to enter mountains where "shepherds appeared dressed as in the first time." And Moriarty "looked to heaven with red eyes," aware that he has made it out of orbit with the cockeyed star of NOW into orbit with "the golden world that Jesus came from." But if this Beat angel journeys through the jazz of the North American night finally to reach a semblance of creation day morning time in the Mexican mountains of the moment, he is much too mad to more than distractedly glimpse, and giggle, and give a wrist-watch to a Mexican creation-day child, inviting her to enter time. "Yes, he's mad," says Sal, and so Quixote gives way to Hamlet as Dean Moriarty ends with stockings down-gyv'd—"ragged in a moth-eaten overcoat"—a parking-lot attendant in New York—which is no way for a con man to live—silent— "Dean couldn't talk any more"—with only his sad Horatio, Sal, to tell his brother's story.

The jazz is in the continuity in which each episode tells a separate story—variations on the holiness theme. And it is in the remarkable flexible style as Kerouac improvises within each episode seeking to adjust his sound to the resonance of the given moment. Some moments come through tinged with the earlier *Town and City* sentimentality. Others rock and sock with Moriarty's frenzy, the sentences jerking about like muscles on an overwrought face. Still others are curiously quiescent, calm. And the melody which unifies the whole and lifts the cockeyed star up into the jazz sky is the holiness of life because this for Kerouac is the meaning of words, the inside of his sound. Dean Moriarty is sweet prince to this proposition. To read *On the* [163] *Road* with attention to the variations Kerouac achieves is to realize something of his remarkable talent for meshing his sound with the strongly-felt rhythms of many and various moments. It is not possible to compare him very closely with other stylists of note because his fiction is the first in which jazz is a dominant influence.

How dominant emerges into clear focus with the third of his published novels, *The Subterraneans*. Here is a typical sentence, the fourth in the book:

I was coming down the street with Larry O'Hara old drinking buddy of mine from all the times in San Francisco in my long and nervous and mad careers I've gotten drunk and in fact cadged drinks off friends with such "genial" regularity nobody really cared to notice or announce that I am developing or was developing, in my youth, such bad freeloading habits though of course they did notice but liked me and as Sam said "Everybody comes to you for your gasoline boy, that's some filling station you got there" or words to that effect—old Larry O'Hara always nice to me, a crazy young businessman of San Francisco with Balzacian backroom in his bookstore where they'd smoke tea and talk of the old days of the great Basie band or the days of the great Chu Berry—of whom more anon since she got involved with him too as she had to get involved with everyone because of knowing me who am nervous and many leveled and not in the least one-souled—not a piece of my pain has showed yet—or suffering—Angels, bear with me—I'm not even looking at the page but straight ahead into the sadglint of my wallroom and at a Sarah Vaughan Gerry Mulligan Radio KROW show on the desk in the form of a radio, in other words, they were sitting on the fender of a car in front of the Black Mask bar on Montgomery Street, Julien Alexander the Christ-like unshaved thin youthful quiet strange almost as you or as Adam might say apocalyptic angel or saint of the subterraneans, certainly star (now), and she, Mardou Fox, whose face when first I saw it in Dante's bar around the corner made me think, "By God, I've got to get involved with that little woman" and maybe too because she was a Negro.

I count seven shifts away from the narrative line. If these shifts are dropped, one has Leo Percepied, the narrator, walk down the street with Larry O'Hara and meet Julien Alexander [164] and Mardou Fox as they stand beside an automobile in front of the Black Mask bar. The side-trips from this simple narrative line lead to: Percepied's drinking habits—a main variation; (2) his energies—another main variation; (3) jazz and marihuana parties in Larry O'Hara's bookshop; (4) a passage of self-analysis—a major variation; (5) circumstances under which the sentence is being written; (6) descriptions of the people Percepied is about to meet; and, repeated from a previous sentence, (7) Percepied's determination to meet Mardou, who later turns

WARREN TALLMAN

out to be part Indian as well as Negro—another major variation. Kerouac's immediate motive is the Bop motive, maximum spontaneity. The narrative melody merges with and is dominated by the improvised details. And, as Percepied emphasizes twice later, "the truth is in the details." The narrative line follows the brief love-affair between Percepied and Mardou while the improvised details move, as the title would suggest, down into the clutter of their lives among the guilts and shames which come up from subterranean depths to steal their love from them. The truth is in the improvisations.

The novel is written with the driving but hungup rhythms of a hurrying man who is also, always, alas, looking back over his shoulder. The finest scenes, I think, are those in which Mardou figures, particularly that in which she is rejected by some friends, loses control of her consciousness, and wanders out naked into nighttime San Francisco, almost insane, to be saved by the realization that she is meant for love rather than hatred and so walks about the city newly discovering and at the same time transforming the world she passes through. This self-conquest makes her able to trust others, to believe that Percepied loves her, and to love him in return. But he is unable to conquer his own guilts and shames, cannot reciprocate, and so is gradually, frantically pulled back into the clutter of his life. A failure of love by reason of deep fissuring guilts emerges from the depths on the rush but not exactly on the wings of Kerouac's spontaneous Bop style. As Percepied says, "I'm the Bop writer." As one might expect, the spontaneity falters in a good many pages. Yet I do not doubt that the method does permit Kerouac to tap his imagination in spontaneous ways. [165] Nor do I doubt but that *The Subterraneans* is his most important novel and a very important one indeed. Of this, more in place.

The easiest way to approach *The Dharma Bums*—the truth bums—is to imagine an exceptionally talented musician trying out a new instrument in an interested but nonetheless very tentative way. The instrument is Zen Buddhism, American fashion. The novel is full of hummed songs, muttered chants, self-conversations carried on in railroad yards, on beaches, in groves of trees, in the mountains. The half-embarrassed, half-serious mutterer is Ray Smith, Zen amateur, and the style which Kerouac floats through the novel is part of an obvious attempt to adjust the practices, the flavor, the attitudes of Zen to an American sensibility.

Jazz is gone, even from the Bohemian party scenes which alternate with the Zen scenes. Moriarty's frenzy and Percepied's rush give way to a slow—and at times a too-slow—pace. It is surely significant that in the opening paragraph Smith travels past the place where the "king and founder of the Bop generation," the jazzman Charlie Parker, "went crazy and got well again." Kerouac might be hinting at the strain of writing eleven books in six years and about the need for a temporary so-long to jazz, hello to Zen. But the hello is most tentative. To put the very best construction on the novel, always advisable when considering a gifted writer, is to read it as a kind of primer of Zen experience. I spare the reader any attempts to explicate the Zen way as Kerouac relays it into the novel via Smith's friend, Japhy, the American Zen adept.[1] Suffice it to mention that the Zen emphasis upon paradoxes which will annihilate meanings is a peculiarly appropriate counterpart to the Beat writer's suspicion of meanings. Put any meaningful thought through the Zen dialectic and come out with one thought less. But if the Zen attitude is consistent with Kerouac's own, it is nonetheless apparent that the meditative world in which this attitude is [166] best cultivated hasn't much affinity with his essentially nervous and agile sensibility. Unsustained by the driving intensities which make *On the Road* and *The Subterraneans* swing, *The Dharma Bums* frequently goes flat. There are dull scenes, mechanical passages. If there is one superb mountain-climbing episode, that is less because Zen catches hold for Kerouac, more because the mountain does. Certainly, representation of the final trip to the Northwest, where the protagonist attempts to live in the Zen way on Desolation Peak, is so sketchy as to amount to a default. And it is here that one touches upon Kerouac's limitations.

In *The Dharma Bums* distinctly and in his other novels in less evident ways, one becomes aware of Kerouac's receptive, his essentially feminine sensibility. Sensibility, I repeat. This receptivity is certainly his main strength as artist, accounting as it does for his capacity to assimilate the rhythms, the sounds, the life-feel of experience into his representation. When Kerouac is at his best he is able to register and project the American resonance with remarkable ease and accuracy. But on the related, weaker side of the coin, he has only a limited ability to project

[1] And just as well, for I have been informed since writing this essay that the Buddhism in *The Dharma Bums* ranges considerably beyond the Zen variety.

this sound up to heights, down to depths. Moments of climax, of revelation, of crisis, the very moments which deserve the fullest representation, frequently receive only sparse representation. The climactic Mexican journey in *On the Road* suffers from this limitation. Beginning with the madcap afternoon in the Mexican whore house, followed by the night-time sojourn in the jungle, the creation-day morning in the mountains, and subsequent arrival in Mexico City, the hipster Zion, where marihuana cascades like manna into the streets, the entire sequence is as brilliantly conceived as any in recent fiction. But representation in these scenes which show Moriarty's life sweeping up to climax, is sparse, fleeting, even sketchy. No reader will be convinced that Moriarty, the true traveller, has made it to a mountain-peak of our present moment from which creation-day is glimpsed. Nor will any reader be convinced that Ray Smith has gained access to the Zen Way in his mountain fastness.

Yet I do not think that this defect traces so much to want of creative force, though that is what it appears to be, as to [167] Kerouac's almost animal suspicion of the meaning values toward which words tend. When his fictions converge toward meanings something vital in him flinches back. His sound is primarily a life sound, sensitive to the indwelling qualities of things, the life they bear. To be Beat is to be wary of moving such a sound into the meaning clutter. It might become lost, the life. So Kerouac draws back. Which is his limitation.

But also his strength. For in the jazz world of the Bop generation where Charlie Parker is king and founder, Jack Kerouac in a different medium is heir apparent. I do not know but would guess that a number of the six or seven books for which Kerouac can't find a publisher are Bop novels. I would also guess that it will not be until they are published and his method more generally understood than now that his likely influence will emerge. For his emphasis upon a from-under sound made spontaneous by adherence to the jazz principle of improvisation is right for our time, I think. The jazz vernacular is just that, a vernacular, and Kerouac has demonstrated that it can be transposed into fiction without serious loss of the spontaneous imaginative freedom which has made it among the most vital of the modern arts.[2] [168]

[2] Since this essay was written, *Doctor Sax* and portions of *Old Angel Midnight* have appeared. Both indicate a far more ambitious attempt than I have suggested to develop a writing style which will spontaneously repre-

Although Kerouac's art is limited, I am convinced that his sound is more nearly in the American grain than that of any writer since Fitzgerald. The efforts of his outcast protagonists to get life into their lives seem more closely related to our actual moment than any since Jay Gatsby, similar across worlds of difference, tried to shoot the North American moon. Gatsby failed and finished like a sad swan, floating dead on the surface of a pool. And Kerouac's protagonists fail too. Dean Moriarty does not make it to creation-day as was his mad desire. Ray Smith fumbles the Zen football. Leo Percepied cannot enter guilt-forbidden realms of Mardou's Negro love. Fitzgerald's efforts got lost in the personal, national, and international chaos from which he summoned Gatsby into presence. But it was only after his energies lost coherence that Fitzgerald woke up in the ruins of that dark midnight of the soul where it is always three o'clock in the morning. Kerouac starts in with the dark midnight and it is his effort to bring his protagonists through the jazz of that night, naked, into something like a new day. He fails too. The moment, NOW, which is the only promised land, shrugs off Moriarty, Percepied, and Smith, shrugs off Kerouac too. Outcasts they began and end as outcasts. But very distinctly Kerouac's protagonists press more sharply close to the truth about our present moment than have fictional protagonists for many years. And that's a help. And very distinctly he has created new ground of possibility for fiction to stand upon with renewed life. And that's a help. [169]

*November, 1958*
*Vancouver, B.C.*

---

sent the nuance of Kerouac's deep-reaching awareness. I say deep-reaching because both works suggest possession of an almost photographic sensibility; he evidently projects his sound from a matrix of directly registered impressions reaching back to early childhood even as they reach down to deep levels of consciousness. These works provide more than a few signs that with the appearance of his yet unpublished works Kerouac will emerge not simply as an important innovator, as I have tried to suggest, but as a major writer. A word more about Bop. University of British Columbia English professor, Elliott Gose, has pointed out how closely Percepied, the "Bop writer" of *The Subterraneans,* is identified with Baudelaire—both writers, both with Negro mistresses, both with compelling mother attachments. And Kerouac elsewhere styles himself "an artful story teller, A WRITER in the great French narrative tradition." To stress these is to stress the obvious implication that although Kerouac's Bop writing style stems from jazz it is doubtlessly heavily influenced by his literary affinities. I do so only in order to counterstress that it is the Bop influence rather than the literary which has been the shaping spirit of his imagination.

# Henry Miller

## PREFACE TO *THE SUBTERRANEANS*

Jack Kerouac has done something to our immaculate prose from which it may never recover. A passionate lover of language, he knows how to use it. Born virtuoso that he is, he takes pleasure in defying the laws and conventions of literary expression which cripple genuine, untrammeled communication between reader and writer. As he has so well said in "The Essentials of Spontaneous Prose" [see pp. 65–67]—"Satisfy yourself first, then reader cannot fail to receive telepathic shock and meaning-excitement by same laws operating in his own human mind." His integrity is such that he can give the semblance, at times, of running counter to his own principles. (*Cancer! Schmanser!* What's the difference, so long as you're healthy!) His learning, by no means superficial, he can bandy about as something of no consequence. Does it matter? Nothing matters. Everything is of equal importance or non-importance, from a truly creative standpoint.

Yet you can't say he's cool. He's hot, red hot. And if he's far out, he's also near and dear, a blood brother, an alter ego. He's there, everywhere, in the guise of Everyman. The observer and the observed. "A gentle, intelligent, suffering prose saint," Allen Ginsberg says of him.

We say that the poet, or genius, is always ahead of his time. True, but only because he's so thoroughly *of* his time. "Keep moving!" he urges. "We've had all this a thousand million times before." ("Advance always!" said Rimbaud.) But the stick-in-the-muds don't follow this kind of talk. (They haven't even caught up with Isidore Ducasse.) [5] So what do they do? They pull him down off his perch, they starve him, they kick his teeth down his throat. Sometimes they are less merciful—they pretend he doesn't exist.

Reprinted from Jack Kerouac, *The Subterraneans* (New York: Avon Book Division—The Hearst Corporation, 1959), pp. 5–7. Reprinted by permission of the author and the publisher.

Everything Kerouac writes about—those weird, hauntingly ubiquitous characters whose names may be read backwards or upside down, those lovely, nostalgic, intimate-grandiose stereopticon views of America, those nightmarish, ventilated joy-rides in gondolas and hot rods—plus the language he uses (à la Gautier in reverse) to describe his "earthly-heavenly visions," surely even the readers of Time and Life, of the Digests and the Comics, cannot fail to discern the rapport between these hypergonic extravaganzas and such perennial blooms as the *Golden Ass,* the *Satyricon,* and *Pantagruel.*

The good poet, or in this case the "spontaneous Bop prosodist," is always alive to the idiomatic lingo of his time—the swing, the beat, the disjunctive metaphoric rhythm which comes so fast, so wild, so scrimmaged, so unbelievably albeit delectably mad, that when transmitted to paper no one recognizes it. None but the poets, that is. He "invented it," people will say. Insinuating that it was souped up. What they should say is: "He *got* it." He got it, he dug it, he put it down. ("You pick it up, Nazz!")

When someone asks, "Where does he get that stuff?" say: "From you!" Man, he lay awake all night listening with eyes and ears. A night of a thousand years. Heard it in the womb, heard it in the cradle, heard it in school, heard it on the floor of life's stock exchange where dreams are traded for gold. And *man,* he's sick of hearing it. He wants to move on. He wants to *blow.* But will you let him?

This is the age of miracles. The day of the killer-diller is over; the sex maniacs are out on a limb; the daring trapeze artists have broken their necks. Day of wonders, [6] when our men of science, aided and abetted by the high priests of the Pentagon, give free instruction in the technique of mutual, but total, destruction. Progress, what! Make it into a readable novel, if you can. But don't beef about life-and-letters if you're a death-eater. Don't tell us about good "clean"—no fall outs!—literature. Let the poets speak. They may be "beat," but they're not riding the atom-powered Juggernaut. Believe me, there's nothing clean, nothing healthy, nothing promising about this age of wonders —except the telling. And the Kerouacs will probably have the, last word. [7]

*Big Sur, California*

# Paul O'Neil

## THE ONLY REBELLION AROUND

If the U.S. today is really the biggest, sweetest and most suc-
culent casaba ever produced by the melon patch of civilization,
it would seem only reasonable to find its surface profaned—as
indeed it is—by a few fruit flies. But reason would also antici-
pate contented fruit flies, blissful fruit flies—fruit flies raised by
happy environment to the highest stages of fruit fly development.
Such is not the case. The grandest casaba of all, in disconcerting
fact, has incubated some of the hairiest, scrawniest and most discontented specimens of all time: the improbable rebels of the
Beat Generation, who not only refuse to sample the seeping juices
of American plenty and American social advance but scrape their
feelers in discordant scorn of any and all who do.

This penetrating threnody has been going on ever since the
Korean War, but it is astonishing how seldom the noise has been
understood. The wide public belief that the Beats are simply
dirty people in sandals is only a small if repellent part of the
truth. Any attempt to list the collective attitudes of Beatdom,
it must be admitted, would be foolhardy in the extreme. Most
of its members are against collectiveness of any description, a
great many of them even refuse to admit there is any such thing
as a Beat Generation, and most of them spend hours differing
vehemently with their own kind. Individual Beats, however, in
the course of what might be described as the Six Year War
Against the Squares, have raised their voices against virtually
every aspect of current American society: Mom, Dad, Politics,
Marriage, the Savings Bank, Organized Religion, Literary Ele-
gance, Law, the Ivy League Suit and Higher Education, to say
nothing of the Automatic Dishwasher, the Cellophane-wrapped
Soda Cracker, the Split-Level House and the clean, or peace-
provoking, H-bomb.

Reprinted from *Life*, 47 (November 30, 1959), pp. 115–116, 119–120,
123–126, 129–130. Reprinted by courtesy of *Life* Magazine. Copyright
1959 by Time Inc.

Beat philosophy seems calculated to offend the whole population, civil, military and ecclesiastic—particularly and ironically those radicals of only yesterday who demanded a better world for the ill-fed, ill-clothed and ill-housed of the Great Depression and who still breathe heavily from proclaiming man's right to work and organize. Hard-core Beats want freedom to disorganize and thus to ensure full flowering of their remarkable individualities. They are against work and they are often ill-fed, ill-clothed and ill-housed by preference. The Negro, it is true, is a hero to the Beat (as are the junkie and the jazz musician), and he is embraced with a fervor which San Francisco's anarchist poet Kenneth Rexroth sardonically defines as "crow-jimism." But it seems doubtful that antisegregationists or many Negroes could take comfort in this fact. The things the Beat treasures and envies in the Negro are the irresponsibility, cheerful promiscuity and subterranean defiance which were once enforced in him during his years of bondage. A middle-class Negro would be hopelessly square. Novelist Norman Mailer, a devoted follower of hipsterism, calls the Beat movement the cult of the White Negro and glibly suggests that its members seek the "constant humility" of Negro life in order to emulate its "primitive . . . joy, lust, and languor. . . ." But the Beat Generation can be much more accurately described as a cult of the Pariah. It yearns for the roach-guarded mores of the skid road, the flophouse, the hobo jungle and the slum, primarily to escape regimentation. It shares these with Negroes, when it does, only by coincidence.

### Squares Are Tragic Saps

Unlike England's Angry Young Men who know what they want of society and bay for it with vehemence, the Beat finds society too hideous to contemplate and so withdraws from it. He does not go quietly, however, nor so far that his voice is inaudible, and his route of retreat is littered with old beer cans and marijuana butts. The industrious square, he cries, is a tragic sap who spends all the juices and energies of life in stultifying submission to the "rat race" and does so, furthermore, with no more reward than sexual enslavement by a matriarchy of stern and grasping wives and the certainty of atomic death for his children. Thus, say the Beats, the only way man can call his soul his own is by becoming an outcast.

Little of this is as remarkable as the Beats like to think. Bo-

PAUL O'NEIL

hemianism is not new to big American cities, and the whiskery bum was a familiar U.S. figure long before the advent of [115] the western railroad. The recluse and the neurotic artist are as old as time, and most of the Beats' more outrageous attitudes were trumpeted long ago by nihilists, Dadaists and a thousand and one convocations of those crackpots and screwballs who have bloomed so luxuriantly down through the American years. There is, however, one enormous difference. While most of the forerunners of Beatdom were ignored by the general populace, the Beat Generation itself has attracted wide public attention and is exerting astonishing influence.

It is seldom out of the news for long, and there are few Americans today to whom the word Beat or the derisive term, Beatnik, does not conjure up some sort of image—usually a hot-eyed fellow in beard and sandals, or a "chick" with scraggly hair, long black stockings, heavy eye make-up and an expression which could indicate either hauteur or uneasy digestion. "Beat talk," a narrow and repetitive argot mostly stolen from jazz musicians, narcotic addicts and prostitutes, is rapidly becoming a part of American idiom. It relies heavily on such words as "cat," "dig," "bug" and "cool," substitutes "Spade" for Negro, "head" for narcotic user, and utilizes the word "like" as a means of beginning almost any sentence.

A Beat-inspired fad for public recitation of verse has not only caught on in big cities and college towns but has given the very word, poetry, a new and abrasive connotation. A calculated vulgarity is part of the Beat act, and a good many of these performances are conducted in an atmosphere not unlike that which attended the bare-knuckle prizefights of the last century. Awareness of the Beat message is almost a social necessity today, and the name-dropper who cannot mention Beat Novelist Jack Kerouac (*On the Road, The Dharma Bums*), Allen Ginsberg (the Shelley of the Beat poets whose *Howl and Other Poems* has sold 33,000 copies) or Lawrence Lipton (author of last summer's best-seller, *The Holy Barbarians*) is no name-dropper at all.

Armies of Americans experience a sense of tongue-clucking outrage at the antics of Beatdom's more strident practitioners, but most of them also experience a morbid curiosity about them. All sorts of entrepreneurs have rushed in to capitalize on this fact. The cellar nightclubs, espresso shops and coffeehouses which have lately sprung up are a direct result of public interest in the Beat Generation. Although they are patronized mostly by young hounds of the Volkswagen and Tweeter-Woofer cliques, they are popularly believed to be the sort of dens in which Beat-niks hang out. In some cases their proprietors keep a tame or house Beat on the premises to shout crude verse at the customers. A radio soap opera, *Helen Trent,* now includes a Beat character, and a Beatnik has been drawn into the comic strip, *Popeye.* M-G-M's motion picture *The Beat Generation* is dedicated to the proposition that Beats are terrible fellows with women, and the cover blurb of the paperback *Beatnik Party* states invitingly that they are "crazed with strange desires" and victims of "sinful passions."

The pervasive rag, tag, and bobtail of humanity which has set off all this uproar is a confusingly diffuse phenomenon, but it can be roughly divided into three main groups. The bulk of it is comprised of those mobs of "sick little bums" who emerge in any generation—the shabby and bearded men, the occasional pallid and sullen girls—who startle the tourists in San Francisco's North Beach section, inhabit the dreary "pads" of Venice West in Log Angeles, and lounge in the doorways and cheap cafeterias of New York's Greenwich Village. [116] People very like them distributed pamphlets for the Communists in the 1930s, or muttered of anarchism and cadged drinks in the speakeasies of the 1920s, and then as now thirsted cunningly for the off-beat cause which could provide them with some sense of martyrdom and superiority. They are talkers, loafers, passive little con men, lonely eccentrics, mom-haters, cop-haters, exhibitionists with abused smiles and second mortgages on a bongo drum—writers who cannot write, painters who cannot paint, dancers with unfortunate malfunction of the fetlocks. Around this bohemian cadre wanders a second group—an increasing corps of amateur or weekend Beats who have jobs and live the comfortable square life but who seek the "cool" state of mind, spread the Beat message and costume themselves in old clothes to ape the genuinely unwashed on Saturday nights.

Both these groups, however, are only reflections of the most curious men of influence the 20th Century has yet produced: the Beat poets. The poets, almost to a man, are individualistic and antisocial to the point of neuroticism. They are dissidents so enthralled with their own egos and so intent on bitter personal complaint that they would be incapable of organizing juvenile delinquents in a reform school. But the Beat Generation is their baby for all that, and the country's current Beat-consciousness is their doing. This is not to say that the bums, hostile little females and part-time bohemians of the Beat Generation would not have been bums, hostile little females and part-time bohemians anyhow. But without the slightest missionary intent the poets have provided them with a name, the fuel of self-justification and attitudes guaranteed to "bug the squares."

The chief architects of the Beat Generation are Poet-Novelist Jack Kerouac and Poet Allen Ginsberg, the only valid guideposts to be used in determining just when it all began. In a large sense Beatdom is a product of postwar disillusionment and restlessness. One Beat poet maintains that the real beginnings occurred as early as 1949 when a good many of today's Beat activators and heroes were living in gritty desolation on the fringes of Greenwich Village and sneering at New York's leftover bohemianism. But since this poet is a narcotic addict who also recalls with vast nostalgia that 1949 was a year when the price of heroin fell from $10 to 30¢ a capsule in New York "and like you could buy it at the corner grocery store," this view must be discounted as sentimentality. Beatdom's year of emergence must be set at 1953. This was the twelvemonth when Ginsberg and a good many other bohemians followed Kerouac (who had begun his western visitations in 1949) to San Francisco, decided this was the place, and began scratching away at works which set much of the tone of the Beat world and steered American bohemianism toward the West.

Kerouac is a husky, dark-haired fellow of French-Canadian ancestry who might be described as the only *avant-garde* writer ever hatched by the athletic department at Columbia University. Impressed by his prowess as a high school star in Lowell, Mass., Columbia football scouts brought him to New York to play at Baker Field—but also brought him within range of big-city bohemianism. Kerouac began reading Thomas Wolfe, grew "black, broody and poetic," tired of his labors as a subsidized halfback and in 1941, his sophomore year, abruptly walked out on the team and higher education. In the years afterward he worked variously as a sportswriter, a gas station attendant, a merchant mariner and a railroad brakeman and bummed around the country with other garrulous wanderers. One of these companions, Neal Cassidy, became Dean Moriarty, the hero of Kerouac's second published work, *On the Road,* and is consequently regarded as a Beat saint. (Cassidy, known to his more jocular intimates as the "Johnny Appleseed of the Marijuana Racket," is currently doing five years in San Quentin for selling same.)

Kerouac's contributions to Beatdom are priceless. In *On the*

*Road* [119] he celebrated the Beat tradition of bumming across the country and the delights of drinking with cheap Mexican tarts, and he is widely heralded for coining the phrase "the Beat Generation." He denies publicly that he has ever rewritten a line (anyone who has sampled the goulash-like texture of his prose would be inclined to believe him implicitly) and has thus contributed heavily to one of the Beat Generation's guiding misapprehensions: that anything which pops into the Beat mind is worth putting down on paper. Kerouac has also been a leader in the use of uninhibited or "natural" public behavior. One of his finest hours occurred one night last fall when he took part, with other Beat poets, in a "reading" at Manhattan's Hunter College. The audience, bored and restive after a half hour of Kerouac reciting Kerouac, called on him to spare them further suffering, and he gave vent to his feelings by lurching noisily back and forth across the stage during the rest of the program, at one point trying on another speaker's hat and later attempting to wrest back the microphone.

Although Allen Ginsberg has been less publicized, his contributions to Beatdom are probably more important than Kerouac's. Ginsberg, a slight, dark, bespectacled and harmless-looking fellow of 33, grew up in Paterson, N.J. Ginsberg's mother was sent to a public insane asylum when he was very young and spent her declining years there (Ginsberg himself spent eight months in a mental hospital in 1949), and this experience seems to have induced in him a wildly articulate and unreasoning sense of terror and protest, which, combined with a shameless exhibitionism, has dominated his life. Ginsberg, like Kerouac, attended Columbia University. He was suspended for writing an obscene and derogatory three-word phrase about Jews on a clouded classroom window with his forefinger. This act confounded as well as mortified university officials ("But he's a Jew himself!" cried one professor) and has caused thousands of man hours of excited Beat conversation ever since.

No Beat work has so startled the public or so influenced the Beat mind as Ginsberg's long poem, *Howl,* an expression of wild personal dissatisfaction with the world which was written in 1955 while he was encamped in a furnished room in San Francisco. *Howl* begins:

"I saw the best minds of my generation destroyed by madness, starving hysterical naked,/dragging themselves through the negro streets at dawn looking for an angry fix . . ." and goes on to discuss "angelheaded hipsters . . . who were expelled from the academies for crazy & publishing obscene odes on the windows of the skull. . . ." *Howl*, as it gathers steam and momentum, reflects Ginsberg's public and repeated boasts that he is a homosexual, and his habit of implying that he is a heroin addict (he is not). It also makes free with perverse allusion in a fashion calculated to make the squares run for the cops. Both its literary style and the fact that it was pronounced fit for human consumption in 1957 after an obscenity trial in San Francisco seem to have made a profound impression on lesser Beats.

Ginsberg's influence, however, extends beyond poetry. He has been one of the first to insist that the Beat Generation is a religious phenomenon and that Beat (*i.e.*, resigned, abject, pooped, put-upon, disgusted) really stands for Beatitude. "I have seen God," says Ginsberg. "I saw him in a room in Harlem." Ginsberg is also among the most vehement of the Beats who insist that U.S. citizens have a constitutional right to all the narcotics they want, a right that is being abridged by the government in Washington. Like most Beats he is a marijuana [120] smoker and is particularly enraged because this weed "which is better for you than whisky" is illegal. He also cries that there is a plot between the Mafia and the Administration to keep up the price of heroin, morphine and cocaine. Listening to him deliver his opinions on this subject is an experience very much like sharing a room with a wind machine. Only political venality, he implies, prevents legalized addiction and cheap narcotics for American addicts. "We're treating junkies," he says, "like the Nazis treated the Jews."

Ginsberg has a built-in sense of the theatrical and can out-embarrass most humans—although he met his match in an odd interview with Britain's equally theatrical Dame Edith Sitwell last year. "My, you *do* smell bad, don't you," said Dame Edith on being introduced. "What was your name again? Are you one of the action poets?" Ginsberg, genuinely taken aback at this beastliness from one he had fondly conceived to be a fellow genius, reached nervously for a cigaret. "Is that a narcotic one?" cried his inquisitor. "Does it contain heroin?" "No," said Ginsberg, struggling like a western badman trying to get a six-gun out of his bedroll, "but I've got some here. Do you want a shot?" "Oh, dear no," said Dame Edith. "Dope makes me come out all over spots." This, however, was only a minor setback.*

---

* [Dame Sitwell's rejoinder, which follows, appeared in *Life*, February 8, 1960: "Sirs: My attention has been called to a most disgusting report in

Ginsberg is the lion of the poetry-reading circuit. He declaims his own startling verse with wild fervor, and hecklers attack him at their peril. At a recitation in Los Angeles last year a man stood up and demanded to know what Ginsberg was "trying to prove." "Nakedness," said Ginsberg. "What d'ya mean, nakedness?" bawled the unwary customer. Ginsberg gracefully took off all his clothes.

Although hundreds of Beats write poetry, or say they do, only about a dozen are of any note. Ginsberg's leading disciple is Gregory Corso, who shares a dingy slum apartment off Manhattan's Bowery with him and a touseled, sheeplike young man named Peter Orlovsky. (Orlovsky, who occasionally writes a poem of his own, is noted mostly for being Ginsberg's constant companion.) Corso, who served a stretch in Dannemora before producing such poems as *Don't Shoot the Warthog* and *Bomb,* is described by admirers as a "charming child of the streets." He boasts that he has never combed his hair "although I guess I'd get the bugs out of it if I did." [123]

### A Fix at the Altar

Philip Lamantia and Mike McClure of San Francisco are leading exponents of a Beat cult which believes true poetic effects are best achieved through an "ecstatic illumination" induced by what Lamantia calls "the heroic medicines": heroin, opium, mescaline, marijuana, peyote. Lamantia is a tiny, erratic and gentle being with dark hair cropped short along his forehead and a pale, delicate, saintlike face. He has been a heroin addict,

---

your paper—one mass of lies from beginning to end—which pretends to describe my meeting with Mr. Allen Ginsberg. . . . There is not one word of truth in a single sentence of it.

Mr. Ginsberg *never* offered me heroin, and as I have never, in my life, taken heroin, it can scarcely 'bring me out in spots' (an affliction from which, incidentally, I do not suffer).

The English upper classes do not use the expression 'My!' (we leave that to persons of your correspondent's breeding). Nor do we tell people who are introduced to us that they 'smell bad.'

This is the most vulgar attack, actuated evidently by an almost insane malice, probably by some person whom I have refused to receive socially, that I have ever seen.

You had better apologise, publically, both to Mr. Ginsberg and me immediately."

*Life* replied, "The anecdote . . . had been widely circulated at Oxford. Mr. Ginsberg joins Dame Edith in denying it and *Life* apologizes to both.]

although he professes to have kicked the habit by smoking opium for nine months. He is a Catholic and an impassioned student of theology who has convinced himself that the use of drugs to obtain visions does not conflict with the canons of the Church ("Philip," say his raffish friends, "is trying to get a fix at the altar"). Lamantia was a contributor to the surrealist magazine, *View*, at 15 and was much praised by its readers. Now 31 and convinced that life has been "a ball," he lives in fleabag hotels on money doled out by his widowed mother. Unlike many of his colleagues, he can be a delightful conversationalist, but his poetry is often close to gibberish. *Christ*, which leads off a volume of his verse entitled *Ekstasis*, begins thus:

Death,            sunrises
Beatific   the   winter's
rise.    Blanch   light
on rivers seen unseen
Born CRYSTAL FLESH
FISH IN A CLOUD
LIGHT            LIFE

McClure, another small, handsome man, is married (to a working schoolteacher) and has a baby daughter. He was employed until recently as an attendant and towel dispenser at Riley's gym, a San Francisco muscle-building emporium, but has abandoned gainful toil and hopes he has "quit working forever." McClure has achieved hallucination by eating peyote buds, but he gave up the practice last autumn on the theory that his new visionary look at the world would last his lifetime without further medication. He has since endured an emotional letdown he calls "my nine-month dark night of the soul." He is convinced, however, that scientists are preparing to alter the chemical make-up of the human race so that everyone will eventually be born with the privilege of "peyote vision." After that? "All will be chaos, carnage and beauty."

For sheer horror no member of the Beat Generation has achieved effects to compare with William S. Burroughs, who is regarded by [124] many seekers after coolness as the "greatest writer in the world." A Harvard man and an offshoot of the wealthy St. Louis family, Burroughs is now 45, a pale, cadaverous and bespectacled being who has devoted most of his adult life to a lonely pursuit of drugs and debauchery. He has, first in Mexico and then in Tangier, dosed himself with alcohol, heroin, marijuana, kif, majoun and a hashish candy—a regimen he once punctuated with a trip to South America to sample a native drug called yage. Between agonizing periods of ineffectual withdrawal he has rubbed shoulders with the dregs of a half dozen races. His works are three, *Junkie*, *Queer* and a last masterpiece, *The Naked Lunch*, recently published in Paris.

*The Naked Lunch* could be described as an effort to communicate the degradations of addiction in epic tones: ". . . you pinch up some leg flesh and make a quick stab hole with a pin. Then fit the dropper *over not in* the hole and feed the solution slow and careful. . . ." Interspersed are hallucinatory scenes indicative of the "peeled nerves of junk sickness. . . ." "Did any of you ever see Dr. Tetrazzini perform? I say 'perform' advisedly because his operations were performances. He would start by throwing a scalpel across the room into the patient and then make his entrance like a ballet dancer. . . ."

To this list of major Beat poets one peripheral figure, Lawrence Ferlinghetti, must be added. Ferlinghetti, a wartime naval lieutenant commander who studied in Paris under the G.I. bill, is the founder of San Francisco's City Lights Pocket Bookshop, which has become headquarters for Beatdom. A tall, quiet, pleasant man, Ferlinghetti encourages, publishes and defends Beat writers—and, ironically enough, writes better Beat poetry than most of them. Dozens of Beats have lately dashed off poems about the Crucifixion, but none of them has produced anything so startling as one of Ferlinghetti's efforts which was delivered before San Francisco television cameras with a dance interpretation by a girl named Avril Weber:

He was a kind of carpenter
　　from a square type place like Galilee
Who said the cat who really laid it on us all was his Dad
They stretch him on this tree to cool. . . .
He just hang there in his tree, looking real petered out and real
　　cool. . . .
And real dead. . . .

The bulk of Beat writers are undisciplined and slovenly amateurs who have deluded themselves into believing their lugubrious absurdities are art simply because they have rejected the form, style and attitudes of previous generations and have seized upon obscenity as an expression of "total personality." They insist that poetry, until they leapt upon the scene, was written

PAUL O'NEIL

simply for other poets "and not for the people," but most of them
not only write for but about [125] each other and regard the
"people" as residents of Squaresville. While bawling of individuality, scores of them mimic each other as solemnly as preschool
tots in play period.

If the general level of Beat writing is appalling, however, it
is impossible to honestly discount all Beat literature. The astonishing views, self-defeating abhorrence of form, and pitiful personal lives of its authors have led a great many critics to do so,
but it is too easy to forget that Poe was a drunk, Coleridge an
opium eater and Vincent van Gogh a madman, and that a great
deal of the world's art has a disconcerting way of getting produced by very odd types. A few Beat writers demonstrate that
gift of phrase and those flashes of insight which bespeak genuine
talent.

Allen Ginsberg, even at his most unreasonable, communicates
excitement like a voice yelling from inside a police car. A young
Negro, Robert Kaufman, who has produced a long, jumbled poem
entitled Abomunist Manifesto, is capable of humor. "Abomunists,"
he announces, "never carry more than fifty dollars in debts on
them," and he adds gravely that "licking postage stamps depletes
the body fluids." Jack Kerouac has been unable (although he
comes close) to disguise a real feeling for life as it is lived along
the truck roads and tenderloins of America. For all his hideous
preoccupation with man's lowest appetites, William Burroughs
has a terrible and sardonic eye and a vengeful sense of drama,
both made more startling by the fact that he has found the will
to write at all. The Beat movement embraces undiscovered talent
too: the young, troubled and dedicated artist often feels, today,
that it is the only haven to which he can turn in his search for
encouragement and understanding.

The Beat Generation, however, is primarily important in the
U.S. as the voice of nonconformity, the fount of what might be
described as a sort of nonpolitical radicalism. The Ginsbergs,
Kerouacs and Corsos, like the dissidents who emulate them, are
social rebels first and poets only second. Even as writers they
seem more intent on revenging themselves on the squares and
yowling at the world than on triumphs of literary composition.
A great deal of their verse is written to be read aloud before
audiences, and the most noted of them are performers, even
demagogues, whose big moments have been public exhibitions of
personal as well as literary eccentricity. If the poets did nothing

242

but influence other lesser Beats, moreover, they would have to be considered the leaders of a social rebellion. It is a curious rebellion—unplanned, unorganized and based on a thousand personal neuroses and a thousand conflicting egos, but it is oddly effective withall. No matter what else it may be, it is not boring, and in the U.S. of the 1950s it is the only rebellion in town.

The Beat message is being spoken in innumerable unlikely places. Knots of self-professed Beats have come to the surface in Paris, Athens, Manchester and Prague—although the members of these overseas lodges, like Belgian baseball players, seem a little unsure of just what is expected of them and are doubtless unlikely to make the double play. In the U.S. there are few colleges without a cell of bearded Beatniks and fewer yet where some overtones of Beat philosophy have not crept into the minds of students in general.

Hairy evangelists of Beatdom have even collected troupes of semi or weekend Beats in the Midwest and South. In Cleveland an ex-sailor, ex-cook, ex-taxi driver named Wil Martin has become the flag-bearer by being "against creeping meatballism and void-ism." Texas Beats are mostly types which California Beats scorn as "tourists," [126] but their espresso shops have been burgeoning like locoweed in Houston, Dallas, Lubbock and Amarillo. Atlanta's Beats are considered by experts to be "not complete in their thinking," but still they work hard at noncornponity after business hours.

Bongo drums are beaten at Atlanta's all-night Beat parties, marijuana cigarets ("left-wing Luckies" in the South) are sometimes smoked and, more daring yet, carefully selected Negroes are invited to rub shoulders with the jean-clad white folks. The Beats mix socially with Negroes in Washington, D.C., too, and as a result embryo nonconformists in both cities sometimes decide they have hopped the wrong rattler. "I was never so completely outraged as at the first Beat party I went to," says one indignant Atlanta belle who had planned to become a Scarlett O'Hara of the local weirdos. "We climbed a lot of rickety stairs, dodging the rats. The first thing I saw was a big smile with about 68 white teeth in a big black face. I was completely bug-eyed. But not the others. They were too far out. They just sat around looking foggy."

Secondary Beatsmanship is practiced, with local variations and an increasing snobbishness, in a good many other U.S. cities. But the true, hard-core Beats (who "put down" part-time Beats—

occasionally—by taking one look and slowly shaping the word "wow" with the lips) hive almost exclusively in New York and on the West Coast, specifically in Los Angeles and San Francisco.

There are no fewer than 2,000 Beats in Los Angeles, mostly in the crumbling suburb of Venice West. They live with such basic furnishings as a mattress, a few cans of tinned food and a record player, recorder or set of bongo drums in abandoned stores or cheap rooms near the hot dog stands which mark the Pacific shore. San Francisco's North Beach section, because of its long tradition of bohemianism and because of its memories of early Beats, must still be considered the capital of Beatdom. Grant Street is its main drag, and two dingy, placard-plastered hangouts, The Co-existence Bagel Shop and The Place, are its Stork Club and "21." There are probably less than a thousand Beats in San Francisco now, some living in industrial districts and some camped in barren rooms over the spaghetti factories and Chinese sweatshops at the foot of Telegraph Hill, but they exhibit that air of uniqueness to be found in inhabitants of any temple. Beat existence and Beat attitudes are roughly similar, however, in both western gathering grounds.

Beat life is not nearly so enlivened by debauchery as the poets might suggest, the public might suspect or the Beats themselves might hope. True Beats seldom have much more money than is necessary for bare existence. Some get allowances from presumably sorrowing parents. Some work from time to time, usually at menial or unskilled tasks, but almost invariably they quit as soon as the rent money is put by or a foundation for unemployment checks adequately laid. Few indulge in heroin or even whisky, if only because they can seldom afford either. By and large they smoke marijuana when they can get it (Chicago "pot" is prized, New York marijuana considered inferior stuff) and drink cheap wine or beer. A bottle of wine or a few cans of beer, in fact, is adequate excuse for a Beat party, which consists, in many cases, simply of sitting on somebody's floor and listening silently to phonograph records.

### The Rare Pad-sharing Chick

Beatdom is largely a male society, perhaps 10% of which is Negro. Few Beats are homosexual, although they tend to regard homosexuality with vast forbearance, and for all their wild talk about sex, the Beat orgy is largely a figment of their imagination.

There are relatively few female Beats, and—girls being the practical creatures they are—the "pad-sharing chicks" about whom Beats talk so fondly and with such vehemence are few and far between. Even then they are usually so dominated by their own jangling complaints that romance seldom blooms for long. The boon Beats really seem to want from femininity, furthermore, is financial support, and the "chicks" who are willing to support a whiskery male are often middle-aged and fat. "The mature bohemian," according to North Beach maxim, "is one whose woman works *full* time."

By their very nature and appearance, Beats make cops nervous and property owners indignant, and no small part of Beat existence is spent in hopeless though wildly vocal scuffling with authority. The Los Angeles police, perhaps out of ennui produced by long acquaintanceship with other curious cults, seem to suffer the Beats with philosophical calm, although Venice homeowners have lately banded together to protest their existence, decry their propensity for making night hideous, and to moan about property values.

San Francisco's police have gone out of their way to give Beats a bad time. At one point they parked prowl cars or paddy wagons in front of the Bagel Shop and The Place for hours on end and [129] pointedly questioned everyone who went in or out. "But," explains Police Captain Charles Borland, "we do that with *any* problem bar." Still, it cannot be denied that cops have problems too. "First the Beatniks came to North Beach," says Captain Borland. "Then the tourists came to stare at them. Then the paddy hustlers and boosters came to work on the tourists. When I was a lieutenant I spent years south of Market [San Francisco's tenderloin]. I wish I could go back to those Third Street bums. On Third Street they get back in the doorways when they see the wagon coming. But these North Beach bums! These Beatniks! They want to argue with the officer. They stand around drinking and throwing bottles on the pavement, and they sit on the curbs—dirty, unsightly and using bad language. How about a woman coming down the sidewalk with a baby carriage? We get complaints. And these Beatniks argue with the officer. They're always arguing with the officer."

Talk—endless talk—forms the warp and woof of Beat existence. Talk and the kind of exhibitionism that almost always moves the average man to uncertainty and embarrassment are the Beat's weapons against the world. Mostly he is incapable of anything else. Beats are seldom ignoramuses—wild or not, theirs is a world of ideas and a surprising number of them have at least some college education. But Dr. Francis J. Rigney, a young San Francisco psychiatrist who has recently completed a massive study of the Beat Generation based on members of the North Beach community, feels that at least 60% of the Beats with whom he communicated were so psychotic or so crippled by tensions, anxieties and neuroses as to be incapable of making their way in the ordinary competitive world of men, and that another 20% were hovering just within the boundaries of emotional stability.

What sort of heirs are these to the long and stirring history of unpopular dissent in America? The 1950s, granted, have not been years calculated to produce a Thomas Paine or to inspire a crusade for the rights of the working man. The Beat Generation has achieved its effects in part by default and in part as a result of the very prosperity it rejects. But, default or no, who ever heard of rebels so pitiful, so passive, so full of childish rages and nasty, masochistic cries? What would an old-time Wobbly have thought if he had encountered one on his way out of town after burning a bunkhouse or dynamiting a tipple? What would Thomas Jefferson, that advocate of the cleansing qualities of revolution, have been moved to say if he had known rebelliousness in America would come to this?

The Beat Generation is not alone in the U.S. in questioning the values of contemporary society, in feeling spiritually stifled by present-day materialism, and in growing restive at the conformity which seems to be the price of security. But only the Beats have actually been moved to reject contemporary society in voicing their quarrel with those values. There they are—crouching at the roadside in rags like those rascally Holy Men of the Orient who may slit purses but nevertheless remind the fat and prosperous that the way to salvation may yet be hard and bitter. There they prance and gesture, living in poverty (in the Age of Supermarkets), rejecting the goodies of the suburbs (in the Age of Togetherness), babbling of marijuana and mescaline (in the Age of Vic Tanny) and howling about their souls, misshapen as their souls may appear to be.

A hundred million squares must ask themselves: "What have we done to deserve this?" [130]

# Herbert Gold

## THE BEAT MYSTIQUE

In Greenwich Village a dreamy young beggar in a tattered Ivy League summer suit and a buttondown collar with both buttons missing turns on an uptown couple to ask, "Gimme a quarter for a Cadillac, hey?"

In New Orleans a pretty little department store model approaches a man at a party, takes off her sweater, then her bra, and says, "Let's ball, dig,"—by which she means, Let's try a new far-out sound on the hi-fi. If he reaches out to touch anything but the tone arm, she will say, "You're through, frantic boy. You are sawed off." He disappears from future guest lists.

In Denver a gaggle of young lads, not knowing what to do on a warm spring evening, steal a car each, drive them to the other side of town, park, steal a few more, drive back to the starting point, park, and then settle down to giggle about the confusion of the owners and the police. Silence. Return of boredom. Yawn. Finally one says softly, "Pops, why didn't we think of picking up on some chicks?"

In St. Louis a girl and her friend, who used to be a drummer with a well-known quintet, both of them suffering withdrawal symptoms—he has been working to support their habits by pimping for the girl—beg an old pal to put them up with bed and fridge for a few days. While the friend is away at work, they telephone a friend in San Francisco, give him the bit, and after gassing awhile, suggest that they both just keep the connection and leave the telephones off the hook. Their friend won't get the bill until they are gone, far gone. Why do this to him? "He's square, *so* square, man."

In Detroit a hi-fi engineer clucks sympathetically at the plight of a young couple [20] in college. It's true love, but they have

This article originally appeared in *Playboy* magazine (February, 1958), pp. 20, 84–87. It is reprinted by permission of the author and James Brown Associates, Inc.

no place to go. The back seat of a car is for puppy love and sprained backs. OK, they can use his apartment. What they don't know is that there is a microphone concealed in the mattress. Their friend invites them to a party where he plays the tape before strangers.

In San Francisco a group of young poets announces Religious Poetry Night, attracting a hall full of the plump, mournful ladies (purple hats, veils, heaving freckled bosoms) who adore such things. The first poet gets up to read. "C—— S————!" he shrieks at the audience.

On State Street in Chicago a frozen-faced grifter stops a passer-by, pushing out his hand and murmuring, "What you say, pop? Give me a piece of skin."

"I'm sorry, I don't know you."

"I don't know you either, man, but you like to have a party?" He slides off and away with a passive dreamy girlish look which has nothing sweet about it: it plots impossible meanness, anything to make him feel something. He doesn't know anybody, and says "man" to everybody because he can't be bothered remembering names.

In midtown Manhattan a writer, Jack Kerouac, prepares for his interview on TV. "We're beat, man," he says. "Beat means beatific, it means you get the beat, it means something. I invented it." For the television audience he announces, "We love everything, Bill Graham, the Big Ten, rock and roll, Zen, apple pie, Eisenhower—we dig it all. We're in the vanguard of the new religion." Jack Kerouac likes to write of Charlie Parker as God and himself as the Prophet.

These are hipsters.

Who is the hipster, what is it? The pure beast is as hard to track as the pure "student" or "midwesterner," but let us follow the spoor of history and symptoms. We will probably find that "pure hipster" is a phrase like "100% American"—an unstable compound with an indefinite content.

Hipsterism began in a complex effort of the Negro to escape his imposed role of happy-go-lucky animal. A few highly self-conscious urban Negro men sought to imitate "white" diffidence, or coolness, or beatness. They developed a style which was both a criticism of their Bible-shouting and jazz-loving parents and a parody of the detached, uninvolved city ofays. They improvised on an unstated theme—like bop—and if you weren't with it, with it and for it, you heard nothing but jangle. The horn rims of the intellectual came to be known as bop glasses. They blew fine abstractions. The joke was a good one.

Then their white friends took up the fashion, complicating the joke by parodying a parody of themselves. Cool music was the artistic expression of this hypertensive chill. However, in order to keep from dancing, keep from shouting, keep from feeling, a further help was needed and it was found in heroin. Some of the earlier hot musicians had used marijuana, many drank; these were springs toward jumping high in a group. There was a strong prejudice against the cats who went on junk, expressed in the superstition that you might mainline a fatal bubble of air into your veins. Uh-uh, no baby, they said: and in practice they found that the junkie blew lousy drum or horn, no matter what he thought he was blowing.

The new generation preferred super-celestial private music, however. Heroin dissolves the group and each man flies alone all the way to Barbados. And without flapping his arms.

Many other young Americans felt beat, wanted to keep cool, and so into the arms of the first hipster society, that still unravished bride of bop quietness, ran three angry herds: 1. Mainstreet thugs with their sideburns, their cycles, and their jeans; 2. college kids and a few literary chappies, finding in the addict's cool stance an expression of the frustration of fluid-drive lives in which the juicebox had gone dry; and 3. Upper Bohemia, tired of Van Gogh, Italian movies, charades, and sex, and so ready to try anti-art, anti-sex, anti-frantic non-movement. These latter comprise the Madison Avenue hippies, models who strip merely to express their hatred of fashion magazines, admen and lawyers who marry call girls, a host of Ivy League symbol-manipulators, bloated with money and debt, pink with General Electric sun tans and shame, who express their benzedrine blues by wigging at night near a blasting rig. "Well, you know . . . Albert Schweitzer doesn't make me climb the wall . . . Is it true he eloped with Kim Novak?"

"Everyone says," remarks the pretty girl who seeks to please, "that I'm exceptionally fastidious, but would you like me to do something nasty for you? I really wouldn't mind. My name is Grape Nuts, what's yours?"

Let us now move in closer to the hipster's harried heart. When the hipster makes it with a girl, he avoids admitting that he likes her. He keeps cool. He asks her to do the work, and his ambition is to think about nothing, zero, strictly from nadaville, while she plays bouncy-bouncy on him. When the hipster makes it with boys, it's not because he's a homosexual and cares for it—it's for money, a ride home, pass the time of night while waiting for the band to come back on. When the hipster steals a car, he doesn't keep it or sell it; he hides it where the squares will have trouble finding it, and writes "Mort à Louis A" in soap on the windshield. When the hipster digs music, Proust, or religion, it's to talk over, it's to carry around in his jeans, it's to hit his buddies with; it makes no sense or feeling, and the weirder it is, the cooler the kick.

In other words, the hipster is a spectacular instance of the flight from emotion. He is like a sick refrigerator, laboring with tremendous violence, noise and heat, and all for one purpose— to keep cool. This refrigerator is powered by crime without economic need; an editor to one of the hipster writers complains, "Jeez, when I slept on park benches and boosted from the A & P, I did it because I had to. My kick was that I needed sleep and food. I didn't do it to tell people about." The refrigerator is powered by sex without passion; the sole passion is for the murder of feeling, the extinguishing of the jitters. The refrigerator is powered by religion without faith; the hipster teases himself toward the black battiness of oblivion, and all the vital refreshment which religion has given the mystics of the past is a distraction from the lovely stupor he craves. Unlike Onan, who spilled his seed upon the ground, the hipster spills his brains and calls it piety. He also wears music, art and religion as a kind of badge for identification. Instead of the secret handshake which got him into Uncle Don's Boys' Club or the Orphan Annie Secret Society, he now says, "You dig the Bird? Proust? Zen?"

"I'm hip," says his friend. This phrase means: No need to talk. No more discussion. I'm with you. I got you. Cool. In. Bye-bye.

The language of hipsterism is a means toward noncommunication, a signal for silence. The truest lingo is narcotics, because this more than anything gives Little Boy Beat what he wants—release from imagination and the body—an illusion not of omnipotence, as we are sometimes told, but of a timeless browsing in eternity. In other words, a cool simulation of death. The sentimental and sensational talk about drugs producing sex maniacs is nonsense. The man on a habit needs nothing more than his fix. Quiet, quiet. He may perform terrible violence to get the drug, but not sex: pleasure has nothing to do with the dreamy high of heroin. The pale soft face of the addict, with his smudged passive eyes and his drooping mouth, is almost ladylike in its sweetness. It has no fight or love in it.

Heroin enables the hipster to stand guard over his soul, dreaming of cool nothing, beautiful beat nothing, while his feet go ratatat and he strokes a switchblade, a hand, or a copy of *Swann's Way*. Needless to say, the proto- and quasi-hipsters do not usually go all the way to the perfection of heroin. [84]

The current fad for the hipster—his language, manners and attitudes—indicates that he is, as that fearful phrase goes, "no isolated phenomenon." Jack Kerouac proclaimed, "Even the Ivy League is going hip." Emerging out of bop, narcotics, and the subtle rebellion of the Negro against the charge of being "happy, excitable, emotional," the hipster takes one of his chief public models from that most authentic American source, the movies. He ignores the injunction of the pious 13th Century moralist, John of Garland, who wrote: "Be not a fornicator, O Student! Stand and sit upright, do not scratch thyself!" The Stanislavsky hipsters scratch as if their soul's unease were actually juicy fleas, slouch as if leaning to catch Marlon's word from earth or James' from vaulted heaven. The movie shadow of Dean or the Brando of *The Wild One* is a part of the image of the hipster, whether he be the smooth pink Ivy League meta-hipster, staring at himself in the mirror of one of those shops where they apparently do operations to remove the bones from men's shoulders, or the long-chinned hairy proto-hipster with a girl jiggling on the behind seat of his Harley-Davidson "74." In many theatres where *The Wild One* played, there was a lineup afterwards in the men's room, the cyclists in their nail-studded black jackets scowling with adoration into the mirror as they rehearsed their public roles. Each man was Brando, distant and violent. Each man was Marlon, cool and beat. They stood in a row without shame, almost without vanity (so pure it was), like neophytes for sacrifice in their penitential leather, silver trim, sideburns, and duck-ass haircuts. Scratch not, O Hipster!

And so the hipster's lines of communication spread from a four-bit movie-house in a small town of the midwest to the chic saloons of New York and the Coast. He reminds us of the teddy-boys of England, the breaking-loose wild brats of defeated Japan, the existentialist zazous of Paris, tootling the petrified dixie they learned from old Beiderbecke records. His apologists, particularly the literary hipsters of San Francisco and New York, are fond of reaching back into history to invoke the criminal gods of French poetry—Rimbaud, who mysteriously vanished into Africa, Villon, who ended up dancing on the gallows, Genet, who is now a poet and playwright hero of Paris after a career of thievery, blackmail, and male prostitution. The very important difference between the American literary hipster and his foreign models is that the great artist-criminals were true outcasts from society: they did not pick themselves up by the seat of their own pants and toss themselves out. They were driven by class differences and economic pressure. A few of the Americans have performed spectacularly—mostly in the loony-bin; one even played William Tell with his wife and blew her head off—but these are individual troubles, not the product of any vast and windy guilt of society. Who ain't got personal troubles? I dig yours, man; but I got mine too.

In any case, the 1958 hipster is not the bold medieval troubadour prince of song and con, nor the romantic adventurer poet of later times, nor the angry driven Depression stiff: he is the true rebel without a cause. No, of course he has a cause—his charred self, but a self without connection or need. He is a reticent boyo with a yen for thuggery, a reluctant visitor to the affairs of men, a faintly girlish loiterer near the scenes of violence. If he can't be a big boom-boom hero in a war, like Gary Cooper, at least he can take the muffler off his rod, like Marlon. Mainly he is afflicted with the great triumvirate disease of the American male—Passivity, Anxiety, Boredom. Individualists without individuality, a sleepy brawl of knowing non-thinkers, the lonely crowd at its grumbling loneliest, the hipsters fall naturally to the absolute submission of a marriage to heroin. Like the submission to boredom in television and all the other substitutes for personal creativeness in American life, narcotics involve an abdication of good sense by men deprived of the will to make their own ways.

"I dig everything, man."

"What do you want to do now?"

"I don't know, man. Get some kicks somehow."

If the description of the hipster as "passive" strikes you as harsh, look up the dictionary definition of the word: "*Med.* Pertaining to certain morbid conditions characterized by deficient vitality and reaction."

The word hipster came in with bop, which is a way of keeping cool musically, at the same time as narcotics addiction burgeoned—a way of keeping cool sexually. The drug-taking hipster is not a sexual anarchist; he is a sexual zero, and heroin is his mama, papa, and someone in bed. (The pusher in *A Hatful of Rain* is called "Mother.") Not every quasi-hipster mainlines into the tattoo on his arm, of course, but the style of life is set by those who do. The coolest boys call each other "daddy-o," as if their passivity extends to thinking of every man as a potential guardian father. Of course, the traveling musician also cannot be bothered to remember names, so everyone is "man," "pops," "daddy-o." They worship the purple fantasy of torn-tee-shirted masculinity created by Tennessee Williams, William Inge, and others who have invented a new theatrical type—the male impersonator. Adorably brutal, stripped of the prime attributes of manliness—intelligence, [85] purpose, control—they are the curvaceous Mae Wests of popular melodrama. Having died, James Dean and Charlie Parker are defined as immortal. Living and growing up a bit, Marlon Brando is a traitor to this myth of saintly suicide by sports car or heroin. They might have forgiven his giving up the bongos, but his receding hairline is a disgrace to the cause. The strong silent hero must also be weak and pretty.

One of the curious bypaths of hipsterism leads to their far-out religious camp. Jack Kerouac says, "We're in the vanguard of the new religion," which is a little like the monk in the story who claimed that he was the world champion for humility. They picked up on St. John of the Cross for a time, Catholic ritual, St. Francis of Assisi (they were St. Frantics); then they moved on toward Byzantine, Greek, and Orthodox fantasies, with ikons and incense; they made the Dostoievsky scene. In recent years some have taken to calling themselves Zen Hipsters, and Zen Buddhism has spread like the Asian flu, so that now you can open your fortune cookie in one of the real cool Chinese restaurants of San Francisco and find a slip of paper with the straight poop: "Dig that crazy Zen sukiyaki. Only a square eats Chinese food." Promiscuity in religion stands, like heroin, for despair, a feverish embracing of despair, a passive sinking into irrationality. Zen and other religions surely have their beauties, but the hipster dives through them like a side show acrobat through a paper hoop—into the same old icy water of self-distrust below. The religious activities of the hipsters cure their unease in the world the way dancing cheek to cheek cures halitosis.

No wonder the hipster says, "Nada, I'm beat—I'm right in there, see—I'm the most religious, the most humble—I'm swinging, man." He stammers because something is missing, a vital part, the central works. His soul, sense of meaning, individual dignity (call it how you like) has been excised as unnecessary by a civilization very often producing without good purpose. He feels that love is not love, work is not work, even protest is not protest anymore. On the consumer's assembly line, in the leisure-time sweatshop, he pieceworks that worst of all products of anxiety—boredom. This is the response of retreat from the cold inanities of his time payments, luxurious discomfort, dread of the successful future. Boredom is a corollary to anxiety. As the middle-class man now buys a brick for the new church (Does God need that basement bowling alley?), so the hipster tries to find himself in intuitions of meaning through the Anchor edition of Zen tales, or through some other fashionable interior decoration. Naturally he stammers, "Cool, mon, real cool." He wants to stop moving, jittering, flittering. He displays himself as exemplary because he has no wife, children, responsibilities, politics, work. The middle-class man both has and does not have these things. Who can call moving bits of paper a job? Most Americans are paper-movers. How is love of wife and children more than a social habit when a man feels *qua* man (not as husband or father) that he has no authority except in his own home?

When a man's house is his only castle, then he has no castle.

Both smugness and ambition are characteristics of human beings, not of animals, though rats and rabbits can be taught despair by repeated electric shocks. Faced by the threat of absolute manipulation, the hipster mobilizes himself for a last stand— and hops about the cage, twitching his tail, bumping the charged wires.

The cliché which tells us that Americans love Things, Possessions, does not go far enough. Americans also demand experiences of power, one way or the other, in person or out of the picture tube. This seems normal enough to be a condition of life, but not when the starved mirage of power crowds out the quietness which gives experience meaning and organizes a man to face his private issues of working, loving, having children, dying. Certain experiences lead *away from* rather than *toward*, and faster and faster we go: the experience does not help; we try wilder experience; this does not help; still more wild, wilder. The extreme of a flatulent submission to the mass media eventually stops all experience in its tracks, in the guise of giving perfect experiences which make it possible to carry on. Television as a medium of entertainment is not the villain any more than good whiskey is a villain; they can both be good friends. It is the bleared submission by depleted souls which destroys. Relaxation is one thing—sharing experience vicariously is a great experience to which the imagination entitles us. To be stunned is another matter entirely. Despair by electronic shock.

Sensitive to all this, the hipster has decided to quit—resign— have no more of it. Instead of being part of a mass audience before the picture tubes, he becomes an audience of one before the hypo. He gives up on the issue of being human in society. He decides that the problem does not exist for him. He disaffiliates. The man who cares is now derided for being "frantic."

But of course the hipster is still a part of a bewildered America in which Tab Hunter confides to an interviewer that he can only sleep with his Teddy bear in bed with him. The hipster is victim of the most hopeless condition of slavery—the slave who does not know [86] that he is a slave and is proud of his slavery, calling it "freedom." Incurable? Nearly. The posture of negation and passivity thinks it is religion and rebellion; instead it is a mob phenomenon. These Nihilists sail dreamy down the Nile of throughway America, spending many a sleepless day figuring out something real cool to do at night, and end up trying to convince themselves, as Jack Kerouac does, that Charlie Parker is God. Kerouac's birdmen in his novel, On the Road, search for coolness within their beatness, hipness within their jeans-and-dirty-hair dream of quickies with marvelous girls (who also wear dirty hair and jeans). Occasionally, as in the Kerouac variety of superfrantic sub-hipster, sex takes the place of dope. This is a kind of sex which also takes the place of sex. The way some men gloat over possessions, he keeps score of his hero's erotic blitzes, forgetting that—if you are the trooper who uses sex as a weapon—every notch in a weapon weakens the weapon.

The hipster is a street-corner, bar, and partying phenomenon, a creature of mobs. One Rimbaud may be a genius; a crowd of them is a fad. An earlier fad for psychoanalysis had this in favor of it: Freud believed in the prime value of emotions, but in a necessary control by the intelligence. In other words, he valued society despite the discontents of civilization. The hipster gives up society, gives up intelligence, and thinks he is doing this in favor of the emotions; but he has already, without making a decision about them, let his feelings seep away through a leaky personality. What is left is a spasmodic jerk, though some of the individual spokesmen also have vivacious talent. No wonder that the madhouse is seen as the refuge of their "best minds." Catatonia, here we come.

These shrill moonbirds turn out to be rigid earth satellites, rocketed by bureaucrats beyond their ken into the air of reality, where they circle in a pattern determined without choice, give out a diminishing signal, draw to earth and burn, crumble, vanish.

When Yeats looked into the future to find a terrible savior, an evolution up from animality into something strange and wonderful:

> What rough beast, its hour come round at last,
> Slouches toward Bethlehem to be born?

—he did not mean James Dean. Perhaps, as they claim, the tunneling hipster's avoidance of feeling can lead to a new honesty of emotion. Perhaps a ground hog might someday learn to fly, but man O man, that will be one strange bird. [88]

# John Ciardi

## EPITAPH FOR THE DEAD BEATS

It wasn't much fun as rebellions go. Heaven knows the young need their rebellions. And let it be said of the Beats that there was a time when they might almost have been taken as an intellectual uprising. By now, however, it seems clear enough that the rebellion has gone for kicks, that what offered itself as intellectual refreshment has turned out to be little more than unwashed eccentricity, and that one more Parnassus has turned out to be a grimy dive not much different from the speakeasy or the back room of the Communist cell meeting.

The fact is that the Beat Generation is not only juvenile but certainly related to juvenile delinquency through a common ancestor whose best name is Disgust. The street gang rebellion has gone for blood and violence. The Beats have found their kicks in an intellectual pose, in drugs (primarily marihuana, but also benzedrine, mescaline, piote, assorted goof-balls, and occasionally heroin), and in wine, Zen, jazz, sex, and a carefully mannered jargon.

There is in all of them an innate fidget. As high-priest Kerouac tried to dramatize—at least to the extent that monotony can be drama—the Beats talk endlessly about serenity, detachment, and mangled Zen, but the last thing they know how to do is sit still. Were it not for the fact that the narcotics squad drives them to secrecy, and that few of them can afford fast cars, they would be off racing from roadhouse to roadhouse in an excellent imitation of their once-flapper and once-flaming parents. The impulse to run away from convention (while remaining close enough to it to flaunt it) is the same as it ever was. Nor is the search for "kicks" finally distinguishable from "making whoopee" back in the supermelogorgeous days of the cat's pajamas.

And like every essentially adolescent rebellion, that of the Beat

Reprinted from the *Saturday Review* (February 6, 1960), pp. 11–13, 42. Reprinted by permission of the author and the *Saturday Review*.

Generation is marked by an orthodoxy as rigid as the blue laws. The Beats wear identical uniforms. They raise nearly identical beards (now beginning to disappear in reaction to the crop of beards being raised on campus by would-be beatnikoids). They practice an identical aversion to soap and water. They live in the same dingy alleys. They sit around in the same drab dives listening to the same blaring jazz with identical blanked-out expressions on their identical faces. And any one of them would sooner cut his throat than be caught doing anything "square."

It is clearly in the nature of all our rebel youth movements to need a touch of the illicit. The flappers and their plastic-age boy friends made a ritual of drinking rotgut, less because the human nervous system is naturally attracted to bad alcohol than because drinking it was against the law. The Young Communists plotted in secret meetings with dramatic precautions against undercover agents and dramatic fears of being raided, or they distributed pamphlets and howled from soap boxes in ecstatic defiance of "the Cossacks." The G.I. generation had its potential rebellion largely blurred by army restrictions and could do little more than grumble or go AWOL on a binge, but that much at least they did manage regularly enough. The Beat Generation has marihuana and the ritual of dodging the "narcos"—the narcotics squad.

The need to be illegal in some way is a simple enough need to thumb one's nose at society. The need to make a ritual of the illegality is as juvenile as the basic gesture itself. Let four Beats gather in a desert to fire up some marihuana and at least two of them will mention the narcos and look carefully [11] in all directions before they bring the stuff out of hiding. It is exactly the ritual of four high school pals about to sneak a smoke in the boys' room.

The Beats have carried their little drama a step further by adding to it their special argot. The marihuana is "tea." The rolled cigarette, looking very much like a paper-wrapped toothpick, is a "joint." The butt is a "roach." You light up, take a deep drag, and pass it on, holding the smoke in your lungs as long as possible. You save the roaches when they get too small to hold, wad them up, pick the tobacco from the end of a "straight" (a regular cigarette), put in the wadded roach, crimp in the end of the straight, and fire it up for one last drag. Meanwhile, the chicks stare off glassy-eyed into the Ultimate-All and keep saying

"Yeh! . . . hyeh! . . . hyeh!"—long drawn out, ecstatic, and aspirate. I mean like real cosmic, man.

Ideally, the Beat plays it cool, talking a great deal about a serene detachment from the materialism of the square and the corniness of the hot hipster. But put him on wheels and he instantly becomes a raging hot-rodder, distinguishable from the leather-jacket boys only by his volubility in discoursing on "the magnitude of the risk" as he spins his way around a tricky curve.

Speed is, of course, another drug, the illusion of one more escape. In the kind of Beat who most resembles the late Jimmy Dean (who was most nearly a middle ground between the Beats and the leather-jacket hoods, and who finally found the big crack-up he had long been looking for) speed is some sort of death wish.

It is, simply enough, a child's game without the easy freshness of the child's imagination. To the Beat, anyone over thirty is "The Enemy." One trouble, of course, is that by now most of the boys and girls Father Kerouac celebrated in "The Subterraneans" are over the line into enemy territory.

But whatever its foibles, and whether "Beat" is taken to mean "done in," as most people seem to understand it, or "beatific," as Kerouac has been insisting, the separation of the Beat Generation from "square" society was conceived as an intellectual and spiritual revolution. The Beat is a Krazy Kat longing to be stoned by the Mouse he loves, who, in his turn, always manages to fling his brick despite the worst Officer Pup can do. He is Charlie Chaplin ridiculously in love and being chased by cops. He is the jazz-man blowing his soul out in a dive, or wailing through the jail bars. He lives in skid-row-under-the-stars in the company of other "personal madmen poets"—the phrase is Kerouac's. He is a soul rescuing its identity from square conformity. His object is to escape the blindness of the square not only by disassociation, but by a systematic flouting of all square values. The rationale of this disassociation, or so he insists, is Zen.

Zen is an ancient way of life whose ends can be achieved only through a lifetime of rigorous spiritual discipline, and I certainly have no notion of posing as an expert on it. Yet, though its method and discipline are profoundly complicated, Zen is profoundly simple in its basic Buddhist goal of achieving absorption into the All. Zen has been called a religion without a creed; yet it has a priesthood and its candidates must undergo a training as demanding as that imposed by any other religion. Its rituals are basically rituals of purification from the dross of matter and of identification with the ultimate life-force.

But though the Beats have cried loud the name of Zen, the boys and girls have never been close to adopting Zen discipline. The last thing they want on earth is a discipline. They have, rather, raided from Zen whatever offered them an easy rationale for what they wanted to do in the first place. What they seem to have found most attractive in Zen is the idea of the holiness of the personal impulse, and the dramatic role of the Zen lunatic.

By ritual detachment from materiality, and by ritual meditation on the All, the Zen disciple prepares to achieve that point at which all trace of the world's dross will be purged from his mind. At that point there is left only the pure, the spiritual, the holy, and the eternal. The self will have been absorbed into the All. And at that point, whatever speaks to the consciousness is ultimate and true. That goal achieved, every impulse of the soul is an impulse of holiness.

The idea is not, of course, uniquely Zen. It is, in fact, common to all religions whose goal is the surrender of reason to faith after proper purification. At the top of the Mount of Purgatory, Dante achieves an identical state of purification wherein he is free to act entirely on impulse, since his every impulse has become holy.

To the Beats, however, Zen purification has been reduced to little more than "get high and let it spill." Drugs, alcohol, long hours of voodoo sessions with jazz or bongo drums, plus a very eager self-hypnosis, make up the way to a "flip," which may be anything from an epileptic seizure to an inner illumination.

Most Beats are careful not to flip too far out. The really cool ones do not want to flip at all, nor even to get too high. What they want is a "low-high," a kind of serene marihuana-float that will induce a heightened awareness of sounds, smells, colors, and time. They are, that is to say, sensation seekers on the trail of a mildly "mystical" experience. I am surprised, in fact, that they have systematically overlooked the possibilities of laughing gas as a stimulus to semi-mystical halucination, and I recommend that they look into William James's "The Varieties of Religious Experience" for some interesting details on this point. With the narcos sending in bearded, poetry-writing undercover men to make the scene and raid the tea parties—as they did recently in New York—it might be useful to know that there is, or so I am advised, no law against the inhalation of nitrous oxide.

On this level, Beat ritual is no more than sensation-seeking which is itself the mark of an overcomfortable and sterile generation. The Beats like to claim the obsessive violence of Rimbaud as theirs, but too much of what they do is much closer to the raveled nerve-ends of a Huysmans. For the Beats are sprung of a generation that had it easy. When someone accused Kenneth Rexroth (an *hombre,* may I say) of being Beat, he answered: "Beat, Hell!—I've been beaten." And certainly the Beats would not be out on their particular limb of the nervous system had they had to face a tougher problem of basic subsistence or of basic survival. Had the Beats reached their early twenties in time for the Depression bread lines or for the army's dreary combination of foxholes and boredom, they would certainly have found other business than the elaborate cultivation of their sensations and of their purified sacred impulses.

The second aspect of Zen upon which the Beats have seized most avidly is the Zen-lunatic. The holy madman is a figure to be found in [12] many religions. In Zen, as nearly as I understand it, the lunacy is cultivated as part of the long discipline of detaching oneself from the material appearances of reality and from the conventions of material rationality. As with Rimbaud, the goal is the deliberate derangement of all the senses in order to open oneself to the larger reality to which convention is blind. One plays the fool for God.

There is an innate nobility in the idea of playing the fool for God. David, as an example of humility, put by his majesty and danced before the Ark (II *Samuel* vi, 14). But these boys and girls come closer to playing the fool for the fun of it, drawing upon the Zen-lunatic as a sanction for their antics. Shedding one's clothes in public, for example, is a well-established Beat prank (the point of which is probably to prove one's purity of all traces of soap and water). Allen Ginsberg has even made the point by stripping naked in the course of a public lecture. Another kind of antic was demonstrated by three beat poets at the end of a long radio interview in Chicago last year. Closing out the program, the announcer (Studs Terkel) asked if they had anything more they wanted to say. They replied that, yes, they had a message for the world, and they were, of course, invited to give it. Their three messages were, in order: "Fried shoes." "Meow." And "Chicago is a wose" (i.e., a "rose" with a lisp).

So much for the intellectual revolution. To the extent that the Beat Generation can be thought of as a literary movement, it has been systematically vitiated by this insistence on the holiness of the impromptu and by the urge to play the lunatic. Whether or not Jack Kerouac has traces of a talent, he remains basically a high school athlete who went from Lowell, Massachusetts, to Skid Row, losing his eraser en route. His method of composition, as he himself has described it, is to put a roll of paper in the type-writer and to bang out eight or ten feet a day. Nothing must be changed because "whatever you try to delete . . . that's what's most interesting to a doctor."

I take Kerouac's particular phrasing of that point as sympto-matic of a narcissistic sickliness in all Beat writing. "This is im-portant," it says, "because it happened to sacred me." The object seems to be to document one's own psyche on the assumption that every reader will find it as interesting as your psychiatrist does. Sorry, boys: I find it zany without illumination, precious rather than personal, and just plain dull.

For the Zen-spill turns out to be simply a license to write with-out revision. "It's a new method of composition," Allen Ginsberg told me over the phone a while back. He was assuring me that the first part of "Howl" was written entirely without revision. He had, he confessed, tinkered a bit with the second part.

Ginsberg, for all his carefully cultivated (and natural) zani-ness, is a writer far above Kerouac in my estimation. I find that first part of "Howl" a compelling piece of writing. I also find it impossible to believe (though I may be confessing my own square blindness in saying so) that any man could put together without revision as tight a catalogue as I find there. By a "tight catalogue" I mean a piling up of specific details that are intimately related, that maintain interest despite lengthy enumeration, that move at a reader-compelling pace, and that mount to a unified effect that is somehow greater than the sum of its parts. Perhaps it was written exactly as Ginsberg says it was. Or perhaps he had pre-pared a great deal of it in his mind before committing it to paper. Perhaps he is simply making a claim for effect. All I can do here is record both my doubts that the catalogue was entirely im-promptu, and Ginsberg's insistence that it was.

But whatever the truth of the matter, and ready as I am to admire that first part of "Howl," I cannot find that Ginsberg has written anything worth reading since "Howl." Nor can I find any vein of poetic gold in Ferlinghetti, in Corso, or in the odds and ends of the less well-known Beats. As the literary heritage of the

Beat Generation, I conclude, we are left the unreadable un-novels of Kerouac and the first part of "Howl." Add in the Beat influence on a few writers such as Norman Mailer who were on their way before the Beats, but took some of their later direction from behind the beard. It still seems a thin enough achievement for what has been the most talked-of "literary" movement of the last decade. Its very paucity serves to underline the fact that even the literary leaders of the Beats have made their careers primarily in personal eccentricity rather than in writing.

There remains William S. Burroughs, whose "Naked Lunch" is a powerful empathetic descent into the Hell of dope addiction. But though Burroughs has been claimed by the Beats and has been featured in collections of Beat writing, he is, in simple fact, his own kind of madman, a lost soul who has skidded through every mud at the bottom of the world in his journey from one addiction to another. A writer of careful horrors, Burroughs certainly has admitted revision as part of his craft. His literary ancestry may perhaps be best described as a combination of surrealism and Henry Miller. The point is that he would have written exactly as he does write had there never been a Beat Generation. And though many readers will find Burroughs's writing revolting, the revulsion is from reality. Its passion has been suffered rather than theorized.

Aside from the frivolity of depending upon improvisation as a method of composition, it is exactly in its tendency to be theorized rather than suffered that Beat writing seems thinnest. It tends too readily to become not intellect but exhibitionism posing as intellect. It talks endlessly about itself (like those endless dull movies about making movies). And it claims even to be a revolution in human values, but the fact is that the Beat Generation is basically the product of a false dilemma.

There is always reason enough for the young to rebel from the patterns of American complacency. Up at 6:30 to punch an eight o'clock time card, [13] and home at five to watch TV on the installment plan can hardly be expected to recommend itself to the young as a romance with the universe. Nor are the patterns of two-car and swimming-pool success much more attractive when it all comes down to sitting around on the patio and small-talking the world from martini to martini.

The young may be blatant, but their rebellions are always essentially noble. At the core of the Beat rebellion there lies a single, simple, all-embracing distinction between what is "square" and what is "hip." It is, in fact, all but impossible for a Beat to speak ten consecutive words without using one or both of those terms. They define the center of his world. By "square" the Beat means "complacent, stodgy, sterile, spiritually dead." By "hip" he means "aware"—aware of the life force, of reality, of the universe.

And were it a simple choice between going Madison Avenue and going Beat, I should certainly insist that the Beat has all the merit on his side.

The beats have permitted themselves the ignorant assumption that they have stumbled on ultimate answers. What they have ignored in their youth and insolence is the simple fact that the human position has always been a middle term between good and evil, and that the simple continuity of man and woman born of man and woman, and seeking to transmit through every confusion a sense of the value of that continuity, is the one human position there is. It is an imperfect position, but it is the enduring one, and it will survive every doctrinaire fad.

What the surviving Beats have yet to learn is that they, too, must in time peter out into a random Bohemianism (as they have, by and large, already done) or take their own places within that continuity, to be accused in time, and with reason enough, by the confusions and rejections of their own young.

Bless their fling. May every child in his mad adolescence find parents who can remember their own madness. Perhaps the Beat Generation's dabble in Zen will even teach that detachment that leads to mercy and compassion. Even had the rebellion of the Beats lacked all theory, the very fact that the young will yet find their rebellion is itself a cause for hope, the point of which seems to become remarkably clear when we lost souls on the faculty wander into a fraternity house for an evening session with our pink-scrubbed future corporation idiots.

And still, as rebellions go, this Beat jazz wasn't really much fun. As a literary movement it began and ended just about nowhere. As a set of antics, it still has a bit of mileage in it. They are still playing at it in the Village, out there at North Beach, and at Venice West. Certainly there is no problem in coming by marihuana in Chicago. In Denver, I noted recently, a joint that bills itself as a Beat dive runs night after night with a fifty-foot line of high school and college kids waiting to get in. But if the Beats had any sort of rebellion going once, there seems to be little enough left of it now beyond a fad for hip-talk and blare-jazz in crumby dives. That's dead enough, as the man said waving away the buzzards, let's bury it.

I hope the next time the young go out for an intellectual rebellion, they will think to try the library. It's still the most subversive building in town, and it's still human headquarters. And even rebels can find it useful to know something, if only to learn to sit still with a book in hand. [42]

# Carolyn Gaiser

## GREGORY CORSO: A POET, THE BEAT WAY

On East Second Street where the Puerto Rican children are haunting the sidewalks looking for lost jelly beans, in a fourth floor walk-up apartment, Gregory Corso can usually be found whenever he's in New York or America. This tiny four-room, smoky-walled, ill-lit apartment belongs to Allen Ginsberg who shares it with a quieter Peter Orlovsky, and an occasional cat but absolutely no telephone. Anyone who wants to get in touch with them quickly must resort to Western Union and piles of opened telegrams are scattered about the kitchen which is the most lived-in room in the apartment. There is a narcissus blooming on the refrigerator, prints of Michelangelo and Da Vinci on the walls and half-finished haiku in the typewriter unless Jack Kerouac has recently been there; then there is likely to be an equally half-finished manifesto stating the inadequacies of Christianity and the attributes of Zen Buddhism.

A visitor dropping in at any time of day is apt to find whoever is at home seated at the table drinking beer and eating, and someone is always remarking happily that this is the first good meal he has eaten in days. While Allen Ginsberg broods over *The New York Times,* planning a cultural trip to Moscow and reading aloud about the recent discovery of the spoons of Ape Men, Gregory Corso proclaims the advantages of taking a freighter to Greece, the Acropolis by moonlight, dreams of Alexandrian conquests, and Peter Orlovsky reads silently on in Dostoevsky. Or perhaps, someone suggests going down to the White Horse Tavern to see if Delmore (Delmore Schwartz) is there, and they all put on raggedy jackets and go out to look for a taxi. Though between them they may have just enough change for

This essay, included by permission of John Schaffner, Literary Agent, is published here for the first time. The appended poem, "The Fleeting Hand of Time," is reprinted from Gregory Corso, *Gasoline* (San Francisco, Calif.: City Lights Books, 1958). Copyright 1958 by Gregory Corso; reprinted by permission of City Lights Books.

the cab fare, nobody would think of taking the subway. Since nobody seems to have a job, the question of their survival remains a mystery. The possible sale of an article on hoboes to *Esquire* and poetry readings at various Ivy League colleges keep them all in high spirits.

The readings at Yale, Princeton and Harvard were organized primarily by Allen Ginsberg who takes his role as prophet of the Beat philosophy more seriously than the other two. He has a kind of missionary zeal to save youth fram a trammeling bourgeois existence, to direct them toward the liberated life of sensation, while Corso, who is more of a clown, chooses to "jest Truth," never losing sight of a certain ridiculousness in the human struggle toward the sublime. Of the three, Jack Kerouac, who has had the greatest commercial success, is the most detached from the movement. He lives in a house in Northport, Long Island with his mother and five cats and only comes into New York occasionally. He has, in a sense, removed himself from the experiential fray, seems to have given up drinking and submerged himself in solitude.

Corso, on the contrary, never stays anywhere for very long, taking off periodically for wild jaunts through Europe. Two summers ago, he was at the Pamplona bullfighting festival with Art Buchwald and spent some time in Venice with Peggy Guggenheim; he has a facility for attracting the patronage of American art-lovers abroad. At present, he is in Europe again, having taken his dream freighter to Greece, and when last heard from was in Paris writing "a funny book" in which all of America gets high on marijuana. Corso, a small, thin and tousle-haired young man, is very much in the tradition of the enfante terrible, perhaps designedly so. If poets put on various masks in their poems, then this is the mask that is most distinctively Gregory Corso's; the mask of the sophisticated child whose every display of mad spontaneity and bizarre perception is consciously and effectively designed. It is the mask he wears most comfortably in private life and the one which produces the greatest charm in his poetry.

He says whatever comes into his head which is usually shocking, displays a studied child-like enthusiasm for everything from Venetian pigeons to blue camels, and at the same time, is excruciatingly sensitive to other people's opinion of him. He is likely to stop in the middle of a reading to ask a friend, "Do you love me, Bob? I gotta know if you love me." He speaks his own incoherent New Yorkese in which certain fixed phrases are returned to again and again for security's sake: "Oh my illuminating angel," "There must be a death and after the rose," and "Man, please don't put me down." He is beset by a dull awareness of beautiful unrealizable phantasy and a terrible down-to-earth irony. At one moment in the guise of the conspirator, he may confide, "Jack and Allen and I are plotting to take over the world in love's name; instead of streetlights we'll have Bach and Mozart and 'rose, thou art sick' will replace 'the pause that refreshes.'" Or immediately after, tragically tugging at his hair, he may remark that "We are all clowns in the Woody Wood Pecker cartoon and when the truck comes and hits me in the chest, I'll die and hear Woody Wood Pecker's terrible ha-ha-ha still laughing in my ears." The clown image is dominant in one of his new long poems appearing in a collection called *The Happy Birthday of Death* recently published by New Directions. Here the poet proclaims "The clown is dead!/ Pass along the highways of 1959—all clowns are dead!/ See the great dumps of them swarmed by seagulls" and yet he concludes with the assurance "But I am an always clown/ and need not make grammatic/ Death's diameter."

About himself, Corso says wistfully, "I long ago put myself in the image of young Julien Sorel; held plans, schemes, great ways to devise Alexandrian conquests, a simple child's dream." Emerging from a bleak slum environment, he learned to make life tolerable by embellishing it with grandiose fantasies, which, with the poet's imagination, he articulates as if they were real. He yearns for the lost gilt and velvet splendors of the Renaissance and one of his favorite possessions is a brilliantly colored, lavishly embroidered French courtier's costume which he bought in Paris. This affinity for grandeur can be even better understood after a closer examination of his background.

Gregory Corso's parents were poor Italian immigrants; his father though alive seems a very shadowy figure to him and his mother is dimly remembered with a painful sense of loss. Thinking of her, he becomes profoundly sad. "I do not know how to accept love when love is given me. I needed that love when I was motherless young and never had it." When he was about eleven, he was sent to an orphanage. At thirteen, he spent a few months in the Children's Observation Ward at Bellevue. At sixteen, he and two friends devised the wild plan of taking over New York City by means of walky-talkies, projecting a series of improbable and complex robberies. Communicating by walky-talky, each of the three boys took up an assigned position—one inside the store to be robbed, one outside on the street to watch for the police and a third, the master-planner, in a small room nearby dictating the orders. According to Corso, he was in the small room giving the orders when the police came. Given Corso's imagination, it is difficult to know exactly how much of this story is accurate. At any rate, he was arrested and sent to Clinton Prison for three years. His second book of poems *Gasoline* is dedicated to "the angels of Clinton Prison who, in my seventeenth year, handed me, from all the cells surrounding me, books of illumination."

After being released from prison, he spent some time in Mexico and then went to Cambridge where he was summoned by his vision agent, a tall stoop-shouldered old man in a black cape who appears to him at decisive moments in his life and directs him. Though Corso had never finished high school, he read voraciously at the Harvard library and pursued a violent course of self-education. He was encouraged in his poetry by one of the editors of the *Cambridge Review* and in 1955, through the contributions of students, his first book of poems, *The Vestal Lady of Brattle*, was published. At about this time he met Allen Ginsberg and Jack Kerouac who recognized in him a kindred spirit. After Cambridge, Corso went off to Europe where he wandered around for a year or so, patronized by kindly dilettantes. Meanwhile his poems were being published in *Esquire, Partisan Review, Contact,* and *The Evergreen Review,* a review that serves as the oracle for Beat literature. In 1958, Gregory Corso returned to America and the task of bringing the message to the American public began in earnest.

Corso is the youngest of the three Beat prophets; he is twenty-eight. Ginsberg is in his early thirties, and Kerouac in his late thirties. And of the three, Corso is also the most genuinely Beat; life as he found it from his childhood was truly hostile and he had only himself to rely on. It's not surprising that he should grow into a rebel. Kerouac and Ginsberg have more conventional backgrounds; both have strong family ties, Kerouac his French-Canadian mother, Ginsberg his father who teaches in a Paterson, New Jersey, school. Both finished high school and went on to Columbia University where they first met and where Kerouac played football. Yet despite disparities in background, the three share the same dissatisfaction with conventional American life, as they see it, its obsessive sense of responsibility, its unimaginative materialism, its monolithic conformity. They clamor for freedom, the freedom of the individual soul to experience all the sensations available in life, a spectrum that includes love, beauty, marijuana, alcohol, freight-hopping, art, cats, the Brooklyn Bridge, poetry, jazz, or more concisely, the absolute assertion of the ego. Very much in the tradition of Whitman, they too call on Americans to "Unscrew the locks from the doors! Unscrew the doors themselves from the jambs!"

As a philosophy the Beat might be considered a brand of hedonism. While demanding the right to fully experience, the three exponents of the Beat are asking that their behavior be not only approved but applauded. And in the absence of universal applause, they applaud each other. Ginsberg says that Corso is "the greatest poet in America today," Kerouac says "I think that Gregory Corso and Allen Ginsberg are the two best poets in America," and Corso says that Ginsberg is the best poet and Kerouac the greatest novelist. When the three are together, each is accepted for the dream image he has of himself; each wish is fulfilled in this three-way friendship.

Ultimately, the Beat movement can not really be classified as a philosophy since it is not a rational position arrived at through a cool intellectual analysis of the human condition. Nor is it in any sense political. Though poems may be written about the evils of "The Bomb," there are no prescriptions for altering the government or re-structuring society. The three spokesmen for the Beat are singularly disinterested in politics and, as for a socialist state, they would be very unhappy to see the hoboes disappear. It seems incredibly ironic that the Minister of Culture of the Soviet Union should praise Jack Kerouac for being the only novelist in America today writing anti-capitalistic novels. The evil they attack is nothing as specific as capitalism; the evil is defined in terms of whatever inhibits experience, or impinges on the spontaneity of the individual soul.

Essentially, the Beat reduces to an emotional attitude; it is the psychology of self-expression, an attempt to murder the superego and liberate the id. It is the desire to break out of the traditional forms for living, to rediscover the innocence of the natural man who lives by instinct rather than reason. Allen Ginsberg, in his prophetic role, speaks in the name of Beauty, saying "If you get interested in Beauty, then you've latched onto something mysterious inside your soul that grows and grows like a secret insane thought, and takes over completely when you die, and you're IT . . . Now it's weird enough to be in this human form so temporarily, without huge gangs of people, whole societies trying to pretend that their temporary bread & breasts are the be-all and end-all of the soul's fate, and enforcing this ridiculous opinion with big rules of thought & conduct, bureaucracies to control the soul, FBI's, televisions, wars, politics, boring religions . . . a false America's been getting in the way of realization of Beauty—let's all get high on the Soul" (excerpt from "Quo Vadis," *Mademoiselle Magazine,* January, 1960).

In Ginsberg's usage, the term "Beauty" suggests more than the aesthetic; it is a sense of the unboundedness, of limitless possibilities in life that can't be crammed into any religious, ethical or political dogma. Man is instinctively drawn toward beauty and only the unfettered soul is free to realize its own uniqueness. This belief in the primacy of instinct as the means of achieving true knowledge explains the attraction of the Beat toward Zen Buddhism. Basic to Zen Buddhism is the conviction that reason is insufficient for the attainment of truth. Man must transcend rationality, if he ever hopes to achieve wisdom. Or in Gregory Corso's words—"Man is great and mad, he was born mad and wonder of wonders the sanity of evolution knoweth not what to do."

As a literary movement, the Beat is an attempt to free writing from the stringencies of stale academic form. Their distrust of form in writing reflects their equally profound distrust of formal codes for human behavior. For them, the criterion of good literature is automatic writing in which the emancipated consciousness pours itself forth on the page with no thoughts about revision. The danger in this rather extreme view is immediately apparent; the artist has no responsibility to structure his perceptions into an artistic entity. The distinction between what is life and what is art breaks down. However, this danger need not be fatal. The unconscious has a logic of its own, and in certain rare cases (the most notable being Thomas Wolfe) this logic can operate to produce genuine art. Gregory Corso's writing for the most part falls into this category; he seems to have a built-in sense of form that protects him from embarrassingly sloppy writing. This and his startling imagination enable him to avoid the tendency of many Beat writers toward undisciplined work. As might be expected, the poems of his which are most vociferously praised by Ginsberg and Kerouac are those which are the least disciplined and the least successful, such as "Bomb" and "Power."

While bathing in sensation may be a fruitless undertaking in the context of every-day life, it may be of positive value to the poet if the raw intensity of his perceptions can be successfully translated into his poetry. Lyrical poetry speaks most eloquently in the grammar of feeling, and Gregory Corso has a talent for feeling. Although his poems impulsively avoid the limitations of rhyme and meter, they show, at his best, the sure control of a poetic intuition. His work is always intensely personal; his lyric sense combined with a Renaissance infatuation and an almost tragic irony gives his poems a strikingly unique tone.

Though he might not admit it, Gregory Corso is a poet in the true romantic tradition of Keats and Shelley. For him, art is not contingent on reality. It creates reality and the poet like a great magician or a Prince Charming comes to waken the sleeping world with the kiss of spring. In the poem "In the Fleeting Hand of Time," he shows the failure of the poet's vision when reality intrudes. The poem is an extremely revealing one in terms of Corso's personality for it expresses his acute sense of the chasm between his Julien Sorel dreams of Alexandrian conquest and the actual world that confronts him. It is a poem about the birth of the poet, describing how, out of all the points in historical time that offer potential lives of grandeur, he is thrust forth into a small room on Bleecker Street to live a life totally devoid of the glory he himself would have chosen.

At the opening of the poem, the narrator is standing "on the steps of the bright madhouse" which symbolize the limbo of pre-natal time. He hears the "bearded bell shaking down the wood-lawn," the bell that signals him into the inner room where the precise moment of his birth will be decided. He enters into the presence of a fiery gathering of knights who are going over "sheepskin plans," the diplomas with which one graduates into life. The knights represent the master-planners whose decision will determine the time and place of his birth. The knight image, the mailcoated fingers suggest a mystic orderliness in their gesture—that all will be duly performed according to a sacred code. The fingers trace his arrival back to "the black steps of Nero lyre Rome," the narrator whose birth is about to take place is engulfed in all the past history which has gone before. As part of humanity and even more important as the poet, he was present at the mad cataclysm that was Rome's destruction. The poet holds truth in his arms like a wailing philosopher who gives "the final call of mad history," or who stands aside and watches the irrevocable marching of a society toward destruction and screams his prophecy.

Suddenly his presence is known; the curtains of past time fall away; the "great windows of Paradise open" to let in flocks of birds, "winged light" signifying the light of birth. Time leads him by the hand and abruptly the tone shifts to the colloquial— "born March 26 1930 I am led 100 mph o'er the vast market of choice" but "the vast market of choice" is irrevocably limited by "March 26 1930."

Leaving his "orange room of myth," the poet leaves the vast potential of history with no means of locking away his "toys of Zeus" or of safeguarding his dreams of power. "I choose the room of Bleecker Street"—from "the orange room of myth" he is plunged into the actual room on Bleecker Street where he was born. It is a "baby mother" who nurses him as opposed to the "Olympian mother" to whom he aspires and on whom he calls in desperation at the unexpected squalor he has been born into. The experienced life offers only drabness and sordidness— "Snows/Decade of icy asphalt/ doomed horses/ Weak dreams/ Dark corridors of P.S. 42 Roofs Ratthroated pigeons." In his new world even the horses are doomed and dreams are weak.

The poet sheds his "Hermean wings" when the glory he envisioned is replaced by the "all too real Mafia streets" of the poor Italian section. In shedding his "Hermean wings," he is obliged to put aside his godly image of himself as Hermes, son of Zeus, and herald to the gods. Yet, in a sense, he will pursue his heraldic role as a poet.

Begging to be thrown beneath a "humanity of cars," he appeals to Time to destroy him by the machinery of modern civilization, a civilization so grossly opposed to the others in which he might have lived. Ultimately, he is forced to "discard his lyre of Orphic futility" as he was obliged to shed his Hermean wings. Though Orpheus' lyre gained him entrance into the kingdom of death, he failed to bring Eurydice back to life with him. And so the narrator poet recognizes that the force of his art is insufficient to reverse the hand of Time.

The second stanza returns to the starting point where the narrator is climbing the stairs toward the room where his birth will be decided. He knows now that his birth will be a betrayal but implacable Time, like a dog chasing its tail in circles, comes and leads him "into conditional life." And so Julien Sorel puts on a clown face and steps into the Woody Wood Pecker cartoon.

Despite all Kerouac's and Ginsberg's screaming against the sterility of form in literature, Corso, himself, isn't quite so certain. When speaking to someone outside the inner circle, he often confides, "They all keep telling me I gotta have form, putting me down because I don't have form," and then looking bewildered, he demands, "Do you think I need form?"

IN THE FLEETING HAND OF TIME

On the steps of the bright madhouse
I hear the bearded bell shaking down the woodlawn
the final knell of my world
I climb and enter a fiery gathering of knights
they unaware of my presence lay forth sheepskin plans
and with mailcoated fingers trace my arrival
back back back when on the black steps of Nero lyre Rome I
    stood
in my arms the wailing philosopher
the final call of mad history
Now my presence is known
my arrival marked by illuminated stains
The great windows of Paradise open
Down to radiant dust fall the curtains of Past Time
in fly flocks of multicolored birds
Light winged light O the wonder of light
Time takes me by the hand
born March 26 1930 I am led 100 mph o'er the vast market of
    choice
what to choose? what to choose?
Oh ——— and I leave my orange room of myth
no chance to lock away my toys of Zeus
I choose the room of Bleecker Street
A baby mother stuffs my mouth with a pale Milanese breast
I suck I struggle I cry O Olympian mother
unfamiliar this breast to me
Snows
Decade of icy asphalt doomed horses
Weak dreams   Dark corridors of P.S. 42   Roofs   Ratthroated
    pigeons
Led 100 mph over these all too real Mafia streets
profanely I shed my Hermean wings
O Time be merciful
throw me beneath your humanity of cars
feed me to giant grey skyscrapers

exhaust my heart to your bridges
I discard my lyre of Orphic futility

And for such betrayal I climb these bright mad steps
and enter this room of paradisiacal light
ephemeral
Time
a long long dog having chased its orbited tail
comes grab my hand
and leads me into conditional life

# Thomas Parkinson

## PHENOMENON OR GENERATION

When the beat writers emerged in 1956 they struck so responsive a chord that they became the most widely discussed phenomenon of the late 1950's. If they represented a "generation," they replaced a remarkably short-lived and little-lamented "silent generation" which had dominated the first five years of the 1950's. Even in the accelerated pace of twentieth-century living, two generations per decade rather crowds things. Whether they represented an entire generation or a spasm of revulsion, the beat writers attained symbolic status, as did the until-then little-remarked Bohemian communities of New York's Greenwich Village and San Francisco's North Beach. When the San Francisco columnist Herb Caen dubbed the members of current Bohemia "beatniks," the derisive appellation stuck. Beatnik life became a subject of general interest, and that special nexus of jazz, Buddhism, homosexuality, drugs, and squalor was graphed and discussed in a wide range of media that reached a large audience.

It was easy to deride the nonconformist existentialist costumes, the sheer unpleasantness of texture in the dreary fakeries of beatnik art, and no one could defend the aimless self-destructiveness and occasional pointless criminality of conduct. But two basic problems were not so easily dismissed. The first was the genuine vigor and force of Allen Ginsberg and Jack Kerouac, the extraordinary wit and hilarity of Lawrence Ferlinghetti and Gregory Corso, the obvious intelligence, learning, and decency of Gary Snyder and Philip Whalen, the hard integrity of Michael McClure—in short, the simple literary expertise of several gifted writers who participated in many of the excitements and obsessions of current Bohemia. The second problem, essentially social, was how to estimate the importance of this extra-official mode of life. Was it spindrift or the point of an iceberg, this sudden revelation of resentment and bad feeling? Was it American Bohemia newly garbed, new beatnik being old bum writ bold? One commentator closed his very unfriendly article with somber tone: "A hundred million squares must ask themselves: 'What have we done to deserve this?'" A hundred million seems a modest estimate, but whatever the census, the refrain of puzzled commentators was a steady and repeated "What's wrong?" To many people the chief force of the beat movement was the suggestion that all was not well with our unrivalled happiness.

If not puzzled, commentators were pleased to see that the tradition of revolt was not dead, and many a patronizing phrase approved of youth having its fling. A surprising number of people seemed to assume that rebellion per se, whatever its means or ultimate goal, is a good thing. After ten years of literary dandies carefully machining their Fulbright poems in a social atmosphere of cold war and general stuffiness, the beats were welcomed. What troubled the most tolerantly disposed critics, however, was the refusal of beat and beatnik to play their proper social role. Their elders had a hazy rosy memory of their own daring youth in which they had been true radicals, that is, left New Dealers relatively active in political affairs. To their sense of things, the true rebel might take his origins in blank resentment of the world, but he went on to formulate his motives in terms of some ideal mode of social organization. But the beat movement simply denied the role of social critic and took an indifferent and passive posture before the problems of the world. Fallout, population, medical care, legal justice, civil rights—the beats were concerned actively with these problems when they impinged on the printing of books with certain taboo words, or on the problems of dope addicts cut off from their source of supply, or on the rights of poets to say slanderous things about policemen. Otherwise their approach was sardonic, apocalyptic, or impudent.

With very few exceptions, the beat and beatnik compose a social refusal rather than a revolt: as Allen Ginsberg announced to his audience in Chile, he is a rebel, not a revolutionist. They take no particular pleasure in tearing down a social fabric that they see as already ruined, and their attitude toward society is suspicious and evasive rather than destructive. When their attitude becomes destructive, the result is pointless antisocial acts; they then cease to be beat and become unemployed delinquents. Many beatniks are college students who, after two or more years of college, are not certain that they intend to go on into the business and professional worlds that swallow up the graduates of American colleges and universities. So they take a year off and loaf and invite their souls on Grant Avenue or Bleecker Street or the Left Bank. Some find the atmosphere so congenial that they linger through several years, and a few of them become permanent Bohemians. In such an atmosphere the tone is naturally antiacademic and antiofficial.

In this sense the beatnik world is a continuation of the Bohemian world already familiar to observers of American life. The beats are differentiated from past Bohemians by their religiosity (Zen Buddhism, Christ-as-beatnik with sandals and beard), experimental interest in hallucinogenic drugs and occasional dabbling in addictive drugs, proximity to criminality (largely through association with drugs), and fascination with moral depravity for its own sake. The traditional antidomesticity of the Bohemian world is still prevalent, as well as the concomitant relaxation of sexual mores in this predominantly male society.

The differences between the intellectual and religious concerns of current Bohemia and those of the 1920's or 1930's are modes of differentiating the attitudes of those eras from our own. It seems to me fairly plain that American Bohemia in reacting against suburbia tends to produce a reverse image of the society that makes the hydrogen bomb, throws its money around in idiot frenzy, and refuses to vote for school bonds; the same moral flaccidity, the same social irresponsibility, the same intellectual fraudulence operate throughout the two worlds that are, finally, not opposed. Freud in the 1920's meant sexual liberation, whereas psychoanalysis in Bohemia and suburbia in the 1950's was primarily a mode of keeping going. The borderline between beatnik and psychiatric patient shifts constantly, claiming one and releasing another, and a surprising number of people in current Bohemia are under psychiatric care. This in turn reflects the rising commitment rate of American mental hospitals and the steady increase in the numbers of people seeking psychiatric aid so that they can continue their business and professional life. The indifference toward politics exhibited by Bohemia is matched by the neglect and cynicism of suburbia. The beatnik contempt for simple comfort and cleanliness is the counterpart of mindless possessiveness, status-seeking, and other elaborate forms of greed.

It would be easy to multiply points of comparison: the grey flannel suit and the existentialist costume, the smiling religious purveyor of togetherness and the egotism of Christ-as-beatnik, ranch house and pad, cocktails and marijuana. But it was not merely the direct parody that attracted so much attention; rather, the illusion of community promoted by the hip jargon, the agreed values, the common rites, and relaxed tone—this was the chief source of attraction and interest. What was sought by commentator and reader alike was a way of life that would answer their feeling of pointlessness and guilt in looking at their own unrewarding accumulation of commodities. The beatniks not only evaded a society that, even its friendliest critics are quick to admit, has lost all community of motive; they went further and created an impenetrable community that turned the well-adjusted member of suburbia into a frustrated outsider. They shaped a way of life at once public and arcane. No wonder that the spectacle of Grant Avenue has produced so many dances of uncomprehending rage.

And yet is it not pathetic that the alternatives of American society should be posed in terms of Beatville and Squareville? If the beat and beatnik are the only answer to the wasteful cupidity of suburbia, then the country is in a very nasty spot. In truth, there is a vast fund of good sense and social responsibility in this country, and the only problem is to allow its voice to be heard more clearly and loudly. And if a rebellion is necessary, it will be fostered by people who have a sense of commitment to the insulted and injured of the world, who feel and act on an ideal of human conduct that sponsors change in individual experience, and who do not waste their substance on pointless conformity and aimless complaint. Some of those people live in suburbia, some in Bohemia, and many of them just anywhere; they respond to and shape their environment, and from such responsible shaping come the seeds of community and, finally, civilization.

In talking about the social phenomenon of the beat and beatnik, I deliberately distinguished between the two terms. The term "beat" I take to be descriptive, and its primary reference is to a group of writers, especially, who participate in certain common attitudes and pursue common literary aims. They may use the beatnik milieu as their subject and their ideas and attitudes may be widely shared by current Bohemia. The beatnik, on the other hand, is either not an artist or an incompetent and nonproductive one. The beatnik provides the atmosphere and audience of Grant Avenue and analogous areas, and he is frequently an

THOMAS PARKINSON

engaging person. He may write an occasional "poem," but he has no literary ambitions.

The beat writer, on the other hand, is serious and ambitious. He is usually well-educated and always a student of his craft. Sometimes, as is the case with Gary Snyder, he is a very learned man, and his knowledge of literature and its history is dense and extensive. Allen Ginsberg's public posture on literary matters is that of an innocent who writes from impulse, but he knows better. And one of my objections to Lawrence Ferlinghetti is that he is much too literary in tone and reference. He writes for the man in the street, but he chooses a street full of *Nation* subscribers and junior-college graduates, that is, Grant Avenue. In fact, the only untutored writer of the lot is Gregory Corso, and in his work this is neither a merit nor a handicap. His stock in trade is impertinence, and he learned that out of his own impish nature.

The reception of the beat writers, the extraordinary interest taken in the novels of Kerouac, Ginsberg's little pamphlet of poems, Ferlinghetti's *Coney Island of the Mind* (which has sold over 40,000 copies), the San Francisco issue of *Evergreen Review* (entering its seventh printing), and the publicity accorded the beat way of life by national magazines—all this has passed into not only social history but also literary history. When Meridian Books put out its anthology of *New Poets of England and America* in 1957, it included none of the beat writers and none of the writers of the San Francisco school and the Black Mountain group. Any anthology of recent poetry now appearing would practically have to include Ginsberg and Snyder, to say nothing of the nonbeat writers who have by accident been associated with them: William Everson (Brother Antoninus), Robert Creeley, Robert Duncan, Denise Levertov, Charles Olson, Kenneth Rexroth, and Jack Spicer, to name only those I take to be most distinguished.

The beat writers are not, in short, the only writers in America who live outside the universities and are not interested primarily in perpetuating the iambic line. This fact needs underlining, for one unhappy result of the publicity attendant on the rise of the beat was, simply, the tarring of all writers with experimental motives with the single brush *beat* or the further implication that the only valid experimental writers *were* beat. The terms "San Francisco Renaissance" (awakening would be more fitting) and "San Francisco writers," for instance, were cheerily applied to any writer who knew Allen Ginsberg or was published by Lawrence Ferlinghetti. As a matter of fact, only one of the writers on the City Lights list was even born in California. The writer in question is Robert Duncan, who is one of the best poets now writing in English and as nonbeat as a person can get.

The association of the beat writers with San Francisco is not entirely fortuitous. From about 1944 on, the area has been distinguished by considerable artistic activity, and during that period it was one of the strongholds of experimental poetry. There was a great deal of other literary activity, and I do not intend to depreciate the products of Stanford's writing program or of the Activist group associated with Lawrence Hart or the numerous writers who simply lived in the San Francisco Bay area because life was pleasant there or because they had jobs in the various colleges. But what especially distinguished writing in the Bay area was a group of people—mainly poets—who were interested in creating and establishing a community of literary interest. They were like coral insects building a reef that might ultimately create the calm and pleasure of a lagoon. They were interested in forming a culture rather than in shaping unimpeachable structures out of the detritus of a museum civilization. The poetry they wrote and liked was deeply religious in tone, personalist in dramaturgy, imagist in iconographic habit, and experimentalist in prosody. With this poetics was associated a loose cluster of concerns and attitudes—anarcho-pacifism in politics, relatively conservative (especially Roman Catholic) religious preoccupations, a generally receptive attitude toward Eastern art and thought that grew naturally out of the Pacific Basin orientation of the great port of San Francisco, intensive interest in the traditions of European experimentalism, and perhaps above all a very deep elegiac sense of the destruction of both the natural world and the possibilities of the American dream (its waste in the great wars and the frozen polity of the postwar period) dramatized in the brutal exploitation of California as its population swelled. Whatever was wrong with the poetry written out of these basic concerns, it was not a poetry that refused to meet squarely the challenges of great subjects.

This was accompanied by a widespread feeling of poetic community that took its center in activities organized by Robert Duncan, George Leite, and Kenneth Rexroth. George Leite's *Circle* magazine appeared first in 1944, and from then until 1950 he published ten issues of work local and international in origin. Its closest analogue in that period was the British magazine *Now*, which included many of the same contributors, and though Leite's editorial taste was far from infallible, the level of achievement was often very high. Some of his contributors—Henry Miller, Kenneth Rexroth, Josephine Miles, George P. Elliott, Robert Duncan, Brother Antoninus—have come to be well-known figures in current American letters, and a surprising number of his other contributors have been consistently productive. The attitudes that *Circle* espoused, both political and aesthetic, were hardly what could be called generally acceptable, and the magazine embodied the blithe indifference to the official culture that marked the early or postwar stages of the San Francisco Renaissance.

During the period of *Circle's* publication, Berkeley and San Francisco woke from their literary sleep of years. The chief figure in this awakening was Kenneth Rexroth. He was a poet nationally known at the time, printed by Macmillan and New Directions, and one of James Laughlin's advisors at the latter publishing house. He was interesting, well informed, friendly to the young. He gave the impression of truly patriarchal longevity. I said to him once that I had lost all my illusions about the Soviet Union at the time of the Finnish war. He said, "That just shows how young you are. I lost *my* illusions with the Kronstadt Rebellion." It was only much later that I came to realize that at the time of the rebellion he was fifteen years old, for he gave the impression that he had turned his back on Lenin with sorrow and withdrawn his counsel from the baby Soviet republics, leaving them to stumble on into disaster. He had a trick of imaginative projection that allowed him to suggest he was a contemporary of Lenin, Whitman, Tu Fu, Thoreau, Catullus, Baudelaire, John Stuart Mill—they were all so real to him. The amount of labor and confusion that he saved younger people was immense; one could be painfully working his way out of Dublin Catholicism, and he would talk of Buber or Lao-Tzu. Or with difficulty one could be moving toward understanding of his locale, and he would make some casual statement about Pacific Basin culture, adducing Morris Graves as exemplar. It would be easy to multiply instances. His recent collection of essays—*Bird in the Bush*—gives some idea of the range of his interests and talk.

Beyond his work as poet and critic, Rexroth organized discussion groups at his home, chiefly on political subjects though he conducted some literary seminars. He was certainly one of the best close readers of texts that I have ever encountered, and his technical knowledge of verse was wide, detailed, exact. I stress this because he has insisted recently on the indifference of such analysis to the study and writing of verse ("I write poetry to seduce women and overthrow the capitalist system"), and the record should be clarified. Chiefly, however, the discussions were political and religious with literary figures (Lawrence, Blake, Yeats) seen in the perspective of Schweitzer, Buber, Berdyaev, Kropotkin, Emma Goldmann, Toynbee, Gill, Boehme, Thoreau, Gandhi—the list could be extended indefinitely. When poetry was discussed directly, it tended to be French poetry since Apollinaire or the most recent British poetry; he was at that time engaged in his extensive translations from Léon-Paul Fargue, Cros, Carcot, Milosz, Desnos, Reverdy and in editing his anthology of British poetry since Auden. In addition to various poets and ordinary people, the discussions were attended by many of the conscientious objectors who after the war migrated in large numbers to the Bay area and had much to do with establishing the range of intellectual interest. For example, many of the founders of the famous listener-sponsored radio station KPFA-B (with branches now in Los Angeles and New York) were among the participants, and now that the station has become more staid and respectable, it is practically forgotten that the title of its governing board—Pacifica Foundation—was not a geographical but an intellectual designation.

In Berkeley too, partly because of the sudden upsurge of enrollment at the University of California after the war, there was a great deal of extra-academic literary activity. *Circle* was published there, and Bern Porter brought out some individual books of poetry. Robert Duncan, however, was most instrumental in organizing discussions and readings of poetry, and he was the first person in the Bay area who gave large-scale public poetry readings. These readings drew on the large and relatively mature postwar student body at the university for audience. As one sour witness put it, every clique must have its claque. Very true, but the extraordinary thing about the poets was their very great variety, their degree of disagreement. Through the poetry readings in Berkeley and San Francisco and—when it began operation in 1949—over KPFA, a fairly large audience was created that accepted and took interest in poetry readings.

From about 1950 to 1953, there was a period of dispersal when this embryonic literary community developed no further, and it was with the opening of the Poetry Center at San Francisco State College that poetry in the Bay area entered its most recent phase, in which the beat writers were involved. Through the Poetry Center, Mrs. Ruth Witt-Diamant brought to the area most of the important poets of the Anglo-American world, and it was largely because of the generosity of W. H. Auden that she was able to start this always precarious enterprise. Through her hard, thankless labor, a fixed center was established for poetry readings where widely recognized poets could be heard and young poets only emerging could get an immediate audience. As the writers associated earlier with the area began drifting back from their travels, things began to quicken again, and a newly emergent group of younger writers revived the earlier excitements. There were continuities between the by-now older poets and the younger, so that Michael McClure was in some ways a disciple of Robert Duncan, and Gary Snyder and Phil Whalen took much of their poetic method from Kenneth Rexroth. Duncan, through his association with Black Mountain College and his participation (by contributing) in *Origin,* helped to bring to the attention of the writers of the area the work of Charles Olson, Robert Creeley, and Denise Levertov; and Rexroth, who remained tirelessly interested in and receptive to experimental writing of all kinds, also kept people informed of the new and as yet generally unknown.

In other words, when Lawrence Ferlinghetti came to San Francisco in 1953 and Allen Ginsberg in 1954, they were not entering a cultural void, even restricting the sense of culture to experimental writing. It seems to me fruitless to argue whether writing in the San Francisco area has been notably original, just as it is fruitless to ask whether the San Francisco painters are really separable from the main currents of recent painting. In both instances it seems more useful to consider the quality of work produced and the extent to which the producers of the art learned from each other. In both painting and poetry, it seems to me perfectly clear that there *are* San Francisco schools, that is, significant groups of artists who have learned from each other profitably and have produced work capable of competing on equal terms with work produced in other cultural centers. In painting—David Park, Elmer Bischoff, Ernie Briggs, Sam Francis, Richard Diebenkorn, Clyfford Still; in poetry—Brother Antoninus,

Robert Duncan, Michael McClure, Kenneth Rexroth, Jack Spicer, Gary Snyder, Phil Whalen. Naturally all these artists have affinities with painters or writers from other parts of the world, and it is for this reason that their names are often associated with those of artists with whom they have nothing in particular to do.

When the beat writers came to the San Francisco area, then, they found a sounding board, so that Allen Ginsberg wrote *Howl* and related poems only after moving out to the west coast and read it first to Bay area audiences. The audience and structure of public address were there, and the literary atmosphere was receptive. Snyder, Whalen, and McClure, who were in effect a second wave of the Bay area awakening, joined forces with him, and when first Kerouac and later Corso made the trip, they also found an amiable reception. The presence of Lawrence Ferlinghetti as publisher also provided an outlet for at least Ginsberg and Corso, and so another phase in the literary life of the San Francisco area began.

In giving the historical background to the association of the beat writers with San Francisco, I am not trying to depreciate the personal role played by Allen Ginsberg in revivifying the poetic life of the Bay area. Too little stressed in all the public talk about Ginsberg are his personal sweetness and gentleness of disposition. He was a person more cohesive than disruptive in impact, and it was largely through his personal qualities, his extraordinary abilities as reader of his own verse, and his genuinely selfless dedication that the sense of literary community was again established. And he wrote well. In spite of all the miscellaneous demurs against *Howl*, it still stands as a moving and important poem, and I suspect that it will hold up for a long time. And Lawrence Ferlinghetti, with his quiet easiness of manner, his very great skill as public reader, and his persistent courage, was a force of equal importance and pertinacity. It takes nothing from either of them to say they were supported by an environment that, in turn, they changed. Their great contribution was in the expression of new motives and their creation—or recognition—of a new audience. The singular force of the beat writers is manifest in the fact that they did not merely reflect the audience of American Bohemia; they substantially altered that audience, and in so doing they liberated and clarified motives until then only imperfectly realized. The intensity of reaction to their work indicates that the motives embodied in Kerouac's *On the Road* and *The Subterraneans* strike some sensitive hidden nerve that is more important than, before the appearance of those works, many had cared to admit.

I have taken such historical pains because there are two confusions that I think should be unraveled. First, the best experimental poetry in the United States is not necessarily beat, anymore than the beatnik pattern of conduct is the only valid response to the life of the organization man. Second, the beat writers, with the exception of McClure, Snyder, and Whalen, are all easterners whose relations with northern California are either fugitive or nonexistent. A person moving from the Left Bank to Greenwich Village to North Beach is not leaving home but is remaining in a basically constant society. The scene changes but the emotional milieu is fixed, existentialist costumes, jazz, and all. When Kerouac writes of the West Coast, he does so with a tourist's eye; it is all copy, raw material to be exploited, not substantial. No one objects to this seriously, but it is a little annoying to Californians to hear William Burroughs described as a San Francisco writer when he has not, so far as I know, ever set foot in the state. It is all the more annoying when the result is a distortion of historical fact that muddies waters.

More important than such minor pique, however, is the question of the association of all experimental writing with the beat movement. What happened in 1956 when the national news media became aware of the beat writers was a taking off of the lid. Laments had been issued because of the dullness and sameness of American poetry, and as the cold war thawed, there seemed room for a little more freewheeling treatment of experience. At the same time, there was no reason for taking such a matter too far, and the beats were suited for a surprisingly moderate role. They presented a spectacle of a romantically dark community that repelled and attracted, that satisfied and thrilled without inviting. It was possible to feel at once sympathetic, envious, and superior to the way of life they embodied. So too with the writing: if this was all that existed outside the finicky preciousness of the dandy and the plodding wholesomeness of the women's magazines, who could seek or be interested in a change of intellectual diet? In effect, it was possible to talk their work to death by considering only their odd habits, and since their contempt for the intellect preserved them from any rational critical self-defense, they could become figures of derisive fun. The fact that Gregory Corso publicly boasted that he has never combed his hair has led to the belief that he could not then have taken much care with his poetry. The quality of the work could then remain unexamined.

Of the writers represented in this casebook, several seem to me important figures, not merely as social phenomena but as literary artificers of some accomplishment. The best comments on *Howl* are probably those made by Kenneth Rexroth and Mark Schorer during the obscenity trial (see pp. 125–135), and they suggest its remarkable qualities quite clearly. I have always felt that Ginsberg is the genuine article, and if he keeps on writing he will probably become a very important poet. Both he and Ferlinghetti are extremely gifted readers—entertainers—and they have been extraordinarily effective in bringing poetry to a widened audience.

A certain amount of ironic comment has been made on the importance of oral delivery and the writer's physical dramatic presence to the full impact of the poetry of Ginsberg and Ferlinghetti. Their poetry, and that of McClure and Whalen (and Snyder, to a lesser extent), attempts notation of the actual movement of mind and voice in full vernacular. It seems difficult to take this poetry off the page largely because the mode of poetic notation that fits the movement of American speech is still in the realm of the nonconventionalized. Accustomed to syllabic stress and foot verse, the normal audience for poetry is not prepared to take into consideration intensity (loudness), pitch, and duration, and the concept of breath pause is far from being ritualized. The usual prosodic assumption is that the precise notation so readily accepted for music is not possible for poetry, that poetry will have to bumble along with concepts that more or less fit the products of another tone and tempo of speech. This seems to me predicated on a happy combination of ignorance and laziness, ignorance of the past and laziness in the face of actual problems of current experience. The primary problem of poetry is notation, through the appearance of poem on page to indicate the reality of articulation. A poem is a score.

Looked on in this way, much of the notation of this poetry ceases to seem odd or frivolous. The capital letters, the broken lines, the long long long lines, the shift from vernacular idiom to lofty rhetoric, these are attempts to shift from conventional idiom to actual, to increase the vocality of the verse. The experiments with jazz accompaniment are more dramatic instances of the stress on precision of notation.

Related to the concept of vocality that underlies much of this poetry and brings it over into the world of performance and entertainment is the concept of intimacy that affects both prose and poetry. The beat poet is best considered as a voice, the beat prose writer as an active revery. Into this revery come past and present, but the revery is chiefly preoccupied with keeping up with the process unfolding outside and inside the narrator. Hence the long sentences, endlessly attempting to include the endless, the carelessness—even negligence—with the ordinary rules of grammatical function, so that noun, adjective, and verb interchange roles; after all, if the process is endlessly unpredictable and unfixed, grammatical categories are not relevant. It is a syntax of aimlessly continuing pleasure in which all elements are "like." Release, liberation from fixed categories, hilarity—it is an ongoing prose that cannot be concerned with its origins. There are no origins and no end, and the solid page of type without discriminations is the image of life solidly continuous without discriminations in value, and yet incomplete because it is literally one damned thing after another with no salvation or cease. There are no last things in this prose whereas the very division of experience into lines compels the discrimination of element from element. Even a poetic catalogue, which is by definition one thing after another, moves in blocks which have weight, and even if each unit weighs the same, the total weight increases with each succeeding integer. Not so in prose, the only limits coming from the size of the page. The ideal book by a writer of beat prose would be written on a single string of paper, printed on a roll, and moving endlessly from right to left, like a typewriter ribbon.

Is there anything especially new about this sense of endlessness in prose or of vocal notation in poetry? *Finnegans Wake* and Molly Bloom's soliloquy at the close of *Ulysses* could also be printed on a ribbon without violating James Joyce's intention, and the classical experimental poetry of the twentieth century had as one chief aim the kind of precise notation that I have suggested as a major motive in beat poetry. There is nothing new under the sun, even the American sun, granted, but this would not disturb the beat writers. They are perfectly happy to place themselves in a tradition of experimental writing, and they are alert to the existence of writers they can claim as ancestors. They assume that this experimental tradition should be consolidated and extended, and they do not consider it as part of the conventional work of English writers. The experimental era could be looked on as an attempt to vivify the conventions of English verse and prose, that is, as extension of the normal performances of, say, Dickens and Tennyson, corrective to it, part of the loyal opposition. In this sense, it can be assimilated into the institution of literature as generally—that is, academically —understood, just as Blake can be memorialized in Westminster Abbey.

In another sense, the experimental writers destroyed convention in order to create a completely new way of looking at experience and cannot be assimilated into the existing institution. In this view, the aim of literary creation is not to enrich the tradition but to expose its poverty and irrelevance so that it can be swept aside in favor of a literature more responsive to the realities of experience. The question raised by this aim has wide implications, for education, for politics, for human understanding. I have heard William Carlos Williams say that the poet who invented a new measure, a new line, would change the world radically. The scientists at Alamagordo certainly did change the world, as did the biochemists who produced antibiotics, and the technicians working on increased automation. Whether a literature proportionate to technological change is in the process of being shaped is certainly a question worth asking. But by the same token, one might also ask whether this literature is not merely an expression of the hopelessness and consequent frivolity that affects a world shaken to its foundations as its population, power, and problems multiply.

These are fundamental questions that may be too large for the context of beat writing. In the history of American life and letters, the phenomenon of the beat may have been a spasm rather than a "generation," and the final importance of the movement will be seen only when a larger *oeuvre* is available from its several writers. The test of literature is the knowledge it realizes, using knowledge in the fullest and least exclusive sense, and literature realizes knowledge by the labor of that intelligent love we think of as art. It may be an unfair comparison, but to read Theodore Dreiser after reading Jack Kerouac—Dreiser knew so much and had so intelligent a love of life and art that he could compose an image of an entire society. He established a norm for American writers, and it is against the measure of human force represented by Cowperwood, Witla, Carrie, Jennie Gerhardt, Lester Kane, and Clyde Griffith that any claim to embodying an image for a generation has to be placed.

The image shaped by the beat writers is partial, but without it any sense of life in these post-atom bomb years is incomplete. The solution is not, as is often absurdly suggested, to add Bohemia to suburbia and divide by two, thus achieving a golden mean or a shabby compromise. The solution is to be, where you are, what you are, with such persistence and courage as can be called to life. The best of the beat writers exemplify precisely that state of secular grace. In this world of shifting conflicts the integrity of the person might not be enough, but without it, all else is lost.

# Lawrence Lipton

## FROM *THE HOLY BARBARIANS*

### THE SOCIAL LIE

"Since all society is organized in the interest of exploiting classes and since if men knew this they would cease to work and society would fall apart, it has always been necessary, at least since the urban revolutions, for societies to be governed ideologically by a system of fraud."

This is the Social Lie, according to Kenneth Rexroth.

"There is an unending series of sayings which are taught at your mother's knee and in school, and they simply are not true. And all sensible men know this, of course."

Does the rejection of the social lie imply a rejection of the idea of a "social contract"?

"This," says Rexroth, "is the old deliberate confusion between society and the state, culture and civilization and so forth and so on. There was once a man by the name of Oppenheimer who was very popular in anarchist circles. He said the state was going to wither away in a sort of utopia of bureaucrats who serve the state. And you are always being told that your taxes go to provide you with services. This is what they teach in school as social studies. There is nothing contractural about it. There is an organic relationship which has endured from the time that man became a group animal and is as essential a part of his biology as his fingernails. That other thing, the state, is fraudulent. The state does not tax you to provide you with services. [293] The state taxes you to kill you. The services are something which it has kidnapped from you in your organic relations with your fellow man, to justify its police and war-making powers. It provides no sevices at all. There is no such thing as a social contract. This is just an eighteenth century piece of verbalism."

Reprinted from Lawrence Lipton, *The Holy Barbarians* (New York: Julian Messner, Inc., 1959), pp. 293–309, 315–318. Reprinted by permission of Julian Messner, Inc. Copyright 1959 by Lawrence Lipton.

And what of services like sanitation, water and, in some communities, also public utilities like gas and electricity?

"These are not functions of the state at all. These are normal functions of the community which have been invaded by the state, which are used by the state to mask its own actual activities, like the mask that the burglar wears. Conceivably a burglar could wear a mask of Kim Novak but this doesn't mean he is Kim Novak, he is still a burglar. The state has invaded and taken over the normal community relations of men. Now, it is true that if the state was suddenly to give this up today, people would probably go out and chop down all the trees in the national forests and kill all the bears in the national parks, catch all the fish in the rivers and so forth and so on. But this is due to six thousand years of exploitation and corruption by the state, not due to anything inherent in the community of man."

In rejecting the social lie, what is the disaffiliate disaffiliating himself from?

"He isn't disaffiliated from society, he is disaffiliated from the social order, from the state and the capitalist system. There is nothing unusual about this. It's just that in America there is an immense myth which is promulgated by the horrors of Madison Avenue and Morningside Heights, by the professors and the advertising men (the two are now practically indistinguishable), that intellectual achievement lies within the social order and that you can be a great poet as an advertising man, a great thinker as a professor, and of course this isn't true. There happens to be a peculiar situation in literature due to the fact that literature —and this is true of Russia too—that literature is the thing that sells the ideology. After all, just as the scribe knew in ancient Egypt, writing and handling words is the thing that sells the ruling class to the ruled. So departments of English are particularly whorish. On the other hand, a philosopher like Pitrim Sirokin can say at a meeting of a philosophical association, of course we are operating on the assumption that politics attracts only the lowest criminal types—he happened to be speaking of the president of the United States—[294]

"The entire pressure of the social order is always to turn literature into advertising. This is what they shoot people for in Russia, because they are bad advertising men."

What is it, then, that holds the natural community of men together?

"The organic community of men is a community of love. This

doesn't mean that it's all a great gang fuck. In fact, it doesn't have anything to do with that at all. It means that what holds a natural society together is an all-pervading Eros which is an extension and reflection, a multiple reflection, of the satisfactions which are eventually traced to the actual lover and beloved. Out of the union of the lover and the lover as the basic unit of society flares this whole community of love.

"Curiously enough, this is Hegelianism, particularly the neo-Hegelians who are the only people who ever envisaged a multiple absolute which was a community of love. It is unfortunate that the Judaeo-Christian wrath of Marx and the Prussianism of Engels has so transformed us that we forget that this is what lay back of the whole notion of the Hegelian absolute. But, irrespective of the metaphysical meanings, this is what makes a primitive society work. The reason that the Zunis all get along together is that they are bound together by rays which are emitted from one lamp and reflected from one lamp to another and these rays are ultimately traced back to their sources in each lamp in the act of the lover and the beloved. So the whole community is a community of lovers. This sounds very romantic but it is actually quite anthropological."

To counter this cohesive social force the state employs the social lie.

"The masters, whether they be priests or kings or capitalists, when they want to exploit you, the first thing they have to do is demoralize you, and they demoralize you very simply by kicking you in the nuts. This is how it's done. Nobody is going to read any advertising copy if he is what the Reichians call orgastically potent. This is a principle of the advertising copy writer, that he must stir up discontent in the family. Modern American advertising is aimed at the woman, who is, if not always the buyer at least the pesterer, and it is designed to create sexual discontent. Children are affected too—there is a deliberate appeal to them—you see, children have very primitive emotional possibilities which do not normally function except in the nightmares of Freudians. Television is designed to arouse the most perverse, sadistic, acquisitive drives. I mean, a child's television program is a real vision [295] of hell, and it's only because we are so used to these things that we pass them over. If any of the people who have had visions of hell, like Vergil or Dante or Homer, were to see these things it would scare them into fits.

"But with the adult, the young married couple, which is the

object of almost all advertising, the copy is pitched to stir up insatiable sexual discontent. It provides pictures of women who never existed. A guy gets in bed with his wife and she isn't like that and so he is discontented all the time and is therefore fit material for exploitation."

To avoid the pressures of advertising and the slanted propaganda of the State in the "news" pages and on the radio and television, the beat generation rarely buys newspapers or news magazines and rarely tunes in to radio or TV. With very few exceptions, all the young people I interviewed said they never read newspapers at all, glance at *Time* or *Newsweek* now and then, but only at the back of the magazine, passing up all the news, domestic and international. They all own radios but listen only to the jazz programs and an occasional newscast when something interesting is going on like the launching of a space rocket. The few who own television sets use them only to watch the two or three programs a month that offer adult shows, like "Omnibus," or a jazz program. If there are any commercials they are never too lazy or too lost in pot or contemplation to get up and cut out the sound till it's over. I have known them to deliberately pass up merchandise that is advertised in favor of an unadvertised brand, regardless of merit.

### The Social Lie of Militarism

To the beat generation advertising is the No. 1 shuck only because it is the most ubiquitous. There are others which are equally if not more important. There is almost universal agreement among them that militarism and war is the biggest shuck of all. As long ago as 1951 *Time* reported that among the younger generation "hardly anyone" wanted to go into the Army and there was "little enthusiasm for the military life . . . no enthusiasm for war." But the draft boards could rest easy, *Time* concluded, for when they are called "youth will serve." By 1956 *Life* was selling military service to the youth as "job opportunities," in line with the official posters—Plan for a Brighter Future, [296] Learn a Trade, etc.—and offering advice on how to "break it up in a number of ways" by serving "as little as six months at one stretch of active duty," by enlisting and getting a choice of duty, etc. For *Time* it was still the Silent Generation, eager to conform and ready to serve.

But the Army knew better. It knew that behind the façade of

silence lay a sullen resistance to soldiering and everything connected with it. It was not confined to any disaffiliated minority. It was quite prevalent among the youth in the armed services. As early as the middle forties Colonel (now Brigadier General) S. L. A. Marshall had called attention to it in the *Infantry Journal* and, in 1947, he published his findings in a book, *Men Against Fire.*

He (the normal American ground soldier) is what his home, his religion, his schooling, and the moral code and ideals of his society have made him. The Army cannot unmake him. It must reckon with the fact that he comes from a civilization in which aggression, connected with the taking of life, is prohibited and unacceptable. The teaching and the ideals of that civilization are against killing, against taking advantage. The fear of aggression has been expressed to him strongly and absorbed by him so deeply and pervadingly—practically with his mother's milk—that it is part of the normal man's emotional make-up. This is his great handicap when he enters combat. It stays his trigger finger even though he is hardly conscious that it is a restraint upon him. Because it is an emotional and not an intellectual handicap, it is not removable by intellectual reasoning such as: "Kill or be killed."

The disaffiliated among the beat generation would not take issue with the general's premise that the teaching of our civilization is against killing, against taking advantage. The preaching and the teaching *is* against it, but in practice our whole civilization is a perfect school for killing and taking advantage, they would tell him.

Line commanders (the general goes on to say) pay little attention to the true nature of this mental block. They take it more or less for granted that if the man is put on such easy terms with his weapon in training that he "loves to fire," this is the main step toward surmounting the general difficulty. But it isn't as easy as that. A revealing light is thrown on this subject through the studies [297] by Medical Corps psychiatrists of the combat fatigue cases in the European Theater. They found that fear of killing, rather than fear of being killed, was the most common cause of battle failure in the individual, and that fear of failure ran a strong second.

It is therefore unreasonable to believe that the average and normally healthy individual—the man who can endure the mental and physical stresses of combat—still has such an inner and usually unrealized resistance toward killing a fellow man that he will not of his own volition take life if it is possible to turn away from that responsibility. Though it is improbable that he may ever analyze his own feelings so searchingly as to know what is stopping his own hand, his hand is nonetheless stopped. At the vital point, he becomes a conscientious objector, unknowing.

The disaffiliated of the younger generation are those who are conscious of their objections long before they are confronted with "Kill or be killed." They have analyzed their own feelings searchingly and know perfectly well what is stopping their hand. If they do not always make conscientious objector it is not from lack of awareness. There is no party line in this matter. "Pacifism is not something you talk about, it is not a matter of 'principle,'" they will tell you. "You don't know what you will do about killing or being killed till you are confronted with it. Pacifism isn't something you believe in or don't believe in. It is something you *do* or *don't* do. It is an *act*, not a statement."

But all the young men I have spoken with are doubtful that they could bring themselves to fire a gun if the enemy were in view, or kill at close quarters unless it became a question of He or I. In this, apparently, they are no different from the majority.

Now I do not think (continues the general) I have seen it stated in the military manuals of this age, or in any of the writings meant for the instruction of those who lead troops, that a commander of infantry will be well advised to believe that when he engages the enemy not more than a quarter of his men will ever strike a real blow unless they are compelled by almost overpowering circumstances or unless all junior leaders constantly "ride herd" on troops with the specific mission of increasing their fire.

The 25 per cent estimate stands even for well-trained and campaign-seasoned troops. I mean that 75 per cent will not fire or will not persist in firing against the enemy and his works. These men may face the danger but they will not fight. [298]

These figures will not come as any surprise to the men who were drafted for service in the Korean "police action" at about the same time that *Time* was assuring the draft boards that they would serve. They did, but with what results? Here are some excerpts from a report by Bill Davidson in *Collier's* of November 8, 1952.

In pursuing the question of why soldiers don't shoot, I spoke with dozens of scientists, Army historians, combat commanders and noncommissioned officers who had just returned from the Korean front. Nearly all told the same story. At Fort Dix, in particular, I had a revealing series of bull sessions with a group of noncom heroes of the U.S. Infantry.

"It was rough," said Master Sergeant Nicholas Smith, of Washington, D.C., a recent Distinguished Service Cross winner in Korea. "Sometimes you sent a squad to cover your flank and, instead of nine rifles firing, you only heard two or three."

"That's right," said Sergeant Thomas McGrath of Haddon Heights, New Jersey (Silver Star, Bronze Star, Purple Heart). "Of the nine men in my squad in Korea, I never could count on more than four or five to fire, even when it meant saving their own lives."

"Time and again," said Master Sergeant John S. Williams of Flushing, New York (two Silver Stars, three Bronze Stars, five Purple Hearts), "I had to expose myself and crawl from foxhole to foxhole to get half of the platoon to fire. Sometimes I'd practically have to sight the rifle and pull the trigger for the guy." . . . One of the most clear-cut cases in Korea involved a platoon of the 38th Infantry Regiment; it had collapsed, allowing a serious enemy break-through. The platoon came back with virtually all its ammunition unfired . . . Brigadier General S.L.A. Marshall, who has been described by high Army sources as "undoubtedly knowing more about this subject than any other living man" . . . recently spent five months in the front lines in Korea analyzing Chinese tactics for the United Nations forces. . . .

Marshall learned that of the more than 1,000 men in the reinforced battalion (the 3rd Battalion of the 165th Infantry Regiment) only 37 had fired their weapons. He just thought the outfit was green. But a few weeks later, on Chance Island in the Marshalls, he did a similar group investigation of a gallant action by the crack Reconnaissance Troop of the 7th Infantry Division. Of the 100 men in the fight, only 14 had done all the firing that routed the enemy. . . . I went to the University of Michigan to talk to two [299] outstanding military psychiatrists: Dr. Raymond W. Waggoner is head of the university's department of psychiatry and an advisor on psychiatric problems of the draft to Director of Selective Service Major Lewis B. Hershey; Dr. M. M. Frohlich is a psychiatrist who, as a lieutenant colonel during World War II, handled thousands of combat-fatigue casualties at the 298th General Hospital. They cited case after case of soldiers developing actual paralysis on the battlefield the first time they were required to fire.

Dr. Frohlich suggested there are at least three ways "preferably to be used in combination" of removing these inhibitions temporarily so that soldiers will shoot. The most efficient is to prompt them to lose their individual identities by promoting a mob psychology. People in a mob override their inhibitions and act as they would never dare act as individuals. A second approach is to make the man feel that because he's in uniform and because he's an integral part of a group of men he likes and respects, somehow it is all right to join them in setting aside one's life-long inhibitions against killing. The third tack is to provide a man with a father-like leader who, he can believe, is supremely strong, wise and just; so that he will accept his leader's orders to set aside temporarily the taboos against killing.

Any member of the beat generation can tell you, without any coaching from a psychiatrist, that the first tack is in regular use in the South, among lynch mobs, but it works only where the individuals of the mob are sure they outnumber the quarry by at least a hundred to one, something you cannot always promise the men on the firing line. Something of the sort was tried, nevertheless, by trying to make out the enemy to be "niggers" of a sort—"gooks" was the name for it in the Korean War; in World War II it was "them little brown monkeys" on the Pacific front. The second approach is to be found in its most successful form among the juvenile delinquent gangs. And the third tack was the one used with the S. S. elite guard by Hitler and with the Red Army by Stalin.

The most dramatic innovation has been talking-it-up—the yelling in combat which has accompanied many of our most heroic actions in Korea. . . . "Let 'em holler," Marshall advocated. . . . "The yelling . . . can stir up chain reactions that will convert lambs into lions on the battlefield." [300]

Grant Flemming, home on Christmas furlough from basic training, had this comment to make on the way Marshall's "Let 'em holler" training technique was working out in the year 1958.

"In bayonet practice we are told to make the bloodthirstiest sounds we can with every thrust. Every now and then the sergeant yells 'What's the spirit of the bayonet?' and we're supposed to yell back 'To kill.' I try to get away without saying it and so do some of the other boys, and when we do we smile to each other when we do it. Like it's just a shuck and we make a joke out of it. Then again they'll turn it the other way around. They'll tell us that the aim of warfare is not to kill but to take enemy-held ground, and to think of the enemy positions as the enemy—trying to depersonalize and dehumanize the act of killing. They tried that in Korea, too. Some of the re-enlisted men at the base went through the Korean action and they tell me that what they did was keep firing their rifles in the air just to make a noise to satisfy their commanding officers."

After three months of basic, much of the time spent in the hospital with ailments that may well be diagnosed as plain malingering, the Army was satisfied to transfer Grant to a medical unit. "Now it's round-about-face for me. Instead of learning how to destroy life I am learning how to save it. How that is going to work out under fire, if it ever comes to that for me, I don't know. It will probably turn out to be the same old shuck."

A somewhat older disaffiliate, who describes himself as a veteran of World War II and who also served his country for a few days in the county jail, turned up in Venice West for a visit and left with me an interesting document of his own version of pacifism as a revolutionary, nonviolence resistance movement.

It is a Questionnaire for a Peacemaker (one of the pacifist organizations) Directory and Personal Resources File which he filled out. After giving his name, address, birth date and other information, he answered the remaining questions in this fashion:

6. Present vocation (specific description):
   Fanning flames of discontent, translating, arguing, speaking.
7. Past employment (specific descriptions): Helped to load junk on and off junk wagon as employee; junked as self-employed paper boy; collector of charges for newspaper delivery; cleaned desks and helped (?) mechanical drawing students as NYA worker; loaded [301] mail bags on skiffs; cleaned canning machines; peeled carrots; loaded cans on conveyor belts; shoveled coal; domestic work (cleaned floors, waxed furniture, etc.); taught the alphabet; picketed for union.
8. Education (how long: where: subjects):
   B.A. June 1952, Roosevelt College. Sociology major, Psych minor.
9. Skills not being used in vocation at present:
   Student skills, if any, are not being used.
10. Avocational interests and skills:
    Table tennis, swimming and digging the sound.
11. Eventual vocational aims:
    Are you kidding? What can one plan for under threat of global thermonuclear war?
12. Do you own your own home? No. Rent? Sort of. Live with relatives? Yes.
13. Do you own a car? No. Truck? No. Farm machinery? No. Tools and machines needed in vocation? Describe:

Pen (preferably ball point) note and address book, English dictionary, more dictionaries, paper, carrying case, literature, envelopes, stamps, chewing gum . . .

14. Do you have room in your home and are you willing to put up traveling Peacemakers? (State any limitations as to time, space, finances, etc.):
My brother Joe has not very long ago returned from Lexington, Ky., where he kicked the habit. He is using the extra bed until he can get back on his feet. Ergo, no room for traveling Peacemaker (at this writing).

15. Are you or were you a draft refuser? Yes. CPS? No. Prison? No. (Give details): I refused to register in 1948; automatically registered in 1950; publicly burned classification card (5-A) and questionnaire in July 1951; I am a veteran of 1941-45 war. (However, I did spend a few days in County Jail in Dec. 1943, occasioned by unwillingness to report for induction. I did not go to big house because I lacked courage to follow thru on convictions.)

16. If over draft age or a woman, do you openly counsel draft refusal? Yes. Does your spouse? I reject compulsory monogamous mating. Affirm free love. Tend toward the sexual revolution theories of Wilhelm Reich. [302]

17. Are you a tax refuser? No, too poor. Would you be if your income were large enough? Yes. If your taxes were not withheld at sources, etc? Yes. I cut out movies two or three years ago in order to avoid the treasury contribution collected at the box office.

18. In what activities do you participate in your local community? (PTA, labor union, Farm Bureau, Rotary Club, church, pacifist groups, etc.)
Peacemakers, CORE, IWW socials and picnics, Liberation Socialist Comm; Washington Park Forum. And when afforded, the wild life at Whitman House.

19. Do you consider yourself permanently settled in your present community, or are you willing to or actively interested in moving elsewhere?
Am considering moving off a target such as Chicago to some place of no strategic value. (A non-violent revolution can alter this perspective.)

20. Would you be interested in joining a Peacemaker Unit of a permanent type? Possibly. Of a training type? Possibly. (Give details):

Am not altogether sure what all this may involve, but do have predilection for this sort of thing. See Ques. 19.

21. Are you interested in any particular state or region in this country? The unexplored wilds of Idaho. See Ques. 19. A foreign country?
    Lower California. See Ques. 19. Would be interested in southern Chile for same reason, only I don't know how I would get there since I don't believe in asking State for permission to travel.

22. Do you prefer to live in a rural area? Small town? Small city? Large city?
    Used to large city. Don't know about other places, tho I expect they might be boring.

23. In what types of Peacemaker activity are you most interested and do you consider yourself most fitted to participate?
    Interested in Direct Action, violating national boundaries, law-breaking aspects of Peacemaker activity.

24. Do you live in or are you interested in living in a status of "voluntary poverty?" A communal set-up where all assets, income are pooled and funds for needs taken from common purse?
    I do live in a condition of poverty which is probably voluntary, [303] since I have not been seeking work. I might be too extravagant to fit in successfully in a wholly communistic set-up tho I am willing to try it.

25. Do you feel personally able to live communally with a group of other families and individuals, perhaps in the same house? Or do you feel you and your family need private living quarters?
    Me and my "family" have no need of private living quarters, which is to say, I would live communally, *sans* family, as it does not share my views enough.

26. Do you belong to some mutual aid group or have you definite plans for your family in case you are sent to prison? No.

27. If both you and your wife were sent to prison, what would you do or want to do with your children?
    See Ques. 16. As for children, I imagine they would be left to the vicissitudes of the American Way of Life, if there were no Peacemaker provision for them.

28. Any additional information which would be of value to Peacemaker committees and to individual members:
    I am anarchist. I think the correct response to arrest is to

go limp and make no distinctions between being arrested and being drafted. Am vet of WW II. I regard myself as a stateless person of the world, cosmopolitan. I make no distinction between anarchism and (the non-violent type of) pacifism.

29. Comments on present Peacemaker program, your part in that program:

The Peacemaker publication is very disappointing to say the least and the kindest. It does not nearly enough reflect the aggressiveness, intransigeance, non-conformity and subversiveness that one should expect from a revolutionary pacifist movement. There is too much God, too much law, and too much World Government. There are too many lifts from *Peace News* and other publications and not enough "internal discussion." Peacemakers should forge toward a bootleg economic system in order to circumvent hidden taxes. Taxation *as such* should be rejected on non-violent grounds.

Our visitor—I am sure he will reject this anonymity and I am doubly sure he would resent any pseudonymity—was dressed as near to Gandhian simplicity as the weather permitted, carrying all his possessions [304] in a cloth shopping bag. He asked for nothing and accepted only simple refreshment. Holy, but no barbarian, he presented the classical picture of the lean, weather-beaten, ascetic desert-prophet of the Bible illustrators. Your true holy barbarian is no ascetic. Some of the answers in the Questionnaire will be better understood by the reader if he bears in mind that the minority status of my visitor is further complicated by the fact that he is a Negro. How the practice of "going limp" on arrest works out in practice the reader can judge for himself by the pictures he has seen in the press from time to time of Direct Action war resisters being carried off limp by policemen and military guards from missile-launching sites and other military installations where they were staging a nonviolent protest demonstration. They measure their success by the amount of publicity such actions produce, depending on the power of action and example rather than principles and manifestoes.

They do not altogether disdain the power of the word, however. One such resister, Albert Bofman of Chicago, carries on a constant letters-to-the-editor campaign and reports the most astonishing results in a mimeographed letter that he sends to anyone requesting it. These letters sometimes run to ten or twelve

single-spaced, legal-size pages and contain news of pacifist activities all over the world, the latest figures on war appropriations,
digests of election platforms of all parties and reams of other information of use to war resisters and their friends and sympathizers. These letters differ from other such literature in the
modesty of their requests for contributions. "Unused postage
stamps acceptable" is the usual request, and the prices of the
pamphlets they offer are rarely over a nickel or a dime. Bofman
reports publication of his "letters to the editor" in hundreds of
newspapers, some of them among the most reactionary in the
country. Editors of such Vox Pop columns are, as everyone knows,
very liberal in what they accept for publication. It all comes
under the heading of human interest, I suppose.

Nonviolent war resisters like my visitor are received hospitably
in beat generation circles and treated with respect as disaffiliates
who are wise to the social lie of war and militarism and practitioners of the dedicated independent poverty. In some respects
they are regarded as squares. Their asceticism does not go with
the Dionysian love of life that the beat cultivate. Their religion,
though anticlerical in some cases, [305] is in the main churchly.
The conscientious objector among the beat may base his objections
on religious grounds but not as a member of any church. A few
have won their cases in the courts on such grounds, although
the law does state that church membership is required as ground
for exemption.

### The Social Lie of Politics

That the typical member of the beat generation does not regard
himself as a citizen in the usual meaning of that term is clear
from all my observations and interviews. He does not value his
right to vote, although he would be opposed to any move to take
it away from those who do. His attitude toward the ballot is
simply that it is usually meaningingless; it does not present such
vital issues as war and peace to the voter nor give him any voice
in—or control over—such important matters as wages, prices,
rents, and only the most indirect and ineffective control over taxation. His choices at the polls are limited by such tricky devices as
conventions, gerrymandering, legal restrictions on party representation on the ballot, to say nothing of boss rule, back room
deals and big campaign contributions. Elections are rigged, he
will tell you, and the whole political game is a shuck.

He does not have to spend a dime for a newspaper or waste reading time in order to document his thesis that politics is a social lie. All he has to do is glance at the headlines as he passes the newsstand. Or listen to any five-minute summary of the news on the radio. Or—the plainest giveaway of all—look at the face and listen to the voice of any office-seeking politician on television. As for national conventions on television, the spectacle is too much for even the squares to take. They turned out by the millions on the last convention broadcasts.

A beatnik busted for smoking pot could entertain you for hours about the lawbreaking of the lawmakers. And the law enforcers. For an apolitical he often displays a surprising knowledge of the above-the-law, around-the-law and against-the-law activities of policemen and politicians.

All the vital decisions, he will tell you, are beyond the control of the electorate, so why go to the polls? The decision makers and the taste makers are nonelective and nonappointive. They elect themselves and their ballot is the dollar. Moneytheism is not only a religion but a [306] form of *Realpolitik*. The moves of power politicians, once covert, are now open. Even the businessman in politics no longer feels constrained to mask his motives or his methods. More and more the show goes on the boards without props and without disguises.

The voter has no control over the uses to which atomic energy is being put by the businessman and the politician. Cold wars are launched without declaration and are well under way in the Pentagon and the State Department before he is told that they are even contemplated. The war machine is fed billions without any by-your-leave on the ballot. He is presented with a choice between a general with a folksy grin and a governor with an egghead vocabulary. Voting becomes a mass ritual, but an empty one without any art or healing in it. It was once a kind of popular revel at least, a saturnalia on a low and vulgar level, with whisky for a libation and broken bottles in place of phallic ikons. But even that is now forbidden, thanks to the prohibitionists who have made Election Day their last stand and only national triumph.

The voter, the beat generation will tell you, does not have any control even over the air he breathes. What's good for General Motors is proving to be poisonous for the American air. And what's good for the defense industries, and is conned up to look good in the employment statistics, is proving poisonous to the atmosphere of the whole globe. "Have you had your Strontium

FROM *THE HOLY BARBARIANS*

90 today?" is a greeting you will hear any morning among the beat.

The list of shucks that the disaffiliate can reel off for you would take many pages to repeat here. A few, on which there is more or less unanimous agreement, will have to suffice.

First in order is the shuck of war, hot or cold, and the "defense" industries that are maintained to feed and perpetuate it, which the beat call Murder, Incorporated.

A close second is the shuck of "business ethics" and the morality of the businessman, the wide profit margin between his pretensions and his practices. Even the youngest among the beat generation are thoroughly familiar with the call girl sell, for instance, the bedroom bribery by which the businessmen bribe (and blackmail) buyers to the tune of millions of dollars. The older ones among the beat have not forgotten the cost-plus racket on defense contracts that created bulging bank accounts for the new war millionaires while the boys were fighting a [307] battle of another kind of bulge in the Ardennes and planting Old Glory on a hilltop on Iwo Jima.

Another widely recognized shuck is the "Our" shuck. *Our* national safety . . . *our* natural resources . . . *our* railroads . . . *our* security . . . *our* national honor . . . *our* foreign trade . . . *our* annual income . . . *our* representative in Congress . . . *our* side of the iron curtain . . . It's *ours* when it's our sweat and blood they want, but it's theirs when it comes to the profits, the beat will tell you.

They didn't need Philip Wylie to tell them about the shuck of Momism—or Popism, either. Academicism was an open book to them long before it became a theme for faculty exposés in novels and what's-wrong-with-our-educational-system articles in magazines.

All of these shucks, and many more, are known to millions. The difference between the beatnik and the square is that the beatnik *acts* on his knowledge and tries to avoid the avoidable contagions.

"Cynical" is a word that the sensation-mongering newspaper and magazine writers like to tag onto their stories about the beat generation. If the beatnik lives in a state of voluntary poverty, he isn't being sincere about it—how can anybody turn down a buck?—so he must be cynical. If he turns his back on the installment-slavery of Madison Avenue's "engineered public consent" and phony "customer demand" propaganda, and tries to do with-

305

out kitchen machinery and keep off the car-a-year pay-and-trade-in treadmill, he isn't being sincere about it. How *can* he be? He must be cynical, just trying to put on a show of superiority by sneering at all the things that make life really worth living and which he secretly yearns for but hasn't got the get-up-and-go to acquire for himself. That is the "party line" and you will find some form of it in all the mass circulation magazines and newspapers whenever they refer to the subject.

Another gambit of the mass circulation media is: They just don't like to work. Out of perhaps a hundred beatniks there may be one, usually an artist, who is so ridden by the Muse that he is utterly unfit for any steady job and tries to make it any way he can without having to punch a time clock. The other ninety-nine are not artists. They chose "the life" because they like it better than what Squareville has to offer. They work, full time or part time, but without any of that good old stick-to-itivness and never-watch-the-clock devotion that was the slogan of the boomtime twenties—and ended for the go-getters in breadlines [308] and apple-peddling. The beatnik of today who adopts the dedicated poverty is simply honoring the old Polish proverb: He who sleeps on the floor has no fear of falling out of bed.

In a society geared to the production of murderous hardware and commodities with built-in obsolescence for minimum use at maximum prices on an artificially stimulated mass consumption basis, poverty by choice is subversive and probably a sin against Jesus Christ who was, according to Bruce Barton, the first Great Salesman. It makes monkeys out of all the soft-soap-sell radio newscasters and commentators who slip so glibly from the horror tales of the mushroom cloud and death on the freeways into the fairy tales of Success by hair oil and Beauty by mud pack, thrill points, homogenized beauty cream or whatever the latest shuck happens to be. It is no wonder, then, that simple-living beatniks come in for vicious tongue-lashings by hucksters posing as reporters and pundits.

It is the voice of Business speaking. Business has its song of Prosperity Unlimited to sing while it picks your pockets, and the razzberry obligato of the holy barbarians and their dedicated poverty is a jarring note.

The editorials and the ads and the speechmakers keep telling youth that the world is his, the future is his, and in the next breath cries out with alarm that "the other side" is plotting to blow up the world with hydrogen bombs. The holy barbarian's answer to

all this can be summed up in the remark of Itchy Dave Gelden
when he dropped in one day with an evangelist leaflet that some
"christer" had shoved into his hand, announcing that the world
was coming to an end—
*"Whose* world is coming to an end?"
Not the holy barbarian's. [309]

GLOSSARY

AX   Any musical instrument.
BALL   As a noun, a good time; as a verb, sexual intercourse.
BENNIES   Affectionate diminutive for Benzedrine pills.
BLOW   To sound (see Sound), to give voice to by word, music
or any aural means.
BREAD   Money, as in "Could you lay some bread on me?" mean-
ing lend or give some money.
BUFF   (also aficionado) An authority on jazz.
BUGGED   Bothered, bedeviled, unstrung.
BUSTED   Apprehended by the Heat (police). Only a cat is
"busted"; a square is "arrested."
CAT   The swinging, sex-free, footloose, nocturnal, uninhibited,
nonconformist genus of the human race.
CHICK   Just what you think it means.
COOL   Said of anything that sends you, whether cool jazz or
a cool chick—unless you like 'em hot (see Hot).
CONNECTION   Contact man for drugs.
COP OUT   To settle down, go conventional, in the sense of "sell
out" or "cop a plea." In some circles you may be charged with
copping out if you shave off your beard.
CRAZY   Anything from mild to wild that meets with a cat's ap-
proval. "Dig that crazy short." (see Short)
CUT OUT   To take one's leave.
DEALER   Drug-seller, pusher. [315]
DIG   Understand, appreciate, listen to, approve of, enjoy, do you
dig me, man?
DRAG   A bore, disappointment. A political convention is a big
drag. An evening with squares is a sad drag (see Drugg).
DRUGG   Brought down from a high (see High). Depressed, bored,
frustrated, blah.
DYKE   A highpower Lesbian. Variants: diesel-dyke, bull-dyke.
FAG   Short for faggot, as in "flaming faggot." A male homosexual.
FALL IN   Arrive, show up, make the scene.

FALL OUT   Pass out from an overdose of drugs.

FAR OUT   If it sends you and you go, you may swing far out, if no one bugs you and you get drugg—or go *too* far out and flip your wig. Also avant-garde, on the experimental frontiers of any art or experience.

FIX   A shot of heroin or some other drug.

FLIP   Anything from a fit of high enthusiasm to a stretch in the laughing academy (mental institution).

FRANTIC   Frenzied. Anything from hot pants to holy vision or any combination thereof.

FROM IN FRONT   First. From the beginning.

FUNKY   Old French, *funicle*, terrible. Latin, *phreneticus* (see Frantic). In the forties, Mezz Mezzrow defined it as stench, smelly, obnoxious. Today it means "that happy-sad feeling," according to some jazz musicians.

GANG-SHAG   The principle of the car pool or the common dish applied to sexual intercourse.

GAS   Supreme, tops, the most. A gasser.

GAY BOY   Homosexual.

GET WITH IT   Comprehend, understand, participate, dig?

GIG   Any gainful employment, as distinguished from work (see Work).

GIMP (gimpy)   Lame.

GO   When you're swinging you feel sent and when you're sent you Go! (see Gone)

GONE   The most, the farthest out. If you go far out enough you're gone—"out of this world."

GROOVE   As in groovey and "in the groove," meaning on the beat, swinging. A hip chick is a groovey chick.

HEAD   A marijuana user, pot head.

HIGH   In euphoric state, whether from drugs, alcohol, esthetic ecstasy or sex.

HIP   To know, in the sense of having experienced something. A hip [316] cat has experiential knowledge. A hip square has merely heard or read about it.

HIPSTER   One who is in the know. A cool cat.

HOLDING   To have marijuana or other drugs in your possession.

HORSE   Heroin. Also called H, and in some circles, affectionately, shit.

HOT   Said of anything that sends you whether a hot lick (jazz) or a hot chick—unless you're a cool cat.

HUSTLE   To engage in any gainful employment (see Gig).

HYPE   A heroin user. A contraction of hypodermic.

JOINT   A place, a penis, a marijuana cigarette, preferably a combination of all three.

LAY   To give, as in "Lay some bread on me."

LATER   When you're ready to leave the pad you cut out and say, "Later."

LIKE   The theory of relativity applied to reality. "Like that's *your* reality, man."

MAKE   To act, as in "make the scene." To "make it" may be said of anything that succeeds, whether a dental appointment or a crazy chick.

NOWHERE   If you're not with it, you're nowhere (see With it).

O.D.   An overdose of drugs.

PAD   A cat's home is his pad.

PICK UP ON   Get hip to, understand, appreciate.

POT (or pod)   Marijuana. Also called tea and at various times and places, muta, muggles, the weed.

PUSH   Sell, handle or purvey drugs. Pusher.

RELATE (to)   Establish mental and emotional contact with a person, communicate.

ROACH   A small butt of marijuana.

SCENE   The world and the lifeways of the beat generation. To "make the scene" is to fit in, to be accepted.

SHACK UP   To cohabit, in every sense and sex of the word.

SHORT   A small, foreign sports car.

SHUCK   As a noun, a falsehood, deception, fraud; as a verb, to deceive, swindle or defraud. I wouldn't shuck you, man.

SLAM   Jail. Also slammer.

SOUND   To voice an opinion, recite a poem. To inquire, as in "I sounded the cat was he holding."

SPADE CAT   Negro. The holy barbarians, white and negro, are so far beyond "racial tolerance" and desegregation that they no longer have to be polite about it with one another. [317]

SPLIT   As in "I've got to split," a form of leave taking.

SQUARE   Conformist, Organization Man, solid citizen, anyone who doesn't swing and isn't with it. Also called Creep and Cornball. Man, if you still don't dig me, you'll never be anything but—

STONED   High, loaded.

SWINGING   Liberated, uninhibited. Like if you don't swing that thing it don't mean a thing.

TURN ON  To get high. To introduce somebody to anything, as in "He turned me on to Zen."

WITH IT  If you're in the know you're with it. If you ain't with it man, you ain't nowhere no how.

WIG  The mind, as in "wig out" or "flip your wig," meaning out of your mind.

WORK  Sexual intercourse (see Gig). [318]

APPENDICES

# BIBLIOGRAPHY

In addition to the works listed below, the various writers who represent the hard core of beat writing have been widely printed in certain magazines, especially the following:

*Big Table.* 1316 North Dearborn Street, Chicago 10, Illinois. The first issue of *Big Table* contained the works originally intended for the Winter 1958–9 issue of the *Chicago Review,* and the preface by the editor discussed the argument over the "suppression" of the material by the university administration. It is further discussed by Albert N. Podell in his article listed under secondary works below.

*Chicago Review.* See the issues of Spring, Summer, and Autumn 1958.

*Evergreen Review.* See especially the issue devoted to the San Francisco Scene (Vol. 1, No. 2), although the beat writers are generously represented in other issues as well.

*Yūgen.* Seven Morton Street, #20, New York 14, N.Y. This little magazine prints extensively works by beat writers and others with consonant motives.

*Ark II, Moby I. Ark III.* These are more properly anthologies than magazines. The original *Ark* was printed in 1947 and is a key document in the early history of the San Francisco Renaissance.

*Beatitude.* Bread and Wine Mission, Grant and Greenwich Streets, San Francisco, California.

These magazines should be consulted in order to see the work of the beat writers presented in a context that helps to define their motives. To trace the work of any individual writer, the standard bibliographical aids should be consulted, especially the *Index to Little Magazines.*

BOOKS BY INDIVIDUAL WRITERS

William S. Burroughs

Under the pseudonym William Lee: *Junkie* (New York: Ace Books, 1953).

*The Naked Lunch* (7 rue Saint-Severin, Paris 5, France: Olympia Press, 1959). Although this book is available only in Paris and cannot be sent to the United States by the publisher, sections from it have been printed in the *Chicago Review* (Spring and Autumn 1958) and *Big Table* (Vol. 1, No. 1 and No. 2). The essay by Burroughs printed above (pp. 98–105) explains his motives in writing *The Naked Lunch.*

*The Exterminator* (with Brion Gysin) (San Francisco: The Auerhahn Press, 1960).

Gregory Corso

*The Vestal Lady of Brattle* (Cambridge, 1955).

*Gasoline* (San Francisco: City Lights Books, 1958).

*Bomb* (San Francisco: City Lights Books, 1958).

*The Happy Birthday of Death and Other Poems* (New York: New Directions, 1960).

Lawrence Ferlinghetti

*Pictures of the Gone World* (San Francisco: City Lights Books, 1955).

*A Coney Island of the Mind* (New York: New Directions, 1958).

*Tentative Description of a Dinner Given to Promote the Impeachment of President Eisenhower* (San Francisco: Golden Mountain Press, 1958).

Translator of *Selections from Paroles* by Jacques Prévert (San Francisco: City Lights Books, 1958).

*Her* (a novel) (New York: New Directions, 1960).

Allen Ginsberg

*Siesta at Xbalba,* privately printed in mimeographed form and reprinted in *Evergreen Review,* Vol. I, No. 4, pp. 29–47.

*Howl and Other Poems* (San Francisco: City Lights Books, 1956).

*Kaddish, Poems 1956–9,* announced by City Lights Books for publication in 1960.

Jack Kerouac

*The Town and the City* (New York: Harcourt, Brace & Company, 1950).
*On the Road* (New York: Viking Press, Inc., 1957). Reprinted by New American Library, 1958.
*The Subterraneans* (New York: Grove Press, 1958). Reprinted by Avon Publications, Inc., 1959.
*Doctor Sax* (New York: Grove Press, 1959).
*Maggie Cassidy* (New York: Avon Publications, Inc., 1959).
*Mexico City Blues* (verse) (New York: Grove Press, 1959).
*Visions of Cody* (New York: New Directions, 1959).
*Tristessa* (New York: Avon Publications, Inc., 1960).
*The Scripture of the Golden Eternity* (verse) (New York: Totem Press/Corinth Press, Inc., 1960).

Philip Lamantia

*Erotic Poems* (Berkeley: Bern Porter, 1946).
*Extasis* (San Francisco: The Auerhahn Press, 1959).
*Narcotica* (San Francisco: The Auerhahn Press, 1959).

Michael McClure

*Passage* (Highlands, N.C.: Jargon Press, 1956).
*Hymns to St. Geryon and Other Poems* (San Francisco: The Auerhahn Press, 1959).
*For Artaud* (New York: Totem Press, 1959).

Gary Snyder

*Riprap* (Ashland, Mass.: Origin Press, 1959). Distributed in the United States by City Lights Books.
*Myths and Texts* (New York: Totem Press/Corinth Books, Inc., 1960).

Philip Whalen

*Self-Portrait from Another Direction* (San Francisco: The Auerhahn Press, 1959).
*Memoirs of an Inter-Glacial Age* (San Francisco: The Auerhahn Press, 1960).
*Like I Say* (New York: Totem Press/Corinth Books, Inc., 1960).

John Wieners

*The Hotel Wentley Poems* (San Francisco: The Auerhahn Press, 1958).

ANTHOLOGIES

Donald M. Allen (ed.). *The New American Poetry, 1945–1960* (New York: Grove Press, 1960). This anthology provides selections from beat writers and other poets experimental in method and temper. It has an extensive bibliography, biographies of the authors, notes on their poetics.

Gene Feldman and Max Gartenberg (eds.). *The Beat Generation and the Angry Young Men* (New York: Citadel Press, 1958). Reprinted by Dell Publishing Co., Inc. (New York, 1959).

Lawrence Ferlinghetti (ed.). *Beatitude Anthology* (San Francisco: City Lights Books, 1960).

Seymour Krim (ed.). *The Beats* (New York: Fawcett Publications, Inc., 1960). A Gold Medal Book.

Elias Wilentz (ed.). *The Beat Scene* (New York: Citadel Press/ Corinth Books, Inc., 1960).


SECONDARY WORKS COMMENTING ON BEAT WRITERS,
BEATNIKS, THE BEAT GENERATION, ETC.

This list is selective and should be supplemented by reference to such standard bibliographical aids as the *Abstract of English Studies, Book Review Digest, Index to Little Magazines, New York Times Index, Reader's Guide to Periodical Literature*, etc. Back files and current issues of magazines devoted to commentary on current literary and social phenomena should also be consulted, for the indexing of book reviews and current magazines is not altogether perfect.

Adams, J. D. "On Writers of Beat Generation," *New York Times Book Review*, VII (May 18, 1957), 2.

Algren, Nelson. "Chicago Is a Wose," *Nation*, 188 (February 28, 1959), 191.

Amis, Kingsley. "The Delights of Literary Lecturing," *Harper's Magazine*, CCXIX (October 1959), 181–182.

Baker, G. "Avant Garde at the Golden Gate," *Saturday Review*, 41 (August 3, 1957), 10.

"Bam; roll on with bam," *Time*, 74 (September 14, 1959), 28.

"Bang bong bing," *Time*, 74 (September 7, 1959), 74.

Baro, G. "Beatniks Now and Then," *Nation*, 189 (September 5, 1959), 115–117.

"Beat Friar," *Time,* 73 (May 25, 1959), 58.

"Beatniks just sick, sick, sick," *Science Digest,* 46 (July, 1959), 25–26.

Beatty, J. "Trade Winds," *Saturday Review,* 40 (September 28, 1957), 6.

"Big Day for Bards at Bay: Trial over *Howl and Other Poems,*" *Life,* 43 (September 9, 1957), 105–108.

"Blazing and the Beat," *Time,* 71 (February 24, 1958), 104.

Bradbury, M. "Review of Lawrence Lipton's *Holy Barbarians,*" *Reporter,* 21 (July 9, 1959), 40–42.

Burdick, E. "Innocent Nihilists Adrift in Squaresville," *Reporter,* 18 (April 2, 1958), 30–33.

Carruth, H. "Four New Books," *Poetry,* 93 (November 1958), 107–116.

Ciardi, John. "Book Burners and Sweet Sixteen," *Saturday Review,* 42 (June 27, 1959), 22.

———. "In Loving Memory of Myself," *Saturday Review,* 42 (July 25, 1959), 22–23.

———. "Epitaph for the Dead Beats," *Saturday Review,* 43 (February 6, 1960), 11–13.

Conmy, P. T. *Wilson Library Bulletin,* 32 (June 1958), 723–725.

Conrad, B. "Barefoot Boy with Dreams of Zen," *Saturday Review,* 42 (May 2, 1959), 23–24.

"Cool, Cool Bards," *Time,* 70 (December 2, 1957), 71.

"Daddy-O," *New Yorker,* 34 (May 3, 1958), 29–30.

Daniels, Guy. "Post-Mortem on San Francisco," *Nation,* CCXXXVII (August 2, 1958), 3.

Dickey, James. "From Babel to Byzantium," *Sewanee Review,* LXV (Summer 1957), 508–530.

Eberhart, Richard. "Richard Eberhart Discusses Group of Young Poets on West Coast," *New York Times Book Review,* VII (September 2, 1956), 4.

Eckman, Frederick. *Cobras and Cockle Shells* (New York: Vagrom Chap Book #5, 1958).

———. "Neither Tame nor Fleecy," *Poetry,* 90 (September 1957), 386–397.

Eliot, T. S. See MacGregor-Hastie, Roy.

"Every Man a Beatnik?" *Newsweek,* 53 (June 29, 1959), 83.

"Far-out Mission; Bread and Wine Mission," *Time,* 73 (June 29, 1959), 38.

Feldman, Irving. "Stuffed 'Dharma,' " *Commentary,* XXVI (December 1958), 6.

317

Fischer, J. "Editor's Easy Chair: Old Original Beatnik," *Harper's Magazine* 218 (April 1959), 14–16.

Fleischmann, W. B. "Those Beat Writers," *America*, 101 (September 26, 1959), 766–768.

"Fried Shoes; Beatniks," *Time*, 73 (February 9, 1959), 16.

Fuller, Edmund. *Man in Modern Fiction* (New York: Random House, Inc., 1958).

Fuller, J. G. "Trade Winds: Ginsberg Trial," *Saturday Review*, 40 (October 5, 1957), 5–7.

Gleason, Ralph. "Kerouac's Beat Generation," *Saturday Review*, 41 (January 11, 1958), 75.

Gold, Herbert. "Hip, Cool, Beat, and Frantic," *Nation*, 185 (November 16, 1957), 349–355.

———. "How to Tell the Beatniks from the Hipsters," *The Noble Savage*, No. 1 (Spring 1960), pp. 132–139.

———. "The Beat Mystique," *The Beats*, ed. Seymour Krim (New York: Fawcett Publications, Inc., 1960), pp. 154–164.

Golffing, Francis, and Barbara Gibbs. "The Public Voice: Remarks on Poetry Today," *Commentary*, XXVIII (July 1959), 63–69.

Green, Jack. "Peyote," *The Beats*, ed. Seymour Krim (New York: Fawcett Publications, Inc., 1960), pp. 94–107.

Hecht, Anthony. "The Anguish of the Spirit and the Letter," *Hudson Review*, XII (Winter 1959–60), 593–603.

Holmes, John Clellon. "The Philosophy of the Beat Generation," *The Beats*, ed. Seymour Krim (New York: Fawcett Publications, Inc., 1960), pp. 13–16.

Howe, Irving. "Mass Society and Post-Modern Fiction," *Partisan Review*, XXXVI (Summer 1959), 420–436.

Hynes, S. "Beat and the Angry," *Commonweal*, 68 (September 5, 1958), 559–561.

Jacobson, D. "America's Angry Young Men," *Commentary*, 24 (December 1957), 475–479.

Krim, Seymour. "A Hungry Mental Lion," *Evergreen Review*, Vol. IV, No. 11, pp. 178–185.

———. "King of the Beats," *Commonweal*, 69 (January 2, 1959), 359–360.

———. "Review of *The Holy Barbarians*," *Evergreen Review*, Vol. III, No. 9, pp. 208–214.

———. "The Insanity Bit," *The Beats*, ed. Seymour Krim (New York: Fawcett Publications, Inc., 1960), pp. 60–72.

Leonard, G. B., Jr. "Bored, the Bearded and the Beat," *Look*, 22 (August 19, 1958), 64–68.

Leonard, John. "Epitaph for the Beat Generation," *National Review,* VII (September 12, 1959), 331.

Lipton, Lawrence. *The Holy Barbarians* (New York: Julian Messner, Inc., 1959).

McFadden, J. P. "Howling in the Wilderness," *National Review,* VII (September 12, 1959), 338–339.

MacGregor-Hastie, Roy. "Waste Land in Russell Square," *Trace,* No. 32 (June–July 1959), pp. 1–5.

Mailer, Norman. "The White Negro," *Dissent,* IV (Summer 1957), 276–293. Reprinted in Gene Feldman and Max Gartenberg (eds.), *The Beat Generation and the Angry Young Men* (New York: Citadel Press, 1958), pp. 342–363.

Mahoney, Stephen. "The Prevalence of Zen," *Nation,* 187 (November 1, 1958), 14.

May, James Boyer. "Flipping the Coin(age)," *Trace,* No. 34 (October–November 1959), pp. 20–27.

Miller, Henry. Preface to *The Subterraneans* (New York: Avon Book Division—The Hearst Corporation, 1959), pp. 5–7.

"Minister for the Beatniks; Bread and Wine Mission," *Newsweek,* 53 (March 16, 1959), 88.

Montgomery, John. "Report from the Beat Generation," *Library Journal,* 84 (June 15, 1959), 1999–2000.

Moore, Rosalie. "The Beat and the Unbeat," *Poetry,* 93 (November 1958), 2.

"New Test for Obscenity," *Nation,* 185 (November 9, 1957), 314.

O'Neil, Paul. "Only Rebellion Around," *Life,* 47 (November 30, 1959), 114–130.

Offen, Ronald. "Editorial: Ginsberg Revisited," *Odyssey,* Vol. I, No. 4, pp. 5–10.

Perlman, David. "How Captain Hanrahan Made *Howl* a Best-Seller," *Reporter,* 17 (December 12, 1957), 37–39.

Pinck, D. "Digging the San Franciscans," *New Republic,* 138 (March 3, 1958), 20.

Podell, Albert N. "Censorship on the Campus: The Case of the *Chicago Review,*" *San Francisco Review,* I (Spring 1959), 71–89.

Podhoretz, Norman. "Howl of Protest in San Francisco," *New Republic,* 137 (September 16, 1957), 20.

————. "The Know-Nothing Bohemians," *Partisan Review,* XXV (Spring 1958), 305–311, 313–316, 318.

Pritchett, V. S. "The Beat Generation," *New Statesman,* August 23, 1958, pp. 292, 294.

Rexroth, Kenneth. "Disengagement: the Art of the Beat Generation," *New World Writing,* No. 11 (New York: The New American Library, 1957), pp. 28–41. Reprinted in Gene Feldman and Max Gartenberg (eds.), *The Beat Generation and the Angry Young Men* (New York: Citadel Press, 1958), pp. 323–338.

————. "Jazz Poetry," *Nation,* 186 (March 29, 1958), 282–283.

————. "Revolt: true and false," *Nation,* 186 (April 26, 1958), 378–379.

————. "San Francisco Letter," *Evergreen Review,* Vol. I, No. 2, pp. 5–14.

————. "San Francisco's Mature Bohemians," *Nation,* 184 (February 23, 1957), 159–162.

————. "The World Is Full of Strangers," *New Directions in Prose and Poetry,* No. 16 (1957), pp. 181–199.

————. *Bird in the Bush: Obvious Essays* (New York: New Directions, 1959).

Rosenthal, M. L. "Naked and the Clad," *Nation,* 187 (October 11, 1958), 215.

————. "Poet of the New Violence," *Nation,* 184 (February 23, 1957), 162.

Roskolenko, Harry. "The Jazz-Poets," *Prairie Schooner,* XXXIII (Summer 1959), 148–153.

Ross, Basil. "California Young Writers, Angry and Otherwise," *Library Journal,* 83 (June 15, 1958), 12.

Rubin, Louis D., Jr. "Two Gentlemen of San Francisco: Notes on Kerouac and Responsibility," *Western Review,* XXIII (Spring 1959), 278–283.

Rumaker, Michael. "Allen Ginsberg's *Howl,*" *Black Mountain Review,* No. 7 (Autumn 1957), pp. 228–237.

Shapiro, Karl. "Poets of the Silent Generation," *Prairie Schooner,* XXXI (Winter 1957–8), 298–299.

————. "Romanticism Comes Home," *Prairie Schooner,* XXXI (Fall 1957), 182–183.

Sigal, Clancy. "Nihilism's Organization Man," *Universities and Left Review,* No. 4 (Summer 1958), pp. 59–65.

Sisk, J. P. "Beatniks and Tradition," *Commonweal,* 70 (April 17, 1959), 75–77.

Solomon, Carl. "Report from the Asylum," *The Beat Generation and the Angry Young Men,* ed. Gene Feldman and Max Gartenberg (New York: Citadel Press, 1958), pp. 153–163.

"Squaresville U.S.A. vs. Beatsville," *Life,* 47 (September 21, 1959), 31–37.

Stanford, Derek. "Beatniks and Angry Young Men," *Meanjin*, XVII (Summer [December] 1958), 413–419.

"Symposium on the Beat Poets," *Wagner Literary Magazine* (Spring 1959). Brief notes by Marianne Moore, Herbert Read, Dorothy Van Ghent, *et al.* and replies from Corso, Ginsberg, and Orlovsky.

Tallman, Warren. "Kerouac's Sound," *The Tamarack Review*, Spring 1959, pp. 58–74. Reprinted in *Evergreen Review*, Vol. IV, No. 11, pp. 153–169.

Tilling, Diana (pseud.). "The Other Night in Heaven," *The Fifties*, No. 3, pp. 54–56. Parody of an article by Diana Trilling listed below.

Trilling, Diana. "The Other Night at Columbia," *Partisan Review*, XXVI (Spring 1959), 214–230.

Van Den Haag, Ernest. "Conspicuous Consumption of Self," *National Review*, VI (April 11, 1959), 656–658.

Wakefield, D. "Night Clubs," *Nation*, 186 (January 4, 1958), 19.

Winn, J. "Capote, Mailer and Miss Parker," *New Republic*, 140 (February 9, 1959), 27–28.

Wolfe, B. "Angry at What?" *Nation*, 187 (November 1, 1958), 316.

"Zen-Hur," *Time*, 74 (December 14, 1959), 66.

## SUGGESTED PROBLEMS

1. Make a bibliography of comments on the recent attempts to read poetry to jazz. To simplify the problem restrict your bibliography to the years 1958 and 1959.

2. What recordings have been made by the following writers:

   Dylan Thomas     James Joyce
   T. S. Eliot     Kenneth Patchen
   Richard Eberhart     Allen Ginsberg
   Kenneth Rexroth     Jack Kerouac
   Richard Wilbur     William Carlos Williams

3. The distinguished English author Aldous Huxley has written a great deal on his experiences with hallucinogenic drugs. Compile a bibliography of Mr. Huxley's writings on this subject, and compile a bibliography of comments on those writings.

4. Make a list of works printed in magazines in 1959 by the following writers:

   Gregory Corso     Norman Mailer
   Lawrence Ferlinghetti     Bernard Malamud

5. Make a list of articles printed in 1958 by Kenneth Rexroth that are *not* on the subject of the Beat Generation. Describe in one sentence the subject of each.

6. Make a list of as many reviews as you can find of one novel by Jack Kerouac.

7. Some of the following authors have been contrasted with writers of the beat movement. Compile a bibliography of the publications, both in book and magazine form, between 1955 and 1959, for *one* of the following:

   Richard Wilbur     Mark Harris
   Donald Hall     Bernard Malamud
   Herbert Gold

8. Prepare a bibliography for the study of censorship of books in the United States in 1957.

9. Make a list of books on Zen Buddhism printed in the United States between 1955 and the present.

10. A group of English writers frequently compared with the "Beat Generation" is called "The Angry Young Men."
    a. Make a list of books and articles that comment on the "Angry Young Men."
    b. Make a list of the writers usually associated with this group, indicating what sort of writing each does (drama, fiction, poetry, criticism).
    c. Make a list of the books printed in the United States by *one* of these men.

11. One of the most famous suppressions of a book in the history of American literature is the suppression of Theodore Dreiser's *Sister Carrie*. Prepare a bibliography on this subject, including five books and fifteen magazine articles.

II. POSSIBLE SHORT PAPERS.

1. Write a description of the censorship problems faced by Lawrence Ferlinghetti after the publication of Allen Ginsberg's *Howl and Other Poems*. Try to make your essay as objective as possible.

2. Using the material in your descriptive essay, write an essay for or against the suppression of *Howl*.

3. Using an encyclopedia article and one book, write an essay defining Zen Buddhism. Include with your essay a bibliography listing five books on Zen Buddhism.

4. Write an essay, using the material gathered for problem 3 and the selections by Gary Snyder in this book, on the importance of Zen Buddhism in his work. It would be well to read in addition one book by Snyder, *Riprap* or *Myths and Texts*.

5. After reading both Allen Ginsberg's "Notes on Finally Recording *Howl*" and John Ciardi's "Epitaph for the Dead Beats," write an essay on the relevance of the

poem's possible mode of composition to its final form and impact.

6. Using the material in this casebook, write a definition of the term "beat."

7. In discussions of beat writers, the terms "Bohemia," "Bohemian," "Bohemianism" are often used. Write an extended definition of the term "Bohemian." Append to your essay a list of five books relevant to the problem of defining the term.

8. The writing of the beat generation has often been described as comparable to the work of the abstract expressionist painters. Write a definition of abstract expressionism. Append to your definition a list of the more prominent abstract expressionists.

III. LONGER PAPERS.

1. Several French writers have been compared with writers of the beat generation. Choose *one* of the following as the subject for a brief report on his life and work. Append to the essay a list of translations of his work which are available in English.

Guillaume Apollinaire    Ferdinand Céline
Antonin Artaud           Jean Genêt

Write an essay in which you compare and contrast the author you have chosen with one of the beat writers.

2. Make a complete bibliography of the published work of Michael McClure and Gregory Corso. Write an essay in which you compare and contrast their work.

3. A complaint frequently made against beat writers is that they are humorless. Using the material in this casebook, discuss the question of humor in beat writing. In shaping the essay, discuss the question in relation to all the writers, but stress *one* of the writers, using material not included in this casebook.

4. Among Walt Whitman's poems is one called "Respondez! Respondez!," written shortly before the Civil War and finally omitted by Whitman from *Leaves of Grass*. Write an essay in which you compare and contrast this poem

with the first section of Ginsberg's *Howl*. Shape your essay in such a way that it will form a general comparison and contrast of Ginsberg and Whitman.

5. Henry Miller admires Jack Kerouac's work, as is evident in his remarks in the Preface to *The Subterraneans*. Write an essay comparing and contrasting one of Miller's books with one of Kerouac's. Append to the essay a bibliography of the writings of the two men.

6. Read *one* of the following works:
   Brother Antoninus, *The Crooked Lines of God*
   Robert Duncan, *Selected Poems*
   Denise Levertov, *With Eyes at the Back of our Heads*
   Kenneth Rexroth, *In Defense of the Earth*
Write an essay comparing and contrasting the poet read from this group and the work of one of the poets directly associated with the beat movement. Append to the essay a bibliography of the two writers discussed.

7. The beat writers have been compared with the "Dada" movement. Write an essay in which you discuss the differences and similarities between "Dada" and "Beat." Append to the essay a bibliography of books and articles relevant to the subject.

8. One of the chief criticisms of the beat writers has been that they lack a sense of social responsibility. Using the material in this casebook and the works of one beat writer, write an essay on the beat writer's sense of political and social reality.

9. One of the chief interests of the beat writers is religion. Write an essay on the importance of religious ideas in the works of one of the writers, analyzing the extent to which his ideas differ from conventional Christian ideas.

10. Norman Mailer, though in many ways different from the beat writers, has expressed favorable opinions of their work. Write an essay in which you compare and contrast the work of Norman Mailer with the work of Kerouac or Burroughs.

11. Many writers have experimented with drugs, both in the twentieth century and earlier periods. Write a his-

tory of the relation between literature and drugs since the French revolution. Since the material will be extensive, try to choose three typical figures from earlier literature and one of the beat writers as the centers of discussion.